Evolving Creative Mindsets

The arts come from a hopeful place, and they forge and mend relationships even in a time of crisis. Words, music, the built environment, movement, images – artistic creation in all their forms inspire us to reflect on who we are and the world in which we live. Arts entertain us, comfort us, and bring us together. Arts nourish our sense of belonging, strengthening our connections to the wider world, as well as to the many communities to which we belong – by origin, adoption, and aspiration. The power of arts endures when everything else falls apart; arts are essential needs.

—Canada Council of the Arts 2021–2026 Strategic Plan

Evolving Creative Mindsets

Thinking Through the Arts

Lynn F. C. Yau

Hong Kong University Press
The University of Hong Kong
Pok Fu Lam Road
Hong Kong
https://hkupress.hku.hk

© 2025 Hong Kong University Press

ISBN 978-988-8900-80-0 (*Paperback*)

The author hereby asserts her moral right to be identified as the author of this work in accordance with applicable copyright laws, including the Copyright Ordinance (Cap. 528) of the Laws of Hong Kong.

All rights reserved. No portion of this publication may be reproduced or transmitted in any form or by any means, electronic or mechanical, including photocopying, recording, or any information storage or retrieval system, without prior permission in writing from the publisher.

British Library Cataloguing-in-Publication Data
A catalogue record for this book is available from the British Library.

Digitally printed

To
WSC, TWL, MYC, and LCD
For your magnanimity

Contents

Foreword	viii
Preface	x
Acknowledgements	xiii
Introduction	1

Part A: Origin

1. Cracking the Creativity Code: The Future Starts Now	15
2. The Power of Imagination: Redressing Poverty?	36

Part B: Passage

3. In Praise of Gaps: Programming with Voids	47
4. Passivity to Engagement: *Sm-ART Youth* Case Study	69
5. Reflections as Assessment: Acknowledging Considered Thinking	90
6. Those COVID Days: The Arts and Well-Being	129

Part C: Bearing

7. Creative Mindsets, Creative City: OECD PISA Creative Thinking Test	157
8. Museums and Performing Spaces: Sites of Creative Learning	190
9. Contextualising Human Resource Planning: A Triumvirate Concept	218
10. Myths and Misunderstandings: Musings and Replies	254

Epilogue: First-Class Humans	263
Appendix	269
References	276
Index	282

Foreword

The title of this book, *Evolving Creative Mindsets: Thinking Through the Arts*, attracted me instantly because it reveals how the arts can contribute to the evolution of creative mindsets. In this age of AI and technology, the cultivation of 'creative mindsets' are high on the agenda of educators and parents. The book summarises the visionary work of the author and the group she founded (AFTEC) fifteen years ago – pioneering arts education and arts-in-education projects which nurture creative mindsets. As readers will discover, it was a fascinating learning journey for her and her stakeholders, with many challenges and rich rewards en route.

Most arts practitioners in Hong Kong are involved in arts education in some way since skill-based arts training is in big demand from parents and schools. It is a pity, though, that there are few arts-in-education programmes where the emphasis is on optimising the educational value of the arts. This book shares both theories, insights and real-life cases of how the arts can be used as a powerful tool to enhance the intellectual and personal development of young people. Depending on the nature of the project, improvement of soft skills such as critical thinking, empathy, resilience, teamwork, self-reflection, and self-learning can in fact be assessed and measured. Creativity learning, which offers no right or wrong answers, can be a useful supplement to the traditional mode of learning (as demonstrated by the success of the Jockey Club Arts-Based Cross Curriculum Creative Learning [JCABC] pilot scheme).

The author urges the arts sector to forge a partnership with the education sector in order to cultivate creative mindsets for society. She believes that the key to this partnership is the training of teaching artists (creative practitioners), who played a crucial role in JCABC. She also points out that nurturing creative mindsets is a key to audience development for the arts. I can't agree more with her that arts companies should pay more attention to the 'impact' their programmes make on audiences (both on site and online). When audiences derive deeper meaning and/or feeling from their arts experience, their commitment to art attendance will no doubt increase. Hence, creative practitioners can also play an important role in our arts organisations.

This book is extraordinary in many ways. First, the author's vision, passion, and determination to strive for excellence in her calling. Secondly, her remarkable scholarship and insights, sharing latest trends, theories, overseas studies, and cases on the subject. Thirdly, her frank sharing of how she implemented arts-in-education and creativity learning schemes in Hong Kong – what obstacles she overcame and the lessons learnt. Finally, her holistic view of the interrelationship between creativity education and future human resources needs, East-meets-West Centre for Cultural Exchange, supply and demand of arts and culture, arts education provision at schools, and teaching artists (creative practitioners). Hence, she made a convincing case that the subject should be addressed at the cultural policy and education policy levels.

I strongly believe that this visionary book should be read by artists, art students, student teachers, arts/cultural administrators, teachers and school principals, academics, and policymakers in education and culture. There is an urgent need to broaden arts students' outlook on how the arts can contribute to society (including education). This book can provide a useful reference in the curriculum of future artists training programmes.

TSENG Sun Man
Adjunct Professor, The Education University of Hong Kong
Member, Culture Commission, HKSAR

Preface

The genesis of *Evolving Creative Mindsets: Thinking Through the Arts* originated from the preparation for AFTEC's fifteenth anniversary celebrations in 2022–2023 as a collection of thinking notes for internal record. After the process began, by coincidence an AFTEC board member was seated next to the publisher, who exclaimed the dearth of writing in arts education in Hong Kong. The rest is history.

Every book has a backstory. After a stint in London pursuing an MPhil scholarship, I realised that I never truly felt at home in any of my varied professional roles despite my initial belief in an academic life. Then I jumped off the cliff, transforming a lifelong passion for the arts into a career that has been a source of exhilaration and fulfilment for decades.

Friends thought it was absolute folly to surrender status and perks for the arts where there is little materialistic reward and where few would understand the nature of the work beyond being entertained. This is issue one for this book: the arts are not really recognised in Hong Kong beyond performances and exhibitions. At best, they are for academic portfolios in schools, or economic and glamour windows to the world. I was intrigued by what else the arts could be.

Nothing has been more uplifting (and dampening) and gratifying (and frustrating) than the arts. Nevertheless, one feels so alive physically (energised yet exhausted), mentally (multimodal yet singular), and emotionally (inspiring yet drained). Perhaps in reading this book, you too can partake in some of the positive feelings, for what is the aim of writing but to connect experiences and deep feelings in the silence of reading. In a world of much artificiality and technology, it is good to be human.

In the years after the deep dive, I am still invigorated by the possibilities of being in as diverse roles as an arts practitioner: as an explorer (continuous), as an educator (armed with some formal knowledge), as an occasional performer (now ceased), as an administrator (out of necessity), and always as an active member of the audience, absorbing, analysing, and experimenting.

I have gained multiple hypothetical perspectives of how the arts can gain a larger audience, how artists can become more involved with the public, why the arts should be integral to all our lives, and how schools can nurture creative mindsets to further embrace the arts beyond practical skills-based learning. These are also issues in the book which, in retrospect, all stem from the bubbling disquietude of two words.

'Arts appreciation', a much-bandied phrase, is a fuzzy concept with insufficient clarity, applied liberally and with the box ticked too easily. What is it? What can it be? A burning question has always been how it is feasible for one to relate to an artwork via factual knowledge alone with minimal engagement, often passive. This has spurred me to investigate the concept of building a pathway to the arts for the purpose of learning through diverse ways of engagement.

The interest in teaching and learning appeared at a later stage, quite by accident. The occasions when I could review the homework of my nieces, Sian and Maya, in a local primary school set off alarm bells. That was a good answer, I thought. Why was it circled in red with marks deducted? What was wrong? An interest was piqued as to what learning is and hence a plunge into understanding primary school education first-hand. By the time I surfaced, it was clear that learning needs to be redefined and the system needs to be reviewed.

This is another concern in the book. In this twenty-first century of VUCA[1] (vulnerability, uncertainty, complexity, and ambiguity), doling out information only does not work. Our IoTs (Internet of Things) provide more than enough facts to enrich and drown us daily. How can schools hope to impart knowledge and teach related skills yet exclude the development of capacities and capabilities? Knowing how to fish is surely more fundamental than being fed fish as a matter of routine.

Gradually, I became increasingly preoccupied with the connection between the arts, and teaching and learning, how the two could meet, be mutually beneficial, and how there might be possibilities for complementary nourishment and contribution.

On this front, opportunities are many. What will make sense within the bounds of AFTEC's limited knowledge? What is achievable given a charity's limited energy and financial resources, and in a field which is peripheral even in the arts? Above all, how can the education and arts communities sit side by side? After all, two heads are better than one. Or are they?

This book touches upon certain ideas that have surfaced from AFTEC's philosophy and programming that link the two fields. I have tried to present and tease out some of the answers here, using the organisation's experiences, achievements,

---

1. 'Where Does the Term VUCA Come From? Role of Nanus and Bennis', *VUCA-World*, 18 August 2023, https://www.vuca-world.org/roles-of-nanus-and-bennis/.

and mis-steps to illustrate the wider adventures and putting forward notions that may kindle dialogues among peers. Most of the time, questions overwhelm answers.

Looking down the road are three thoughts. One, for universities to develop undergraduate and postgraduate degrees in creative teaching and learning through the arts, because this is where the bottleneck is ultimately. Two, that a creative learning fellowship can be inaugurated to nourish future leaders in creative learning spanning the arts, education, and elsewhere. Finally, the idea of a network, one in which regional and international collaborators excite each other and extend their practices to meet challenges creatively.

Acknowledgements

This book would not have been possible without the generosity of a host of professionals and friends over the years.

I am profoundly indebted to AFTEC's board of directors for their unwavering counsel and steadfast support of this value-driven charity. Your belief in the organisation's potential and your willingness to embrace risk have been instrumental in shaping AFTEC into what it is today.

I am very grateful to Professor Lois Hetland, Jean Ho, Marissa Fung Shaw, Dr and Mrs Arthur van Langenberg, Professor Samuel Leong, Robert Li, Jonathan Meth, Professor Tseng Sun Man, Dr Richard Whitbread, and my sister Amanda for their invaluable feedback on my draft manuscript. Special thanks to AFTEC's artistic director, Dr Vicki Ooi, for her editing, wisdom, and staunch support throughout the writing process.

Thank you to my current and former colleagues – Calvin Co, Natalie Ting, and Ebona Yeung – for your dedication to AFTEC during the challenges of the COVID years. To all colleagues, your efforts made AFTEC stronger during and after the pandemic.

Special thanks to Ally Wong and colleagues who undertook research for the book, especially Calvin Co and Cat Lai, who were very meticulous with details and always with a smile.

To all sponsors and donors who made AFTEC's work possible, our gratitude runs deep. Special thanks to the Government of Hong Kong, the Hong Kong Jockey Club Charities Trust, Jean C. K. Ho Family Foundation, Lee Hysan Foundation, and Swire Properties for your deep trust and substantial support.

To Sue Hoyle and Sir John Tusa at the Clore Leadership Programme in London (2010–2011), you affirmed and further excited my understanding to explore learning in the arts and cultural sector.

I am grateful to Michelle Chawla, CEO of the Canada Council for the Arts, for allowing the use of a quote from their Strategic Plan, and to artist Shilpa Gupta for permitting the use of her artwork. My thanks also go to Hong Kong University Press, Michael Duckworth, and Yasmine Hung; your support for an arts-in-education publication has deeply encouraged us at AFTEC.

Lastly, I am deeply honoured to have collaborated with all stakeholders over the past sixteen years – the audience, schools, participants, and graduates. Special thanks to the professionals in the arts and education fields, especially Dr Priscila Chu, Grace Cheng, Dr Tong Choi Wai, and Tse Chun Sing, for your hard work in exploring the arts and creative learning. You have truly made a difference.

Introduction

Setting the Scene

Imagine three pieces of data are given to you. How will you make sense of them?

1. Cultural and creative exports totalled HK$618 billion (US$79.4 billion) in 2018, accounting for 15% of Hong Kong's total exports. The largest component was audiovisual and interactive media (HK$442 billion/US$56.8 billion), followed by performing arts (HK$82 billion/US$10.5 billion), and then visual arts and design goods (HK$72 billion/US$9.3 billion).[1]
2. 'In my regular classes, when the teacher calls on me, I often shy away and avoid answering. But in AFTEC's classes, I raise my hand without hesitation. Whether I get it right or wrong, I feel a sense of accomplishment just from putting myself out there and trying.'[2]
3. 'As a teacher in a creative classroom, I allow students to firstly observe, encourage them to ask more questions and express themselves more. The classroom is not solely led by the teacher inculcating knowledge and skills. It is one in which students are able to discover for themselves, after which I facilitate learning through their findings.'[3]

---

1. 'The Cultural and Creative Industries in Hong Kong', Census and Statistics Department, Hong Kong Special Administrative Region, accessed 17 June 2024, https://www.censtatd.gov.hk/en/data/stat_report/product/FA100120/att/B72406FA2024XXXXB0100.pdf.
2. Lai Tsz Yu, interview by AFTEC project team, *Spotlight on Students 2023–24*, YouTube, https://youtu.be/x5LJV_HK8jE?si=zT6uKewVqU-ORdeD.
3. May Wong, *Jockey Club Arts-Based Cross Curriculum Creative Learning Project* teacher focus group interview by GeoDimension InfoSolutions Limited, 2024.

Item 1 is quantitative facts and easily understood. Item 2, from a student, suggests a frame of mind from a child. Item 3 is taken from the perspective of a professional educator who has taken on the mission of incorporating creative teaching approaches through the arts into traditional classrooms. The latter two quotes are less palpable than hard facts are, but they furnish a qualitative side to how human beings are nurtured. While item 1 is undoubtedly important, the other two values are equally significant.

The powers of the arts often seem more immediately accessible through numbers. However, qualitative data provides in-depth, contextual information that can complement and enrich the understanding gained from quantitative data. The extraordinary capacities of the arts are diverse and provide richer pictures than metrics alone.

In our experiences, the arts have twelve innate powers:[4]

1. Kindle the imagination
2. Empower creative thinking and expressions
3. Make connections
4. Promote interactivity
5. Ignite feelings
6. Foster introspection
7. Probe ideas
8. Tell stories
9. Communicate
10. Offer perspective and further understanding
11. Affect the broader environment
12. Be transformative

The wealth of knowledge flowing from the arts is unfathomable. How much attention do we pay to its abundant harvest? This is what *Evolving Creative Mindsets: Thinking Through the Arts* aspires to do.

Qualities

This book hopes to convey a range and variety of thoughts from direct experience grown with colleagues in the past sixteen years at The Absolutely Fabulous Theatre Connection, or AFTEC. This is one case study seeded during the early days of this century.

---

4. If we compare these twelve powers to the generic skills promoted by the Education Bureau, clear overlaps can be seen.

The frontline experience draws together two disciplines – the arts and education. The arts are roughly divided into the performing and visual arts. Performing arts refer to dance, drama/theatre, music, and any art form that occurs on stage and/or in front of an audience, live or online. The visual arts include 2D renditions (drawing, painting, photography, graphics, etc.) and those in 3D (sculptures, installations, ceramics, printmaking, craft). Nowadays, the digital realm is also included.

Education is taken in its usual form, teaching and learning within structured parameters. In this publication, the focus is on formal education and non-formal education in the school system.

The arts and education are often perceived as quite disparate unless understood as 'arts education'. Arts education is defined here as the *intrinsic* purpose of teaching skills and imparting knowledge, to understand art forms. In this city, teaching students how to play the piano for that sole purpose is considered arts education. Being taught how to look at a painting though its lines, patterns, and shapes is another example. We had a signature project in acting coupled with life skills. That was in arts education, a segment of the total arts equation.

We work in the 'arts-in-education' in the main. This is where the properties and nature of the arts are mobilised to support teaching and learning. It also refers to the characteristics of the arts (the twelve powers) being deployed for the *extrinsic* purpose of teaching and learning and not for their own sake as in arts education. Through looking at a painting on a moment in history, students are guided to think critically, enabling them to compose better essays, for example. This is the arts-in-education. The outcomes are not to improve drawing skills or to astound with remembered facts. They are for developing a reflective habit of mind.

There is confusion, nevertheless, that participating in the arts will make anyone creative, creativity often being interpreted as the ability to conceive of and create, express, and make something which was previously absent.[5] This may occasionally happen although the awareness may not be direct.

Definitions

For the purpose of this book and its discussion, creative learning is identified as 'the ability to question, make connections, innovate, problem solve, communicate, collaborate and to reflect critically, the skills young people will need if they are to take responsibility for their own learning'.[6]

---

5. 'Durham Commission on Creativity and Education', Durham Commission on Creativity and Education, accessed 4 November 2019, https://www.artscouncil.org.uk/sites/default/files/download-file/Durham_Commission_on_Creativity_04112019_0.pdf.
6. Creative Partnerships (2002–2011) is now known as Creativity, Culture & Education, https://www.creativitycultureeducation.org/.

These are, undoubtedly, inherent qualities of the arts, both visual and performing. We believe that creative learning and teaching in schools are able to empower creative thinkers. And by exploring and putting forward the attributes of such a thinker, we have immense opportunities to cultivate and expand creative mindsets.

Creative thinkers are those who can come up with ideas, who explore possibilities through asking questions. In the process, they extend their thinking, connect their own and others' ideas and experiences in inventive ways, locate alternative solutions, follow ideas through, and adapt ideas as circumstances change.[7] Like children and young people, adults can become creative thinkers as well if the 5Cs – creativity, critical thinking, communication, collaboration, and contribution – generic skills commonly found in Hong Kong's official curriculum guides, underpin school as well as lifelong learning.

The nurturing of creative thinkers is grounded on the ability to *teach creatively* through a diverse range of ways and approaches instead of top-down prescriptive teaching. It also means uncovering *teaching for creativity* at the same time, explicitly using pedagogies and practices that cultivate creativity in young people.[8]

Much of the time, our work is dependent on the dedication and commitment of professionals. These are teachers and those whose practice is arts- or culture-based. Normally, and broadly speaking, this second group, that has an educational interest, is referred to as arts educators (the British term) or teaching artists (the American term). They are referred to by either name in the publication.

We have opted for a third reference, creative practitioners, to portray a wider definition. They include arts educators or teaching artists and any professionals who exhibit and use creative behaviour and those who work in the creative field. At its broadest, this can even encompass architects, designers, scientists, journalists, and hybrids from a range of professionals.[9] In our pilot creative learning project from 2021 to 2024, one school collaborated with an architect and another with two artists who are designers and paper engineers.

A Pressing Concern

A lot of great work is happening in the arts sector in performances and exhibitions in Hong Kong, as there is much to celebrate in education institutions. We have met and

---

7. Adapted from the definition from 'A Framework of Personal, Learning and Thinking Skills 11–19 in England', Qualifications and Curriculum Authority, Department for Education, the UK, https://dera.ioe.ac.uk/id/eprint/7268/3/PLTS_framework_v2_tcm8-936-1.pdf.
8. 'Durham Commission on Creativity and Education'.
9. 'Lead Creative Schools Prospectus for Creative Agents', Arts Council of Wales, accessed January 2017, https://creativelearning.arts.wales/sites/default/files/2022-07/Prospectus-for-Creative-Agents.pdf.

are still working with many dedicated, first-rate artists and teachers whose practice is as yet unseen and unheard but who still passionately contribute. Much is happening in both sectors. What, then, is the exigency?

Hong Kong is some twenty years behind the UK in the approach to arts education and arts-in-education, and creative learning is inaccessible to many who are both inside and outside of the arts sector. Why should these fields matter, you will ask? You are already straining to produce work to fulfil grant requirements amidst a lack of space and 'musical chairs' human resources availability. As a principal in a school, you do not lack funding at all; yet keeping the teaching team cheerful and optimistic in spite of an increasing workload (plus keeping the parents happy) is a job and a half, if not two. What is the point of arts learning? I hope to answer some of these questions from our organisation's singular perspective.

In which areas is the UK more advanced? It is way ahead in research (focus on the arts and collaboration with higher institutions), in partnerships (arts-based and cross-sector), in advocacy, in training the trainers, in programming depth, and even in discussions on the whys and hows.

As an example, *The Arts in Schools: Principles, Practice and Provision*,[10] a policy document published in 1982 by the Calouste Gulbenkian Foundation, contributed to a new ecosystem of education teams in cultural organisations. Forty years later, in 2022, A New Direction with the Foundation produced *The Arts in Schools: Foundations for the Future*,[11] urging policymakers to review the values attributed to the arts as part of a rethink of the education sector.

Like the first, this second report is non-governmental. The data spring from a series of round-table discussions with schools, academics, arts educators, and young people. In other words, those who are in the front line of the arts and the beneficiaries.

It is indeed true that the UK is suffering from diminishing funding support in the arts and some closure of arts organisation as I write. Since COVID in particular, schools and universities are also eliminating arts and humanities subjects. In addition, in some UK regions, just making the arts available in schools is in itself a real challenge and an ongoing concern despite the nation's overarching thought leadership.

The point is certainly not that we need to duplicate the UK's efforts just because they are one of the vanguards. The days of copying should long be over if we want

---

10. Ken Robinson, *The Arts in Schools: Principles, Practice and Provision* (Calouste Gulbenkian Foundation, 1982).
11. 'The Arts in Schools: Foundations for the Future', Pauline Tambling and Sally Bacon, Calouste Gulbenkian Foundation and A New Direction, March 2023, https://www.anewdirection.org.uk/the-arts-in-schools.

to be a truly creative city. But to what extent are we original? Again, I will leave this question to the book itself, for each reader to interpret what is relevant.

Context Matters

The crux of the issue is not about arts programming and practices in our city. We have a cornucopia of events here, so much so that one can attend two performances a night, zipping in and out at intermission and still not touch the surface of offerings in a month. For exhibitions, we can all do a fast-paced, 'been there, done that' tour in large and small museums filled with local and international fare yet not managing much at all before eyestrain and brain overload set in.

The heart of the matter is who we are as a city and what we would like to become in the face of geopolitical developments, human-made disruptions, climate change, mass migration, and economic imbalances. Closer to home, three issues matter. First, the *2023 Global Innovation Index Report*[12] placed Hong Kong seventeenth under the Income Group Ranking, or fifth in the Region Rank, Singapore standing fifth and first respectively. Second, China's National 14th Five-Year Plan would like to see the city as an East-West Centre for International Cultural Exchange by 2030. And third, our local wealth gap is widening between the poorest and the well-off.

Cultivating the quality of minds, creative mindsets, may offer one approach to innovation, cultural exchange, and redressing the wealth gap. We need to consider a macro ecosystem where different stakeholders are involved for the arts and education sectors and how that will make an impact. We should no longer be focusing on programming alone but how these very artistic endeavours can grow and be sustained beyond a two-hour performance which will be forgotten in a matter of months as we chase the next cultural fix. And we are not referring to digitalising the shows or archiving the visual masterpieces online to pop up on digital platforms on demand.

Goal number one is to be able to extend the shelf life and morph shows plus exhibitions in ways that will advance the impact of the arts further via the arts-in-education and creative learning. The second goal, equally vital, is to ensure the enhancement and the quality of creative minds at a young age continuing into sustained development for professionals. The third goal, and possibly the paramount, is to take reference from international good practices, then localise. Any intent to globalise will look after itself afterwards.

---

12. The index takes the pulse of four key stages in the innovation cycle: (1) science and innovation investment, (2) technological progress, (3) technology adoption, and (4) the socio-economic impact of innovation. Soumitra Dutta, Bruno Lanvin, Lorena Rivera León, and Sacha Wunsch-Vincent, *Global Innovation Index 2023: Innovation in the face of Uncertainty*, World Intellectual Property Organization (2023), https://doi.org/10.34667/tind.48220.

Macro View

One visual (figure a) introduces the book's overarching framework. It elucidates the relationships that we need to build, quickly but deeply.

Education needs to be a formidable partner to the arts and for the arts to better support schools in delivering arts-based teaching and learning that underpin intellectual and personal development as a matter of policy. This clearly needs extra resources from funders who are able to understand the forcefulness of the arts-in-education and not the arts solely for productions.

One of our sponsors regularly asks us for recommendations for innovative work by arts organisations in Hong Kong. The answer to having more of these is to fund differently, to grow ideas in the arts *and* education as essential, intrinsic fundamentals; then there will be new approaches galore.

Expressed differently, we need to move away from discrete, independent structures, remaining in our familiar territories trying to survive or outdo perceived competitors. Hong Kong itself needs the competitive edge in this complex world of sudden changes. Our best resource *is* our creative mindset, hence the cultivation of our people. We should not entertain a 'copy-and-paste' cooperative attitude in which each party offers a piece of a puzzle and prays that it works. We could embark

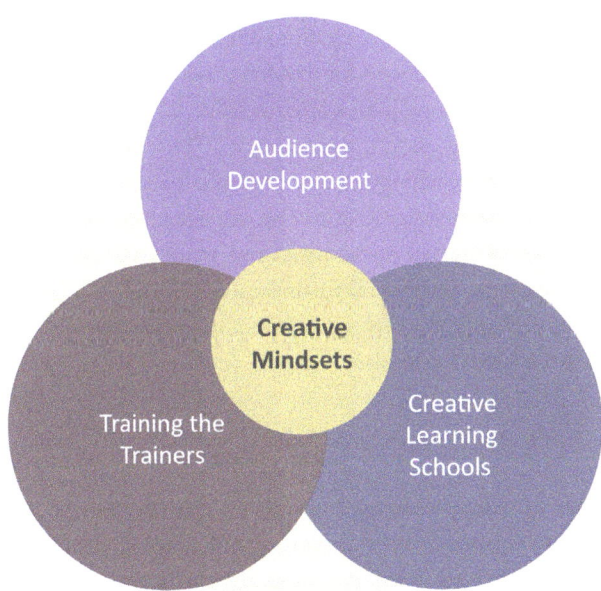

Figure a: Evolving Creative Mindsets. Image from AFTEC, 2023.

on a strategic approach for collective and collaborative engagement that paints one integrated canvas, finding a language of understanding, learning from each other's strengths, and shoring up common gaps. It is hard, as we have witnessed in our own very limited endeavours, but not impossible and well worth the effort.

Quick fixes often stem from present bias, providing a temporary sense of achievement but failing to address long-term challenges. In contrast, fostering ecosystem resilience requires a future-oriented perspective that prioritises sustainable, systemic solutions.

In the past decade and more, as an arts-in-education institution that has taken small steps to pilot the arts' less acknowledged features. We have gone into classrooms for children and young people, providing support to teachers' professional development in the arts, and managing arts practitioners' needs in understanding education.

We have even ventured – perhaps somewhat innocently – into non-arts territory. Our core perception is this. One, schools have very basic knowledge of the powers of the arts. Two, very few arts organisations seem to have seriously reflected on arts teaching and learning outside of skills training, let alone have learning teams in place or a framework that integrates productions and teaching.

As I write, we sent a territory-wide survey to all primary and secondary school heads to understand the nature of arts provisions in schools.[13] The next step, should the opportunity arise, is to enact the same for arts companies.

What can the city's cultural policy do to effectively develop and reinforce arts educators at early to mid-career and for those that may be emerging? The organisation's arts learning and training path hopes to make further inroads as a grant for an extension project kicked off in the autumn of 2024 with a collective of creative practitioners that include teaching artists as well as educators.

The creative mindset belongs to everyone. We need to write that value proposition together. To do that, what resources can be made available for advocacy, for framework development, for intercollegiate arts-referenced dialogues, for teaching artists as a recognised and prospering workforce to join forces with incoming lead creative learning teachers in schools?

Laying Out the Thinking

Evolving Creative Mindsets: Thinking Through the Arts focuses on processes that unfold, ones which constantly need to update and adjust themselves. Indubitably, that is the very basis of creative minds, constantly reaching out like an octopus with its many brains seeking information to adapt to and interact with their surroundings.

---

13. Framework based on chapter 9, table 9.1.

The phrase 'thinking through the arts' encompasses two meanings: how creative mindsets are grown via interaction with the arts and, secondly, the process of thinking about different aspects of the arts over a period to understand the relationship to and implications for learning.

This book is for those in the arts who may wish to understand how meaningful and valuable it is to add a serious learning component in your routine, to understand why investment of time and effort in proper training for current and potential teaching artists predicates the chance for purposeful audience development and as evidence that the arts-in-education is not only workable and feasible but can be highly valuable.

For arts and culture policy formulators, there is a clear need for creative minds, not only in the arts but where creativity is needed in many other areas of the city to move forward. Hopefully, overseas examples may be the catalysts to growing the arts in new directions.

This publication is also meant for educators (current and future) to witness the prowess of the arts, the potentials as yet latent and hidden to a pragmatic society. The incessant pressure to get on with the teaching can obfuscate the fact that times have changed drastically for everyone, and human catastrophes seem to increasingly present themselves. Creative mindsets mean more solutions.

To school heads and teachers, for all the constant calls to generic skills building in official documents, I hope the book will give some authentic examples by offering a preliminary glimpse into how the arts are potent vehicles for creative thinking and well-being outcomes.

I encourage educators at all levels, arts companies, and freelancers to explore this interconnection as I would push funding bodies to offer special grants beyond just programming to provide time and space for research to understand the correlation between the arts, learning, and cross-sector discourse.

Chapters at a Glance

This book is divided into three major sections: *Origin*, *Passage*, and *Bearing*.

Eponymously, *Origin* starts with the beginning of the company, with what caught our attention at the outset.

Chapter 1, 'Cracking the Creativity Code: The Future Starts Now', uncovers arts education in the context of the education reforms in early 2000. Springboarding from four narratives tracking the progress, or otherwise, the chapter continues into future jobs and learning.

Chapter 2, 'The Power of Imagination: Redressing Poverty?', paints a picture of passive local students who mostly come from disenfranchised backgrounds. Poverty is discussed on two levels: the generally understood economic interpretation and the less noticed, hence seldom discussed, realm of the imagination, the one affecting the other. A habit of mind from a deficit model of learning is introduced, leading to ideas on the importance of an asset model of being framed by the imagination for better futures.

The imagination is often linked to the arts and the possibilities that can surface.

The next section, *Passage*, travels through four chapters: from a single programme to across a collection to wider implications and the COVID pandemic that swept normalcy away.

Chapter 3, 'In Praise of Gaps: Programming with Voids', works on the premise that omissions are as much opportunities for change and development. This chapter looks at AFTEC's decision to locate gaps for purposeful programming as opposed to creating programmes as a matter of annual routines. Through actual examples, subsections carry the themes of creative learning in theatre productions, collaboration with professionals to capacity-build young people, and the importance of the arts in the non-arts sector and sustainability.

Chapter 4, 'Passivity to Engagement: *Sm-ART Youth* Case Study', reviews and investigates this seminal project from which the concept in aligning the arts, education, and creative learning eventually developed. The children whom we observed in chapter 2 became part of a creative learning process which we embarked on with the arts at the core of classroom activities. Five segments come into play: pedagogy; the cognitive, mental, and affective environment; an emphasis on building parent-child relationships; the meaningfulness of cultural outings; and the importance of training the trainers.

A core feature of any learning is assessment and evaluation. In education, assessment is expected. In arts education, to assess or not to assess, that is the question and a bone of contention at times. Chapter 5 dives into one approach for arts-based programmes. Through five case studies in 'Reflections as Assessment: Acknowledging Considered Thinking', various ways and means of assessment in the arts are implemented and put forward for discussion. This chapter emphasises the importance of reflections as the entry point for self-enquiry and understanding.

Introspection connects the inner self and gives shape to thoughts and feelings otherwise buried deep. Over time, we have witnessed the opening of minds and resultant flowering of individuals.

In chapter 6, 'Those COVID Days: The Arts and Well-Being', we trace company reactions to the traumatic period, from internal considerations on emotions to outward manifestations of problem solving and resolutions as part of collective learning. This throughline continues into the connection between mental well-being and the arts, using other case studies as examples.

In every journey, there is a starting point, the sojourn, and the end of the passage. This final leg does not happen in this book, as the arts-in-education as an integrated concept, indeed the arts and education as two separate forces, are never-ending because they are constantly evolving to be at their best and freshest. The final section of the book is thus constituted as *Bearing*, because there are futures.

Taking a cue from *The Oxford English Dictionary*, 'bearing' is a compass direction and a determining position. It is also how one carries oneself, the manner in which one behaves, and a part of a machine in which another part turns or slides.[14]

The results of the first OECD PISA Creative Thinking assessment (2022) released in 2024 forms the basis for chapter 7, 'Creative Mindsets, Creative City: OECD PISA Creative Thinking Test'. From countries in every compass direction, results for four domains with three key performance indicators (KPIs) are revealed. The chapter analyses Hong King's relatively lacklustre performance in creative thinking and offers some reasons for this.

In chapter 8, 'Museums and Performing Spaces: Sites of Creative Learning', envisages diverse spaces – museums and performing venues – as regular sites of creative learning beyond classrooms. Through scoping the similarities and divergences of the physical, mental, and emotional components in museums and performance venues, the chapter relates thinking, feeling, and learning to the whole experience, one which works towards audience development.

Chapter 9, 'Contextualising Human Resources Planning: A Triumvirate Concept', returns the wheel to the introduction's illustration of the arts and education sectors' potential to propel Hong Kong forward in audience building and creative mindset development tied to sectorial professional development in training teachers and teaching artists. With three views of layered development in these areas, I look to this possibility for determining the city's position as a focal point of East-West exchange via a phased-in approach.

The concluding chapter 10, 'Myths and Misunderstandings: Musings and Replies', takes a macro view of my experiences in the arts, specifically in conversations, or overheard, at arts events.

Divided into three categories – general, learning, and sector-based – this final segment aims to address some common misconceptions about the arts. The goal is to shed light on at least the most prominent of these misunderstandings, in the hope of dispelling the pervasive chill and instead kindling greater warmth and appreciation for the arts within people's hearts and minds.

In every chapter, the aspiration is to raise awareness, convey stories, and, above all, champion the dedicated professionals who passionately devote themselves to the arts for educational enrichment.

---

14. 'Bearing', *Oxford English Dictionary*, accessed 18 August 2024, https://www.oed.com/search/dictionary/?scope=Entries&q=bearing.

Part A: Origin

1
Cracking the Creativity Code
The Future Starts Now

Summary

Chapter 1 offers a sweeping overview of the intersection between arts and education since 2000, focusing on formal school learning. It navigates various levels of discourse from researchers, prompting the reader to reflect on the vital role of creativity through the arts in our future growth and development. This lays the groundwork for the subsequent chapters, which will delve deeper into the rationale behind a creative learning project's initiatives and the essential role of arts and culture in shaping the future of this city.

Part I explores the past from the education reform in the early twenty-first century according to the macro education policy and for arts education. Part II reviews reform achievements and the challenges faced along the way, with analysis on disparities between the arts and school learning. Part III looks at reasons for a status quo two decades later. Part IV takes an economic perspective on jobs, automation, and future trends. Part V emphasises the importance of creativity and its related constructs for future learning and jobs, highlighting how key characteristics of the arts drive this change.

Part I

What did the year 2000 mean to you? Irrespective of backgrounds, the turn of the millennium was undeniably a massive milestone, humankind celebrating the completion of a century and welcoming the next. On a more fathomable scale, one momentous change that was anticipated was how education needed to anticipate the needs of the twenty-first century.

Globally and locally, the educational future was planned meticulously. Hong Kong was no exception. In 2000, the Education Commission[1] gave macro rationales for sweeping changes given unprecedented worldwide shifts, the return of sovereignty to China in 1997, and the rapid development of information technology that will affect the city economically and socially, opening up new domains in all aspects of lives, creating new challenges along the way.

The commission's education blueprint highlighted key tools for addressing the challenges of a changing world. Notably, the term 'creativity' appeared early and frequently throughout the document – a rare emphasis at the time – which signified strong support for innovation and change.

The main goals of education were clear: to help everyone develop in the five core Chinese concepts of ethics, intellect, physical fitness, social skills, and the arts,[2] based on their individual strengths. This way, they could become lifelong learners, think critically, adapt to change, be confident team players, and work for the betterment of society and the world. Learning, as such, should be enjoyable for our students as they improved their communication skills and fostered their creativity and commitment.

In the arts, music and the visual arts were, and still are, minor subjects in formal education from primary to secondary school. For the first time, however, in the reform, policymakers stated unequivocally that the arts are intrinsic to education and are thus embedded in the five core Chinese concepts. Arts education was no longer external to core subjects but coaxed into the fold as one of eight Key Learning Areas[3] through the *Arts Education Key* curriculum guide[4] and complementary documents that first appeared in 2002.

As with twenty years ago, when arts education made its debut as a principal actor on stage, the updated versions until the current one in 2017 (at the time of writing) portray four curriculum aims. They include the fostering of creativity, critical thinking, and aesthetic sensitivity; building skills, knowledge, and positive values in the arts; enjoying participation in arts-making activities; and cultivating a lifelong interest in the arts.

The arts were called into action by policymakers as having a crucial role to play, because it is through the process of integrative learning that students are able

---

1. 'Learning for Life, Learning through Life: Reform Proposals for the Education System in Hong Kong', Education Commission, Hong Kong, September 2000, https://www.e-c.edu.hk/wp-content/uploads/2000/09/Proposal_Edu_Reform_2000.pdf.
2. In Chinese, 德智體群美.
3. The others are Chinese language education, English language education, mathematics, science, technology, personal social and humanities education, and physical education.
4. The Education Bureau speaks of the arts-in-education within the concept of arts education.

to acquire a holistic understanding and deeper insights into what is being learnt.[5] Out of the nine prescribed generic skills, we have teased out four as foundational: creativity, critical thinking, communication, and collaboration. We added a fifth, contribution, as the belief to plough back to society is a fundamental value to us.

Policy formulation is challenging, but implementation is even more daunting when theory meets practice. A key result of education reform is the introduction of school-based management, decentralising decision-making to principals and teachers. Due to diverse school backgrounds, cultures, student abilities, and teaching styles, interpretations of the policy document will vary, even as they align with the education master plan. As global shifts affect city dynamics, schools will also experience changing environments that influence their outlooks.

How have we fared to date in arts education and the arts-in-education? What have we missed? One can consider answering the questions from a few perspectives: formal education (structured, sequential learning with timetables for young children to higher education), non-formal (structured activities outside the formal school system), and informal learning (not organised, no structure, and unintended education).

However, one chapter will not do justice to the realm of the arts and the multiple layers. The decision is therefore to take a bird's-eye view of arts education and the arts-in-education in formal learning settings in schools from the start of the reforms. In the hope of enabling amelioration and future possibilities, the investigation will then move into present necessities in the light of living in tumultuous times arising from worsening global impacts as we live in the fourth Industrial Revolution – climate change, mass migration, socio-political upheavals – and most recently, COVID.

Part II

Probabilities and Possibilities

Four Perspectives

Four key documents shape our understanding of the past in arts education. These papers are interlinked, revealing similar concerns across different areas. They will be referenced in the chapter.

---

5. 'Learning to Learn – Life-long Learning and Whole-person Development', Curriculum Development Council, Hong Kong, June 2001, https://www.edb.gov.hk/attachment/en/curriculum-development/cs-curriculum-doc-report/wf-in-cur/CDC_LtL_Report_2001(web)_e.pdf2002b: 61.

Lau and Tam[6] explored the impact of performing arts education on teachers, artists, and student learning. While not directly connected to recent education reforms, their findings update us on the reforms' effects twenty-two years later. Cheung Yung's studies[7] focused on resource partnerships and how integrated arts learning has progressed in schools since the reforms.

The Bamford, Chan, and Leong team provided a detailed analysis of arts education in Hong Kong,[8] examining its effectiveness in various settings – formal, non-formal, and informal – ten years after the initial reform.

Finally, Whitbread conducted a comprehensive investigation into the way arts education and cultural policies interact, shaping the desired cultural landscape that the government aims to establish.[9]

The Achievements

What did the reforms achieve?

After the education reforms in 2000, Cheung Yung identified patterns of cross-subject integration, particularly in English language learning through drama. She focused on a significant Arts-in-Education programme, which ran for three years starting in 2000.

This programme created a bridge in which artists and arts organisations collaborated closely with schools to develop an integrative curriculum in and through the arts and to explore various integrative approaches. Organised by the Hong Kong Arts Development Council, co-organised by the then-Hong Kong Institute of Education[10] and the Education Bureau, the programme was undertaken during formal school hours to integrate the arts with other Key Learning Areas.

Students showed noticeable improvements in motivation and interest in learning. The integration of different subjects created more meaningful and coherent experiences, especially through interactive activities. As a result, students developed better cooperation, communication skills, and self-confidence.

Bamford et al.'s survey of schools found that about half of the respondents viewed the curriculum reforms positively for the arts although 43% remained

---

6. Chung-yim Lau and Cheung-on Tam, 'Examining Performing Arts Education in Hong Kong', *Arts Education Policy Review* (2022): 1–12, https://doi.org/10.1080/10632913.2021.2023933.
7. Wai Yee Jane Cheung Yung, 'Integrated Arts Education in Hong Kong', APERA Conference (2006), https://citeseerx.ist.psu.edu/document?repid=rep1&type=pdf&doi=0f02cc11eaddc39517307036cf4cc1934aa949cb.
8. A. Bamford, R. Y. J. Chan, and S. Leong, *Quality People Quality Life: Developing Hong Kong into a Creative Metropolis Through Arts Education* (Home Affairs Bureau, Hong Kong, 2011).
9. Richard Whitbread, 'Cultural and Arts Education Policies in Hong Kong: Two Wings of the Same Bird?' (EdD dissertation, Education University of Hong Kong, 2016).
10. Now the Education University of Hong Kong.

neutral. The report also indicated that the new reforms received 'overwhelming support' and were seen as a 'positive step'. These changes made the curriculum more flexible, at least in some schools. Additionally, new programmes for continuous professional development for teachers were initiated.

On another success front, the new senior secondary school offered space for more arts, culture, and creative learning. Additionally at the same level, in the early 2000s, schools tested out a new set of applied learning courses that were career-oriented. These encouraged the development of generic and vocational skills across six areas, creative studies being one of them with the inclusion of design, media arts, and two performing arts disciplines, in theatre arts and dance.

At the macro perspective on arts education policy, there was an elevation of arts education within the wider curriculum including the relevance of the arts for whole-person development especially in life skills such as cooperation and problem solving. Whitbread, like Cheung Yung, pointed out that the Arts Development Council's contributions made a difference in raising the profile of arts education.

The Gaps

Over the past two decades, achievements in arts education have increased, leading to a positive outlook and strong support for new programmes. There has been greater awareness of the arts and creative learning in education and the public sphere. However, researchers have consistently identified gaps in these developments, leading to discussions about common challenges.

A common discovery in our work is what Whitbread calls the 'artificial silo-ing' of rationales and skills in stakeholder partnerships. We view this as an administrative convenience. He sees these silos hinder true integration between cultural and arts education policies.

Whitbread identified this problem as stemming from a lack of strong leadership, a clear strategic vision, and reluctance to embrace the interdisciplinary nature of arts education. He also noted a shortage of meaningful partnerships both within and between sectors. Whitbread did not hold back in describing these issues as 'mismatches, misconnections, disconnections, gaps, and contradictions'. Those of us on the front lines understand that these policy gaps directly affect stakeholders, especially at the formal school level.

The mismatches and misconnections stem from the way major cultural and arts education policies influence our understanding of the arts. While there is broad support for the arts, Bamford et al. highlight an important distinction: the school system views the arts primarily as curriculum-based learning for *academic* purposes, whereas artists interpret the arts more broadly as central to Hong Kong's *cultural* life.

This artistic perspective focuses less on education and more on the quality of artistic experiences. As we will explore further, this disparity has many ripple effects.

Gaps as Maps

For effective cross-sector collaboration between the arts and education, a mutually agreed-upon conceptual framework is essential. In our collaboration with schools and artists, we have identified a gap: conceptual thinking is often unfamiliar to both schools and some artists. A conceptual framework functions like a mini policy document, outlining the foundation for teachers and artists to come together on shared objectives, outcomes, and activities.

In our experience, however, there is one exception: when the end result requires a product, such as winning competitions or performing at year-end showcases. In these cases, there is clear alignment as educational meaning shifts towards creating high-quality productions for local or overseas competitions. These objectives are certainly valid.

This raises the age-old divide between focusing on the *extrinsic* qualities of the arts-in-education – using arts education for other purposes, as in how drama supports language learning – and the *intrinsic* qualities focusing on the dynamics of singing, acting, or dancing. Without a strong consensus on a conceptual framework, values will vary, leading well-intentioned learning experiences to become merely mechanical or tokenistic integrations of education and the arts.

When foundational matters diverge, it leads to system-wide inconsistencies in planning and implementation. For instance, schools focus on practical learning objectives, while artists prioritise producing high-quality artworks for schools over effective arts education activities.[11] For artists, the emphasis is on artistic experiences rather than the educational values schools seek. Although economic development affects education, artists often resist this focus and retreat into their artistic work.

Thirdly, partnerships between schools and arts organisations are often short term, primarily occurring outside of school hours and the curriculum. Bamford et al. support this view. While there have been improvements in the theatre sector since 2011, such collaborations remain relatively rare.

Artists in general are not sympathetic to assessment, as they genuinely do not appreciate the point of evaluating the amorphous nature of the arts and believe that outcomes cannot be defined let alone quantified. In our experience, the route to acceptance of assessment by artists is a long one though not without success. The basic need is to cultivate artists' understanding of education components and demonstrate the worthiness and meaning of the arts for the purpose of teaching and

---

11. Chung-yim Lau and Cheung-on Tam, 'Examining Performing Arts Education in Hong Kong', 7.

learning and, in the mid- to long-term, illustrate that such a route, albeit seemingly longer, benefits the development of artists and the arts in the end. This persuasion is ongoing.

Likewise, the training provided for artists in tertiary institutions appears to take insufficient account of the education system, assessment, and evaluation beyond artistic creations. Their artistic work matters predominantly, as they are what artists live for. Principally, in our experience, artists do not focus on words[12] but on diverse human expressions. Added on to this is the fact that assessments are almost always text-based even for focus-group interviews. Verbal evaluation is always preferred to anything in the written form. This is not to say that artists dislike words; this is to say, however, that there is a major difference in the approach taken in cultivating mindsets and between valuing the product and process.

Additionally, artistic endeavours, by their very nature, are very much based on processes, while schools are very clear about the end goals in the curriculum or the products. This is not to say that products are unimportant. We have witnessed on many occasions that, when processes are genuinely considered, the product will take care of itself. For schools, the products are the ultimate prize. These seemingly opposing ends of the spectrum make the development of a consensual teaching framework arduous.

Over the years, we have sought to bridge this binary mindset. Caught unambiguously in the middle are teachers, particularly those who are more adventurous and willing to take some risks as they locate alternatives to teaching in the arts, through the arts, and integrating the arts in creative learning.

What might have slowed down progress? Back in 2005, Cheung Yung pointed out that teachers were not given models or strategies for combining different art forms or integrating them with other subjects. At the same time, there was a lack of guidelines and hands-on training for using arts in the curriculum. As a result, schools and teachers became disconnected from understanding policy intentions, focusing instead on working things out on their own. This led to feelings of inadequacy when it came to designing and implementing an integrated curriculum.

If we think about the origins of teachers as learners, it does come down to the habits of mind nurtured in the larger education environment. Often the single-subject textbook culture transmitted through traditional convergent thinking pedagogy means ingrained practices are deeply rooted. In AFTEC's most recent *Jockey Club Arts-Based Cross Curriculum Creative Learning* pilot project[13] (2021–2024), nothing could be clearer than this phenomenon.

---

12. Literary artists being the exception.
13. Project details in the appendix.

Cheung Yung truly understands teachers when she says that they often struggle to see the benefits of diverse thinking in integration. When integration happens, it is usually just surface-level teamwork, where subject teachers meet, split up the lesson plan, and teach their parts. Consequently, teachers' confidence in teaching across subjects remains basic, and they often do not embrace more creative and integrated approaches.

From an arts perspective, integration in teaching and learning involves a different way of thinking that alternates between and merges divergent and convergent approaches. But in local schools, how much of this actually happens, given the packed curriculum, tight schedules, and exam pressures?

Bamford et al. note that, by international standards, children in Hong Kong are highly skilled in the arts, particularly in music and visual arts. However, she points out a lack of emphasis on developing creative and critical thinking, only superficial attention given to critical reflection and understanding the arts in context. To foster subject integration and cross-curricular learning, teaching mindsets must change, as evidenced by the creative learning pilot, when a shift in habit of mind to incorporate creative learning is possible.

This suggests that the goal of holistic development and incorporating essential skills has often been treated as checkboxes rather than genuine commitment. As a result, interdisciplinary learning is largely absent, except for some drama integration in language learning. While arts appreciation is frequently promoted as a stepping stone, it requires deeper consideration and more support. This responsibility falls equally on teaching artists and the government's cultural and education arms.

According to Bamford et al., a key reason schools are not adopting more creative approaches is the lack of recognition of the connection between arts education and creative learning. Although the arts education policy discusses creativity, it remains inadequate and largely theoretical. Compared to schools and teachers in mainland China and Taiwan, those in Hong Kong struggle to grasp the role and value of creativity in arts education.[14]

Part III

Understanding the Creativity Code

As this chapter is being written, the status quo seems dominant still. Creative learning is still discussed albeit training is thin on the ground. If the seven researchers mentioned in previous pages were seated at a table right now, they might be surprised

---

14. Bamford et al.; Lau and Tam; Cheung Yung.

that parallels and paradoxes abound today and still echo the issues raised in part II. The key question is why. One could hazard several guesses.

First of all, the definitions of creativity in research and subsequent implementation are so diverse that the concept appears to be slippery. Reading research on the topic is not easy, making practice difficult to place.

A second reason is that on-the-ground implementation is far more challenging than is policy formulation, and the latter cannot be expected to accommodate all possibilities. That is not its purpose. Additionally, policy documents are wide open to interpretation by multiple stakeholders in their understanding, unique circumstances, and stages of development in the arts vis-à-vis the entire holistic reform.

This includes the Education Bureau which adopts the official line and only peripherally connects with arts policy, unlike in Singapore where the Ministry of Education's Arts Education branch works hand in glove with its National Arts Council. There is also a very fine balance between macro guidelines in a policy and actual details in a school curriculum that integrates the arts into other disciplines.

Thirdly, the training afforded to principals and teachers in tertiary institutions is only as well-rounded and as thorough as the curriculum design on offer and as university expertise permits. Although in recent years there has been growth in creativity as a research interest, there are too few academics that understand and work through the arts.

In addition, many creativity portfolios are in science, technology, engineering, mathematics (STEM) education. Given the scarcity of dialogue on the arts-in-education and the continual focus on core subjects in school, the trickle-down effect on parents in the past two decades is that many still champion academic excellence, high-stakes exams, and grades rather than become the standard–bearers for a wider picture of education that is creative. Changing mindsets is, ultimately, time-consuming.

As a fourth point, what permeates Hong Kong's culture in the arts primarily is founded on a high proportion of performances and exhibitions as *the* face of the arts (see chapter 9). Outreach/arts education/arts-in-education trail a far second. In the city, the environment of the arts as spectacle has probably led to an ecology that defines the arts as mainly just that: tangible, visible performances, and exhibitions.

Scintillating products succeed at the expense of the city's understanding of the inherent values of underlying processes. Until policy leadership understands that the arts are not purely entertainment or economic drivers, they will be less able to appreciate that there is an influential third layer of creative teaching and learning.

A fifth point is that there is but a small critical mass of arts professionals rooting for and advocating arts education and arts-in-education consistently and widely. A case in mind is how the awards meted out annually by the Hong Kong Arts Development Council – of which we a grateful recipient – redefined the Arts

Education prize to become the Arts Promotion accolade at one point. However, it did rescind this decision and has, to date, merged the two awards into one award for the arts sector. One reason overheard is that applicants were unable to differentiate between them.

To borrow Whitbread's 'mismatches, misconnections, disconnections, gaps and contradictions' once again, I would like to culminate with a sixth point as to why creative learning has made little headway in the past two decades.

In the year 2000, when the education reforms were promulgated, Hong Kong was simply not ready for the kind of momentous change demanded for a more progressive type of creative learning. After all, there was no urgency then. We were a leading international hub, economically very sound, and the 2008 financial crisis was eight years down the road. All in all, we were exceedingly comfortable.

In hindsight, the Education Commission in 2000 had indeed been prescient in its key reform document. 'The world is undergoing unprecedented changes, and Hong Kong is no exception' (2000, 3) is such a foresight. They would have never contemplated how prophetic they have been. By 2023, as we lived through regularly occurring natural and human-made calamities, perhaps the city is ready to seriously reconsider that creative teaching and learning via the arts is of the essence? There are too many issues that need innovative mindsets (and not simply in the arts) to solve, and many need to be creative, not merely artistic.

Part IV

Tagging Along the Economic Path

The many layers of the arts and culture are unlikely to be understood by the majority as a general rule, except in key countries and cities where the social fabric is woven together by arts and culture. In Hong Kong, a financial hub with economics at the leading edge, the quantitative is unceasingly and proportionately more distinguishable than is the qualitative, too easily regarded as intangible and invisible.

An example lies in the tongue-in-cheek comment of the bifurcation of the arts overseen by the former Home Affairs Bureau (where money is expended) and the creative industries that are situated in the Commerce and Development Bureau (where money is earned). Fortunately, this changed in July 2022, when the creative industries and similar entities came under the wing of the Culture, Sports and Tourism Bureau.

I believe this city fears abstractions, and the arts are best in that. Where there is little understanding, there is little desire to grow. Albeit 'thinking out of the box' is bandied around regularly, it is more a buzz phrase.

Perhaps one possible solution to induce more people to understand the arts is to turn the tables here by looking at the more utilitarian and economic aspects of life to gauge if creativity does have a role to play.

The Role of Creativity

Three publications can assist with that: a research report from Oxford University's Oxford Martin School, *The Future of Employment* (Frey and Osborne, 2013), the Canadian consulting and software firm Quantumrun[15] Foresight's research in the futures of education and work, and *The Future of Jobs Report 2023* from the World Economic Forum. We will begin with the last report and work backwards to the two academics who actually show us, quantitatively, that those in the arts and creativity matter.

All of these reports speak of the fourth Industrial Revolution, where the melding of technologies is obscuring the lines between the physical, digital, and biological spheres. The practicalities of current jobs and the change brought about by this latest ongoing revolution have been researched widely, COVID evidently playing a substantial role in accelerating and transforming work.

The Future of Jobs Report 2023 illustrates pandemic-related disruptions and provides the expected outlook for technology adoption jobs and skills in the next five years. Predictably, its capture of pandemic-induced lockdowns and the ensuing global recession revealed a highly uncertain outlook for the labour market and one which has accelerated the arrival of the future of work.

One of the eleven findings in the executive summary speaks of skills gaps. The basic premise listed throughout the three publications is that the fourth revolution's technological advancement is increasingly witnessing the replacement of jobs by AI.

One of the main consequences of COVID has caused what is termed 'The Great Resignation' in the US due to burnout from the pandemic (particularly in the tech and health care sectors) and the realisation that the meaning of life matters more. Due to the growing frequency in mass displacement and expanding AI dominance, how skilled one is is pivotal to survival and living in a world order that has been turned on its head.

As demand skills across jobs change in the coming years, the finding also states unequivocally that skills gaps will continue to be high. The way to address the situation is to develop and enhance human skills and capabilities through learning and meaningful work. These, in turn, will drive economic success, improve individual well-being, and grow social cohesion.

---

15. 'Future of Work P1', Quantumrun, accessed 19 June 2019, https://www.Quantumrun.com/series/future-work.

Figure 1.1 from the *World Economic Forum Report*[16] shows perceived skills and skills groups of increasing importance based on the share of companies surveyed. The top three skills are critical thinking and analysis, problem solving, and self-management.[17] Further up the figure, the top fifteen skills by 2025 reveal that creativity is a major item, seven others being directly associated with the arts: analytical thinking; active learning and learning strategies; complex problem solving; critical thinking and analysis; originality and initiative; emotional intelligence, resilience, stress tolerance, and flexibility; and reasoning, problem solving, and ideation.

Why is creativity so important in future jobs? How can those in the world of economics understand that it is essential? To recognise its vital role, we can turn to how teaching and work will be transformed in the next few decades as the fourth Industrial Revolution affects our lives.

Data Explosion and Automation

If we look at the data that have been created since the internet was released to the public, it is little wonder why rote learning or traditional classrooms will no longer be manageable and we all need to adapt and change.

Figure 1.2 exemplifies the exponential growth of data and more. Reading from left to right, by 2040, some 50% of jobs in the US will be automated, a reflection of things to come globally. It is plainly not possible to learn by rote the amount of new data and knowledge being generated online daily. How much factual knowledge can teachers impart year on year at the touch of a button? How much can students continue to memorise when a few clicks away is information more than textbooks can supply?

In Quantumrun's research on the future of teaching, one common misconception on automation is clarified. Robots are not competing to take over human jobs; they are automating routine and linear tasks.

From another perspective, aspects of blue- and white-collar jobs that have a narrow and repetitive set of skills will be replaced sooner rather than later. By definition, the remaining jobs that will be relatively unscathed by automation will be those with the requisites for relationship building, creativity, research ability, discovery, and abstract thinking. These are jobs for people who can experiment, jobs with aspects of 'randomness that pushes boundaries to create something new'.[18] If this

---

16. *Future of Jobs Report*, World Economic Forum, May 2023, https://www3.weforum.org/docs/WEF_Future_of_Jobs_2023.pdf.
17. Data here are supported by metrics partnerships from LinkedIn and Coursera.
18. 'Future of teaching: Future of education P3', Quantumrun, accessed 19 June 2019, https://www.Quantumrun.com/prediction/future-teaching-future-education-p3.

B. Top 15 skills for 2025

1	Analytical thinking and innovation	9	Resilience, stress tolerance and flexibility
2	Active learning and learning strategies	10	Reasoning, problem-solving and ideation
3	Complex problem-solving	11	Emotional intelligence
4	Critical thinking and analysis	12	Troubleshooting and user experience
5	Creativity, originality and initiative	13	Service orientation
6	Leadership and social influence	14	Systems analysis and evaluation
7	Technology use, monitoring and control	15	Persuasion and negotiation
8	Technology design and programming		

A. Relative importance of different skill groups

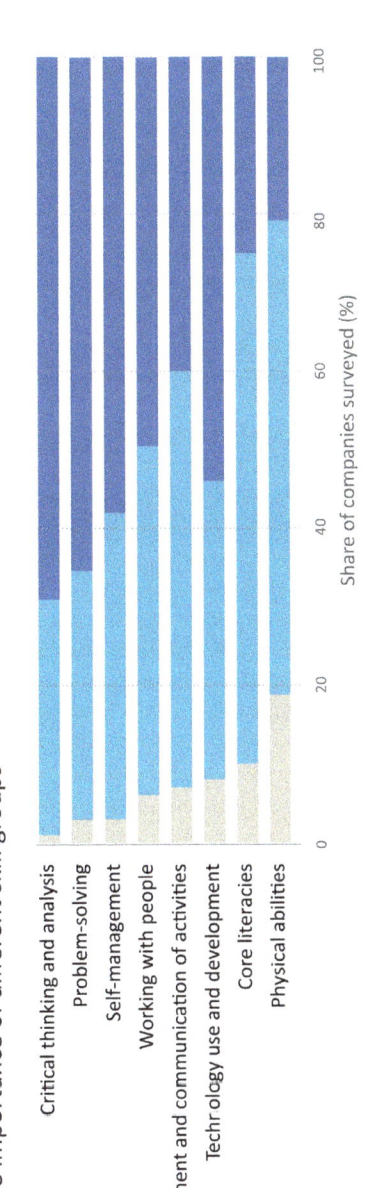

Figure 1.1: *Important Future Skills*. Image courtesy of the *World Economic Forum Report*, 2023: 36.

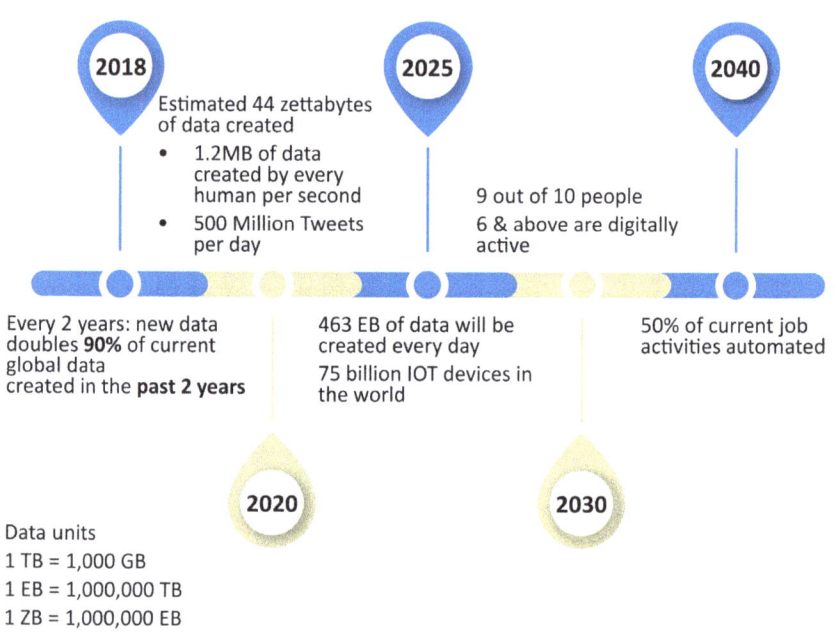

Figure 1.2: Exponential Data Growth. Data from various sources. Image from AFTEC, 2022.

sounds familiar, it is. This is a general definition for creativity.[19] Rote learning cannot save jobs. Adaptability and flexibility to deal with suddenness are crucial.

This is another way of saying that siloed teaching and learning based only on single disciplines in traditional classrooms will not be as influential and that cross-disciplinarity shall become the main theme in education. For the future economy, more sophisticated workers will need to be nurtured, workers who are educated, creative, technologically adaptable, and socially adept. STEM subjects shall be vital, yet STEM without creativity is the equivalent of following a manual step by step to produce the final product.

---

19. See introduction.

Quantumrun affirms that 'pushing young people to learn STEM without a balance of humanities courses can leave them unprepared for the interdisciplinary requirements of tomorrow's labour market'.

Quantumrun offers sobering statistics.

- By 2020, over 50% of students in Western countries will register in at least one online Massive Online Open Courses or MOOC in their transcripts.
- By 2025, virtual reality will be integrated in some form into teaching at top universities.
- By 2025, AI systems will be commonplace.
- By 2030, most universities will offer degree-backed MOOC.
- By 2040, 47% of all current jobs will be automated.

Fortunately, not all current jobs will disappear. Quantumrun on the *Future of Work* offers some examples. Persons who are specifically accountable for their actions such as judges, doctors, and other health and safety professionals will be some of the last to go the AI way. Careers in which people can build, handle, and maintain complex relationships such as caregivers, coaches, or executives in strategic planning will also not be replaced. In these jobs, analysing a large amount of data is a prerequisite; being able to handle both verbal and non-verbal cues to make sound judgement on application with high emotional intelligence mean AIs taking over will be much delayed if at all possible.

This is also to iterate that the creative profession will likewise be one in which replacement by robots will be challenging. The consulting firm supports this. In the visual arts, for example, humans still prefer to purchase human-created art forms. Clearly, even with NFTs (non-fungible tokens), humans still have the edge.

One conclusion drawn from Quantumrun is that polymaths will be very much sought after by employers for jobs that matter. A polymath typically needs several key skills to thrive. Curiosity is essential, as it drives a strong desire to learn and explore various subjects. Critical thinking allows people to analyse information and connect ideas from different fields, while adaptability helps them switch between topics and approaches as needed. Creativity is crucial for generating new ideas by combining knowledge from diverse areas.

Time-management skills are also important for effectively balancing the learning and practice of multiple disciplines. Finally, strong communication abilities enable a polymath to share knowledge and ideas clearly, whether in writing or speaking. Together, these skills empower a polymath to integrate knowledge across domains and innovate in unique ways.

Part V

Future Jobs

Frey and Osborne[20] began by recalling the various industrial revolutions (figure 1.3) and how technological progress affects the composition of employment from agrarian societies to artisanal to manufacturing, service, and management occupations.

Specifically, the first revolution involved deskilling labour, as agriculture gave way to mechanisation. Into the second one, the massive technological advancement resulted in upskilling with the invention and proliferation of new energy (electricity, gas, oil), communication (telegraph and telephone), and assembly lines (Ford motorcars), together rewriting the meaning of work and lives.

In the twentieth century, the advent and expansion of computers and the internet created office systems that lowered the cost of information-processing tasks and enhanced the demand for employees who are well educated. This third revolution hastened the pace of IT to a large extent. Now into the fourth revolution, it has given us a strong edge. It has increased productivity because of a higher level of skilled workers and a demand for higher-quality products at a faster pace.

The research by Frey and Osborne, updated in 2017, investigated the kind of actual jobs susceptible to computerisation[21] to gauge 702 occupations that currently exist in the second decade of the twenty-first century. Although their focus was on the US, findings provide general illumination in advanced and developing cities. Each occupation investigated is based on one overarching key question – whether tasks of specific jobs could be sufficiently specified enough to be automated.

Figure 1.4[22] illustrates AI takeover when problems can be clearly delineated with quantifiable criteria that can be easily evaluated. As a result, 47% of jobs in the US are at high risk of computerisation, whereas 33% will be less so. In the former category, this will include workers in production, transportation and logistics, and office administrative support, in a first wave of changes. Included in the latter are education and the arts. What we are witnessing in this report as well is that humans can excel without being overtaken by AIs and can support economic activities where the human touch is at the forefront.

---

20. C. Frey and M. Osborne, 'The Future of Employment: How Susceptible Are Jobs to Computerization?' Working Paper (2013), Oxford: Oxford Martin, https://www.oxfordmartin.ox.ac.uk/publications/the-future-of-employment.
21. The Gaussian process classifier is a classification machine learning algorithm.
22. Frey and Osborne discuss the ideas of Acemoglu and Autor (2011), highlighting the impact of automation on the labour market and the evolving nature of job susceptibility to computerisation. They explore how certain jobs, particularly those requiring creativity and human interaction, are less likely to be automated compared to routine tasks.

Figure 1.3: The Four Revolutions. Image by Queenie Ng for AFTEC, 2022.

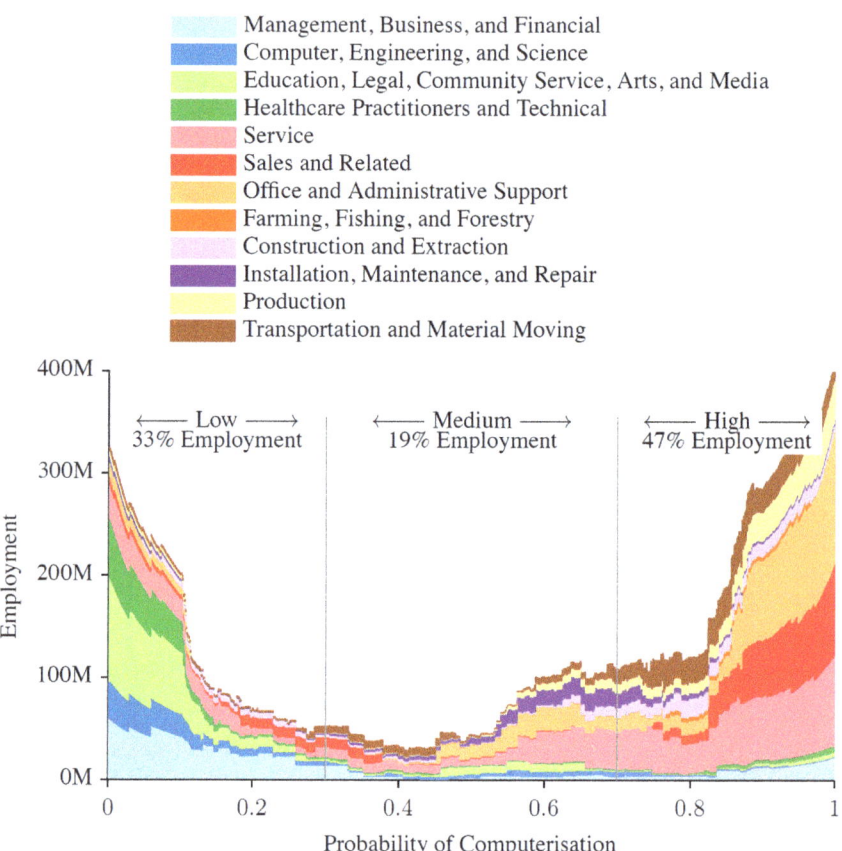

Figure 1.4: Low- to High-Risk Jobs. Courtesy of Frey and Osborne, 2013.

Table 1.1[23] is an extrapolation of details from the research giving actual jobs that may or may not be assimilated by technology. The top five resilient, low-risk occupations and bottom five easily replaceable high-risk jobs have been selected for commentary. In addition, the table includes thirteen occupations that the researchers drew from the arts out of a total of 702 estimations.

The occupations are ranked according to their probability of computerisation, from the least probable, depicted by 0 to 1 as being highly computerisable. It is compelling to observe that professions in the arts are among the former, some at relatively high positions of not being able to be computerised.

The above job estimations were predicated on three criteria and their accompanying questions:

---

23. Frey and Osborne, appendix, 57–59.

Table 1.1: Arts Jobs with Low Susceptibility to Computerisation. Image courtesy of Frey and Osborne, 2013.

Rank	Probability	Occupation
1	0.0028	Recreation therapists
2	0.003	First Line supervisors of mechanics, installers & repairers
3	0.003	Emergency management directors
4	0.0031	Mental health & substance abuse social workers
5	0.0033	Audiologists
13	0.004	Choreographers
27	0.0055	Set & exhibit designers
34	0.0068	Curators
50	0.01	Make-up artists, theatrical & performance
68	0.015	Multimedia artists & animators
72	0.015	Music directors & composers
91	0.021	Photographers
95	0.023	Arts directors
116	0.035	Craft artists
123	0.038	Writers & authors
131	0.042	Fine artists including painters, sculptors & illustrators
179	0.13	Dancers
259	0.37	Actors
698	0.99	Insurance underwriters
699	0.99	Mathematical technicians
700	0.99	Hand sewers
701	0.99	Title examiners, abstractors, searchers
702	0.99	Telemarketers

Source: Frey & Osborne 2013:37

- Dexterity
  - To what extent can employees accurately coordinate hand-eye movements to grasp, manipulate, or assemble objects?
- Creative Intelligence
  - How able are employees to come up with original ideas?
  - How able are employees to find and nurture creative ways to solve problems?
  - How able are employees to create, produce, and perform in the performing and visuals arts?
- Social Intelligence
  - To what extent are employees aware of others (verbal and non-verbal skills) and understand the reasons?
  - How able are they in negotiating human relationships?

Creative intelligence is not the sole purview of the arts although the arts are a formidable contender to be the very first port of call because of their nature. Frey and Osborne have distinctly seen this. Their interpretation is undoubtedly that the higher the dexterity, creative, and social intelligence required in occupations, the more likely job retention is assured.

To the three criteria, we can add key elements from the four major research papers in part II of this chapter. These are: relationship building; creativity; research ability; discovery and abstract thinking; analysis of a large amount of data; handling verbal and non-verbal cues to make sound judgement on application with high emotional intelligence; and complex, strategic, productive, abstract, and creative tasks or projects.

Jobs and the Arts

Reviewing the thirteen occupations pertaining to the arts (table 1.1) and then aligning them with the main research characteristics in the seven skills groups from the *World Economic Report*, it seems that these arts-related jobs have the majority of all characteristics, the difference being in emphasis based on the nature of the art form.

1. The arts naturally promote **relationship building** on the human level for the work to be achieved. This includes working professionals across the arts sector, as they create and interact with the audience and participants as part of the approach. In order to create, a deep understanding of the artistic elements in the performing and visual arts and their intricacies are important. As there are multiple perspectives to creating, the possibilities created both in the works and the understandings thereof mean there are constantly shifting relationships and adjustments.
2. Handling **verbal and non-verbal cues** to make sound judgement on application with high emotional intelligence is part of the essence of the arts, as they form the very basis of human nature. In theatre and dance, for example, choreographers, dancers, directors, and actors all communicate through dialogue for the joint objective of expressing verbal and non-verbal cues (acting) and generally non-verbal cues (dance). Reading body language is integral to the two art forms and thus expands expressive platforms to understand and build relationships. Those in fine arts and photography may speak with a client, but the eventual works through canvases or photos are non-verbal and powerful articulations of inner and outer perceptions and worlds.
3. At the very basic, **creativity** involves the physical, cognitive, and emotional human combination to realise what was not originally present. Creative professionals are highly competent in divergent–convergent thinking, and

their work reflects the inspiration, materials, and circumstances as they evolve, making these professionals highly adept in handling change.
4. Perhaps unknown to those in the non-arts sector, **research ability** is a regular skill deployed by many arts professionals, for example, in set and exhibition designers, curators, music directors and composers, writers and authors. Although inspiration is foundational to artistic creations, the basis upon which quality work is achieved is through fact-finding, probing, analysis, and iteration. The mindset will be different from that of social scientists, for instance, but the process is as rigorous, if not more so, due to the layers of nuances involved.
5. **Discovery and abstract thinking** must be counted as the strongest abilities in arts professionals. Their curiosity and inquisitiveness are formidable catalysts to push and persevere in their work, oftentimes in the face of substantial challenges, be they circumstantial or financial. Abstract thinking is the ability to capture and reshape ideas, imbuing them with a freshness that others may not see. Ambiguity is not resisted, but it is embraced as a general rule, for within the grey areas lie enormous possibilities and opportunities.
6. The daily preoccupation of make-up artists, multimedia artists and animators, and craft artists, to name a few, involve 360 analyses of a **large amount of data**, as these professionals may very well be taking the cue for creative work from broad-based concepts from directors, choreographers, conductors, and composers who begin the ideas.
7. For all thirteen professions in the arts from table 1.1, a routine is being regularly practised, one which involves **complex, strategic, productive, abstract, and creative tasks**. The interaction among front- and backstage professionals in the performing and visual arts, in literary publications and events, and in multimedia is seldom a linear path. These professionals live and flourish in constant transformations of the self because of their involvement in artistic creations.

If the arts are deemed soft and ephemeral, it is due to a lack of knowledge about their substance. With some understanding even as brief as in this discussion, it is clear that they have incontrovertible strengths and should therefore be earnestly reappraised as the core to school and professional training, including recurrent on-the-job requirements for the future.

The skills in the twenty-first century are those that speak to what the *World Economic Report*, Quantumrun, and Frey and Osborne refer to, skills that are fundamental to self-regulated learning (known as self-directed learning in Hong Kong), adaptability, flexibility of mind, social, emotional, and creative intelligence.

The arts can be powerful partners in driving creative learning forward.

2
The Power of Imagination
Redressing Poverty?

Summary

This chapter reviews poverty in its usual sense of economic deprivation and suggests that the poverty of imagination can be even more detrimental. It traces the current deficit model in learning to one which is strengths-based, deploying the imagination as a key approach.

Impressions

Shortly after AFTEC was established in late 2008 and began operations in early 2009, we were able to connect with primary schools that our artistic director, Vicki Ooi, and I, were familiar with, to understand their needs. One impression was indelible: as far as the eye could observe, in many classrooms, we witnessed children quietly and obediently learning. Subsequently, the question of *what* learning meant became the central preoccupation and many hours of thought.

However, deeper in our psyche was a second, and, in retrospect, more crucial, aspect of classroom observation. Because we are in the business of the arts, we intuitively read body language which reverberates into how we feel about witnessing children in classrooms. We felt a blankness as we recalled those classrooms. Blankness, we believed, was on two levels: expressionless faces and the uncertainty of whether the children were truly engaged in learning. Accordingly, the question of *how* students learn became the catalyst for even longer hours of discussions and eventually evolved into the company's prime focus for the arts in creative teaching and learning as a generic concept.

In 2012, the *Sm-ART Youth* project took shape as a pilot in one primary school in the heart of Wong Tai Sin, considered an economically deprived district in Hong

Kong. The eponymous chapter (chapter 4) will delve into our interpretation of learning and early thinking approaches which, over the next decade, evolved into our foundational pedagogy.

Poverty

The classes we visited were in schools that catered to children of working-class families to a large extent, children who, by definition, were far from economically well off. In this context, poverty once mentioned is almost always immediately taken at face value, of being financially poor. As of 2020, the total population living under the poverty line in Hong Kong was 1.65 million[1] or 23.6% of the population before government intervention.

Figure 2.1 shows that, in 2020, there were 274,900[2] young people below the age of eighteen living under the poverty line. Out of that, 50,000[3] lived in severely cramped conditions or subdivided flats.

From a total of eighteen districts in Hong Kong, figure 2.2 offers data for the top ten where these young people live. The graphic visualises the poverty of agency due to a lack of space.

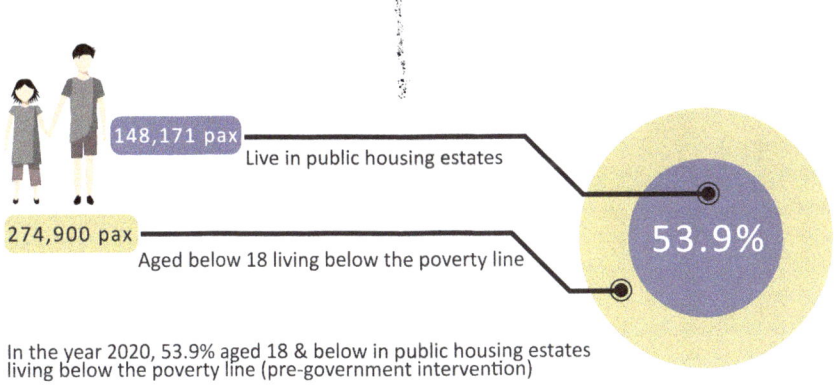

Figure 2.1: Under 18s Living in Poverty. Image from AFTEC, 2022.

---

1. 'Hong Kong Poverty Situation Report 2020', Office of the Government Economist Financial Secretary's Office and Census and Statistics Department, Government of the Hong Kong Special Administrative Region, 10 November 2021, https://www.censtatd.gov.hk/en/data/stat_report/product/B9XX0005/att/B9XX0005E2020AN20E0100.pdf.
2. Office of the Government Economist Financial Secretary's Office and Census and Statistics Department.
3. 'Children's Right Project', Society for Community Organisation (SoCO), accessed 20 February 2022, https://soco.org.hk/en/projecthome/child-rights/.

Figure 2.2: Top 10 Districts with Highest Number of Young People Living in Poverty. Image by Queenie Ng for AFTEC, 2022.

Hong Kong currently has a population of 7.5 million living in approximately 1,043 sq. km of land, the majority of whom are in Kowloon and the New Territories (near the mainland border) and fewer on Hong Kong and outlying islands.

Building upwards has been the only option. Consequently, lack of physical space is a recurrent theme and often denotes mental stress as well as a lower level of well-being. One can imagine how economic poverty, long working hours for the parents who are blue-collar workers, and their absence at home, can generate a negative impact on children. Poverty, on this level, creates vicious and intergenerational cycles that are challenging to overcome except when there are public or private interventions, generally short-term and/or palliative.

Could that be all, we wondered? Might expressionless faces also indicate disengagement, being present physically but mentally absent? In time, these vacant faces led us to conclude that another kind of poverty was in operation, one that was seldom discerned let alone considered.

By getting acquainted with the children and their parents/guardians[4] year on year with different cohorts, we gleaned a few common and recurring characteristics in their lives.

- Most come from single-parent families, some being cared for by grandparents or even guardians.
- Most live in public housing estates or subdivided units near their schools.[5]
- Most walk to and from school daily.
- Many attend after-school activities in schools as they are free or, for those who could manage, tuition in core subjects.
- At weekends, they usually play near their homes.

From this, other discoveries surfaced:

- For many, their social lives are restricted to districts where they live.
- Many have not been out of their districts very much, Hong Kong Island being a little-known part of the territory, and trams[6] are novelties.
- Gaming on smartphones is a routine way to pass time.
- Aside from music and visual arts subjects in schools, they seldom attend cultural outings.[7]
- On cultural outings we engaged them in, they are often carsick, perhaps as a result of not being in vehicles often.

---

4. Three times a year.
5. Forty per cent of local schools in Hong Kong are inside public housing estates or beside them.
6. Trams run only on Hong Kong Island and are the least expensive form of transportation locally.
7. AFTEC's internal survey of 107 students in October 2021 revealed that those who attended cultural outings did so no more than twice per year.

In other words, in addition to economic poverty leading to a shortage of physical space, the paucity of mental stimulation and exposure has cultivated a limited habit of mind and, in time, of being. Aside from financial hardship, cognitive disadvantages and spiritual[8] absenteeism may be the cause of 'poverty of imagination'.

When one is in a fixed routine over a long time – and early childhood constitutes the formative years – habit becomes a great deadener. The habit of mind is linear, hopes and aspirations few and far between. Reception and replication of information become the norm. With this habit come other related responses.

Poverty of Imagination

One frequently given response to various questions asked of the underserved children we know is 'I don't know'. Opinions are sparse and articulation negligible. Feelings are challenging to locate, much less to express. On days, the children can be so physically tired their eyes glaze over with an 'out to lunch' sign prominently displayed. As dismal as economic poverty is the poverty of the imagination. In the end, these children may not see alternative ways of living, ways to gain a better quality of being because they are not exposed to, nor do they understand, possibilities and probabilities.

What might be the cause?

Education systems in many advanced cities take a second Industrial Revolution approach (see chapter 1) of creating mass education cutting across a range of socio-economic status. One phenomenon in many Asian cities, which is pervasive in Hong Kong too, is the single-minded idea that academic results matter above everything else in young lives. After school, tuition is very much alive as a result, all in the name of getting ahead in examinations. While this is not always detrimental, the mindset is habituated to one in which the willingness to take risks is low and the intent to find correct answers high.

This somewhat linear habit of mind dictates that 'more is best'. Learning is necessarily fast-paced, and teaching to the test or offering post-school tuition is often a requirement for low performers in weak subjects. By and large, teaching is prescriptive. Learning is often at lower-level thinking, as time is of the essence. Teaching is along the traditional paradigm of mainly closed questions, single correct answers, and the teacher is the single harbinger of knowledge. Learning results in surface, formulaic information, giving rise to the addiction of present bias and developing a habit of mind that is attuned to short-termism.

This vicious cycle of ever-expanding teaching to the test and tuition concludes in what we refer to as a 'deficit model of being' (figure 2.3), in which getting the

---

8. In the secular sense.

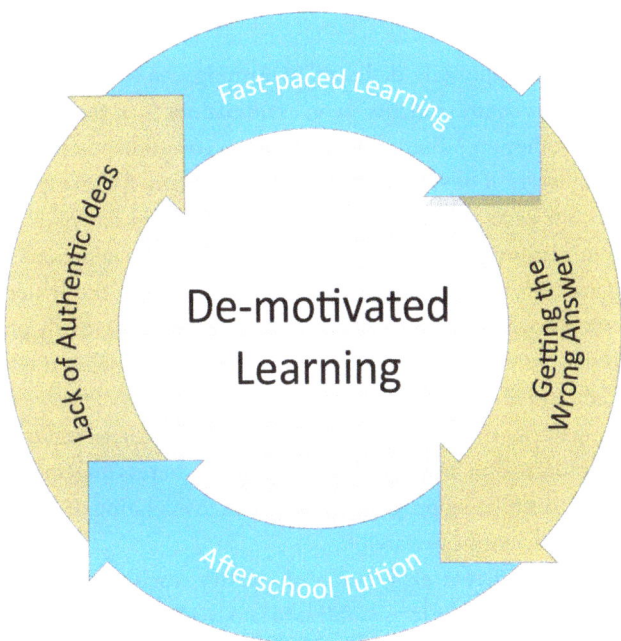

Figure 2.3: Deficit Model of Being. Image from AFTEC, 2024.

wrong answers and not being smart in core subjects in examinations at school indicate a student of 'lower' ability. Unsurprisingly, de-motivation often happens. For many, there is just no point. The world of electronic games is a far better place to be.

While studying hard for academic achievement is not in and of itself negative, a more well-rounded approach is often better for a population of students of different abilities and interests.

Who is responsible for the poverty of imagination? It is perhaps, first and foremost, the cycle of life – from agrarian to industrial society, efficiency, and looking after the burgeoning population – we manage breadth better than we do depth. In school systems that oftentimes cater to the average student population for administrative exigency, we prioritise basic provision for the here and now in favour of a future we are unable to imagine positively. Thus, we train the trainers in a certain way. Hence, parents have certain aspirations. We are all responsible.

If a narrow habit of mind is straitjacketing in some ways, an expansive one is a balance we are in need of. Instead of a *vicious* cycle of demotivation, is it possible to generate a *virtuous* one, in which a fixed mindset gives way to one of growth?

Imagination

If a young person is supposedly 'deficient' in learning, can we create an 'asset model of being', where how *smart* students are in examinations is, at the very least, viewed next to *how* smart they are? There are many known government strategies for alleviating financial poverty. If poverty of imagination is ingrained in many young people, how then does one develop strategies to rise above and break free of it? One solution is to offer them a large palette of imagination. Yet, what is imagination?

The Oxford English Dictionary defines the imagination as 'the power or capacity to form internal images or ideas of objects and situations not actually present to the senses'.[9] This may be misconstrued as meaning that the imagination is solely in the realm of the arts and the sole property of artists whose flights of fancy take off easily.

Debunking the myth is Einstein's often quoted lines which attest to the imagination in the scientific realm: 'For knowledge is limited, whereas imagination embraces the entire world, stimulating progress, giving birth to evolution. It is, strictly speaking, a real factor in scientific research'.[10]

Relevant to the current exploration of creative teaching and learning is this decoding by one of the most formidable educators/philosophers of the twentieth century, the late Maxine Greene, founder and director of the Center for Social Imagination, the Arts and Education at Teachers College, Columbia University.

In *Releasing the Imagination: Essays on Education, the Arts, and Social Change*,[11] she explains that the 'imagination is what, above all, makes empathy possible. It is what enables us to cross empty spaces between ourselves and those we teachers have called "other" over the years.' Greene strongly asserted that, of all our cognitive abilities, imagination is the key that allows us to believe in alternative realities. The purpose of creative learning, empathy, and other realities matter hugely, for it is they that tie the arts closest to being human and transport us to beyond the immediacy of physical living for future possibilities.

Far beyond imaginative skills being the staple of artists and scientists, there is one further sphere of influence with implications for our future. The profusion of challenges that the human race finds itself in in this century is urgently in need of better, more, and diverse solutions, particularly in the light of the COVID pandemic that has become endemic.

---

9. 'Imagination', *Oxford English Dictionary*, accessed 22 February 2022, https://www.oed.com/search/dictionary/?scope=Entries&q=imagination.
10. Albert Einstein, *Einstein on Cosmic Religion and Other Opinions and Aphorisms* (Philosophical Library, 1940).
11. Maxine Greene, *Releasing the Imagination: Essays on Education, the Arts, and Social Change* (Jossey-Bass, 1995).

While many are turning their attention to global change, Mulgan of Demos Helsinki believes it is the deficit of social imagination[12] which is central to human problems and the reason we are struggling to envision positive alternatives.

Due to the ever-increasing complexities in life, we need imagination and its wealth of possibilities to help us solve issues. Children today are the adults of the future. Poverty of imagination will be detrimental not only to their personal growth but more imperatively to the societies they live in and the generations to come. An imaginative society can create far more opportunities for a brighter future. One with an impoverished imagination will continue living in its own 'subdivided flat'. One with the power of imagination opens doors to becoming a creative city.

---

12. 'The Imaginary Crisis (and How We Might Quicken Social and Public Imagination)', UCL Science, Technology, Engineering and Public Policy Working Paper Series, April 2020, https://www.ucl.ac.uk/steapp/sites/steapp/files/2020_04_geoff_mulgan_swp.pdf.

Part B: Passage

3
In Praise of Gaps
Programming with Voids

Summary

Chapter 3 gives an in-depth view of AFTEC's programming rationale, which began as nothing more than a concept. Using analogies of nothingness, diverse signature projects and insights are introduced.

Part I focuses on gaps being regarded as opportunities with four questions as guiding principles for development. Part II explores learning in a proper theatre for authentic experiences and where arts education is as valued as programming. Part III interprets voids as the intellectual need for role models and the development of plays from fifteen global jurisdictions for creative thinking.

Part IV takes first steps into cultivating a habit of mind that is reflective, to enrich passive mindsets. Part V crosses sectors into health care, where medical undergraduates embrace the arts in an otherwise pure scientific space. Part VI examines a problematic and a successful cross-sector project, calling for further collaboration to pool professional expertise. Part VII concludes the chapter by lamenting the lack of local research for programme planning, a blank that needs to be filled.

Part I

The London tube is a historical icon. Opened in January 1863, as a result of the first Industrial Revolution propelling the advancement of steam engines, the Metropolitan Railway became a pioneer in underground travel. It was not until 1969 that the now familiar announcement 'mind the gap' at tube stops was heard, reminding passengers of the space between the train and the platform.

That announcement alerts the public to a possible risk, that of falling into the void which we have to be cautious about. Gaps need not be ascribed as failings; they can be opportunities to create something of substance to fill the void. We believe that the arts have a civic role to play and a positive impact to make. This chapter gives the backstory to the potential of gaps for change.

The initial consideration was the venue that we are resident in for eight weeks a year. We were awarded a venue by the government's Leisure and Cultural Services Department in 2009 through its Venue Partnership Scheme. That was first time ever in Hong Kong's history when performing venues were opened for bidding by professional performing arts organisations[1] to produce work for a short time annually on a three- to four-year cycle. Considering that City Hall, the grand matriarch of venues, opened in 1962, and fourteen others were built since then, venue partnership was a very long time coming.

Opened in December 1990,[2] the Sai Wan Ho Civic Centre is one of the oldest multi-use facilities in the city. The venue was, until 2009, primarily a focal point for amateur Cantonese opera performances and concerts. I clearly remember that, after one year at the venue, a somewhat relieved sound technician candidly proclaimed, in hushed tones, that he had grown weary of the same sounds day in and day out and was all too glad to have programming diversity. This was one change we had not anticipated though delighted it offered respite to someone.

One of the considerations for the civic centre as the desired venue is geographical. We found potential in a venue located in the Eastern District, where 40% of the population on Hong Kong Island lived. It was, however, the demographic features that are the greater pull, or rather, where the gap is situated. Social economic status varied widely in this area, from those living under the poverty line to the very privileged, to more of those in the mid- to lower status than those in the higher income brackets. We wondered what we could do about those who had little exposure to the arts and, more importantly, how the gap could be narrowed.

To date, we have welcomed almost 300,000 participants and members of the audience, both in the theatre venue and in external sites. The majority are from lower socio-economic backgrounds.

In a city where market trend, and hence market demand, was and still is, by and large the vanguard for driving ideas, the immediate discussion with Vicki Ooi, our artistic director, was to follow or not to follow. After some soul-searching, the decision was to provide alternatives. The third rationale for choosing the civic centre was our desire to become a learning organisation and not a producing theatre.[3]

---

1. Quota for venue partnership ranged from fifty-six days per annum in urban sites to 140 for regional ones, the larger companies commanding more days.
2. Major renovation of the building started in April 2022, thirty-two years after the building initially began operations.
3. A producing theatre creates and produces its own theatre productions, and this is mainly its core work.

Eponymously, a learning organisation learns from what it is unfamiliar with and/or is currently non-existent, be it knowledge or skills or attitudes. As such, even in those early days, programming was already learning-based and -led. Theatre productions were, of course, integrated into the plan, but they too were the means to educational ends.

A list of questions followed. Taking the population fabric as the key motivator, what might be essential? How could we create more opportunities for those who are unable or unwilling to come to the arts? How could we transform the once sole operatic vibes in the venue into one with a panoply of learning in and through the arts? How could we advance the deeper aspects of the arts – and not just performance – by making arts-in-education and creative learning the cornerstone of who we are in the longer term instead of focusing on arts promotion to fill seats in the shorter run?

In other words, we were exploring how we could sow the seeds to cultivate an audience of active participants and not passive consumers distanced from the magic, meaning, and value of the arts.

The answer we eventually arrived at was to spend time and energy locating the missing links as opposed to continuing the prolific programming that many arts organisations were already growing with success and gusto in the arts scene. Gaps could be large ones, as they could likewise be crevices. Ultimately, they are passages from what is not there to unknown prospects. These are the ones we were and still are very interested in.

Gaps can also be interstices, a word applied in medicine, meaning 'a small space between things, especially between things that are usually closely spaced, such as cells'.[4] The interstitial space, therefore, is where fluids filter, flow, and are reabsorbed into the body. In our realm, the body represents the integrity of the arts, and while performances and exhibitions have their formidable and recognised presence, arts teaching and learning are the crucial interstices which are less pronounced and less thought of yet of immense importance. Like the fluids, learning in and through the arts are interstitial places of possibilities, without which the body does not function to the best of its potential.

In retrospect, since 2009, four key questions evolved as guiding principles:

- How can the general concept of theatre productions find space for learning?
- What has fallen short in schools and other institutions in arts education, and how are we able to help?
- Why is it that non-arts sectors do not seem to embrace the arts?

---

4. 'Interstice', MedicineNet, accessed 1 July 2024, https://www.medicinenet.com/interstice/definition.htm.

- How can the intention for deep-seated arts learning be realised and sustained?

There is a fifth interstitial concern since COVID-19 surfaced in 2020: the way digitalisation may be explored. For the purpose of this chapter, gaps and resultant opportunities are discussed in the following sections to chart our trajectory, each illustrated by specific projects, leaving descriptive factual details in the appendix.

Part II

Theatre Productions and Creative Learning

From Page to Stage, Classics for Juniors

From Page to Stage, now in its seventeenth year in 2025, began life as an experiment to situate learning at the core of theatre productions. Since its launch in 2009, with an adaptation of Bram Stoker's *Dracula*, learning elements, including a pedagogy, formed the core for schools' participation alongside pre-show and post-show sessions in school premises, with the addition of onstage interactive learning after each show.

In Hong Kong, before 2009, venues for longer runs for the arts-in-education were impossible. With the venue partnership scheme, the situation improved somewhat. From an initial five shows in 2009, the last *Page to Stage* production before COVID exploded clocked twenty-eight sell-out school shows. Numbers, at any rate, are secondary. We wanted to begin nurturing a critical mass of teachers and students who would return year on year[5] and grow to love the theatre and its learning moments. Often in the arts, learning is perceived to be secondary to main theatre productions and thus given a much lower priority. We wanted to see if a more positive outlook would be possible.

Whereas schools mainly saw AFTEC as the platform for English learning through drama, we felt that the theatre with all its professional facilities could provide even more learning beyond simply language acquisition. Of course, drama could be toured in schools, but since we have the actual provision of a ready-made professional theatre venue and professionals to boot, the experiences could be so much more engaging if learning and staging were on equal footing. As such, in the past decade and more, the principle was that we would not tour schools but rather attract them into experience and engage in an authentic theatre setting.

---

5. Schools have been returning to the *From Page to Stage* programme on average for seven years, some from ten to thirteen years.

As a learning organisation, we realise that learning will need to be developed, bolstered, and integrated into the arts. The advantages of this move are

- to ensure the alignment of the stage and learning, enabling the latter to become as definitive as the productions themselves; and
- to explore how a pedagogy can be developed from productions that will benefit teachers and learners at various levels to meet their needs.

After a few years of experience and feedback, we realised that a more elementary level of theatre in English would be helpful to younger audiences (Primary 4 to 6) and those with more basic English language comprehension ability in secondary schools. The gap here was one of comprehension and grasp of concepts.

Classics for Juniors (figure 3.1) for upper primary to junior secondary was created in 2014 as complementary to the secondary level of *From Page to Stage*. As another foundational quality principle, there was every consciousness not to lower the level of difficulty or the quality of the production and its ideas. We felt that being condescending would be detrimental to the value of authentic theatre with the audience and learning undermined in the end. As a result, for both programmes, we offered diverse content levels.

Figure 3.1: *Classics for Juniors' Walking the Amazon*. Photo by Cheung Chi Wai for AFTEC, 2021.

As the theatre programme grew, we began to appreciate that, although there was interaction in schools with students and teachers, actual application before and after being at performances was crucial to more engaged learning. In 2015, the *Creative Box*, a non-venue partner programme, was added in tandem with *Classics for Juniors*, so that role-modelling by professionals became the catalyst and subsequent inspiration for young people as they turned their minds and hands to theatre.

Modelling Through Professionals

Plays for Young People

As part of the strategy to complement essential learning in the arts, we considered connecting theatre productions with currently unavailable yet related facets to shore up theatre learning further. If theatre production at different levels for the *provision* of theatre knowledge is regarded as the horizontal axis on the graph, then the gap on the vertical axis is the *cultivation* of that knowledge in critical thinking and the analysis of plays.

This seems the natural extension, one that will enrich learning about, and through, theatre to a level not previously imagined for us. Being able to learn earlier than formal academic courses in drama and theatre will mean participants getting ahead, growing in understanding of the greater values of theatre. We felt, and still feel, that readiness is not always equated with age; when there is the chance, programmes need to be offered. Additionally, plays are so much more than entertainment and enjoyment. They support the cultivation of a discerning audience (see chapter 9).

In our sojourns into secondary schools, we witnessed an abundance of plays written by students and/or teachers as part of the language arts curriculum. As an adjunct, these plays are frequently performed in schools and for the purpose of inter-school drama competitions, an event popular with schools. Their efforts are truly commendable, especially given that many teachers are neither trained in playwriting nor are they necessarily from a drama background. To date, many enquiries still come from schools asking how more plays can be made available, as ideas from teachers are somewhat finite and themes ever diminishing.

We could have easily directed teachers to online plays and bookshops, and the matter would have been solved. Notwithstanding that easy solution, we considered whether we could support learning diversity by introducing plays that were at once relevant to young lives with themes that went beyond a simple black-and-white plot. These plays would accommodate issues to be analysed and discussed among students, all written to a high standard. Hong Kong is a compact city and with decades of intense focus on Japanese and Korean cultures, we likewise wondered if horizons

Figure 3.2: Turkish Playwright Hasan Erkek with Emerging Translators. Photo by Cheung Chi Wai for AFTEC, 2018.

could be widened by encompassing other cultures since we live in a globalised world. In other words, what about plays from the international stage?

Plays for Young People materialised as a result of these questions. It is now into the third series,[6] and fifteen international playwrights, including our own artistic director, have since travelled to Hong Kong, one play each explicitly written for young people. Themes range from friendship to divorce to the environment to identity and internet fixation, fantasy to real worlds, monologues to those with a large cast.

Playwrights were invited to the city to discuss their plays in-depth over days with emerging translators (figure 3.2), another loophole in the city. Much more serious attention can be paid to this group of potential professionals by the sector. In translation degrees and courses, play translation is seldom a core focus, and Hong Kong's core of quality translators is still comparatively few and far between.

This entire sector of potential professionals has not been given due regard although translated plays[7] are of much value to us in Hong Kong. Through translators, we are all the more able to expand our knowledge, views, culture, and understanding

---

6. Launched in 2016, a second series was completed in 2018; the third started in 2021 online as a pandemic measure.
7. Vicki Ooi with Jane Lai were two of the earliest proponents who imported Western plays for translation into Hong Kong. Cantonese was the core dialect used, as this is spoken here.

of others. While fiction and non-fiction abound in Chinese, plays in translations are comparatively sporadic though the scene has been developing in recent years.

On this front, we have been attempting to deal with somewhat embarrassing feedback from overseas playwrights not once, but twice: that emerging translators here have only superficial interest and understanding of plays and of theatre, let alone arts and culture.

While more have been encouraged to attend the five-day intensive learning and discussions with the playwrights, eventually prior to the playwrights' arrival, an in-house workshop and pre-tasks were developed to be part of the mandatory training. This ensures that, at the very least, emerging translators are able to meet some of the expectations.

It is, finally, a lacuna that affects all of Hong Kong if we are intent on higher-quality arts learning. How do we ensure that arts education and arts-in-education programmes offered are sequential and go beyond merely passive audienceship or the singular post-event talk a few times a year at performances and exhibitions, culminating in minimal understanding? Chapter 10 discusses these issues.

Young Theatre Makers

The route that we have undertaken to plug this omission is through *Young Theatre Makers*, launched in 2017. Engaging young people through these plays felt like the natural next step.

There were two approaches: stage the productions ourselves with professional actors and have young people as the audience or, the better and more fulfilling step of giving these international plays to young people to experiment with the text, explore their thinking alongside the intentions of the playwrights and their perspectives on common issues.

Due to a limited quota of days at the venue partnership and restricted resources, the first idea of extending *From Page to Stage* was not feasible. Even if it had been, the decision was that direct engagement by young people with the plays would be the richer and more meaningful alternative.

To achieve this, *Young Theatre Makers'* objective is in textual understanding and critical thinking rather than just performance. Discussion is the core (figure 3.3), and therefore only excerpts, and not the full play, are staged by students. It is the interaction between teachers and students across institutions that form the backbone of the programme. This has turned out to be much needed and appreciated.

Figure 3.3: *Young Theatre Makers*: Pairing Schools for Collective Thinking. Photo by Cheung Chi Wai for AFTEC, 2019.

Capacity-Building in Young People

Sm-ART Youth

AFTEC is the acronym of The Absolutely Fabulous Theatre Connection. Our co-chair, Marissa Fung Shaw, subsequently in a brilliant stroke, coined a second interpretation to reimagine the acronym delineating our mission: Arts for Transformative Educational Change.

While we are cognisant of the fact that transformation is a huge concept and aspiration, over the course of time, the evidence means that transformation is possible. It just needs constant planning, unfailing perseverance, and continuous implementation with no mission drift.

For this to occur, we concluded that one-off events and activities should be kept to a minimum. For our purpose, to measure shifts in a two-hour workshop seems disingenuousness, because change does take time. In addition to the three-year timeline of the venue partnership, which allowed us to experiment over a longer period in theatre in the main, *Sm-ART Youth*,[8] was the first formal, non-theatre-based learning platform to explore changing mindsets.

Programming per se is a relatively straightforward endeavour once the concept is sound. Implementation is always the greater and harder reality. In all our experiences in filling gaps, changing mindsets has recurrently been the hardest undertaking. Hong Kong being a pragmatic if not sometimes utilitarian society makes the task more.

Sm-ART Youth has its own dedicated chapter (chapter 4), as it is the foundation upon which our fundamental beliefs are conceptualised, explored, revisited, and adjusted. That project's life span from 2012 to 2020 and its inquiry into attendant gaps are analysed there.

Bravo! Hong Kong Youth Theatre Awards

Fully realising that upper primary to secondary school are the crucial years to support young people's creative learning, we created the next project to influence young lives aged between thirteen and nineteen. *Bravo! Hong Kong Youth Theatre Awards* was a nine-year journey from 2013 to 2021, delayed by the pandemic by a year.

Sponsored by the Lee Hysan Foundation, an equally strong strategic partner, *Bravo* was conceived because we believed that even more solid training in schools for young actors was in demand, particularly for those who wished to elevate their abilities to higher levels from Hong Kong to overseas.

In its early stages, the Hong Kong Academy for Performing Arts accepted applications in theatre training from diploma onwards and then later, from foundation to bachelor and then master of fine arts degrees. Application was only for those who were completing their secondary schooling and as such would not have included those who were unsure if they would be suited for degree programmes. Hence, *Bravo* became one golden opportunity to test one's mettle.

For us, the second and greater reason for the project was how capacity-building in life skills could likewise be incorporated into acting.

From *Sm-ART Youth*, we were made keenly aware of the need to support young children to deal with life's challenges, offer expressive platforms, know themselves, and seed experiences to understand their personalities and abilities for personal growth. In *Bravo*, the age cohort was older, and hence the ability to coexist well with others socially – especially in times of duress – was a fundamental skill given the seeming increase in the stresses and strains all round.

---

8. For nine- to eleven-year-olds in upper primary.

Theatre and plays are mirrors held up to life. Irrespective of language or culture, plays portray human beings as they relate to themselves introspectively (monologues), and to each other in an array of relationships (dialogues), wonderful, conflicting, disastrous, and uplifting.

Very broadly, through staged plays, we see human successes and failures at work. Guarantees of the former and/or alleviation of the latter are beyond our control. Perhaps living vicariously through others (characters) may give young people a route into understanding and change. Could we not attempt to extricate examples *of* life from theatre to support young people *in* life through acting? The life skills we believed that would stand the young people in good stead included perseverance, commitment, discipline, communication, motivation, open-mindedness, and others (see chapter 5).

In the schools we know, we did not see many life skills at work on a regular basis. Experiences in the arts and learning reveal that performance-based teaching is often the singular aim for acting. Primary and secondary education are the normal nurturing ground for initial interest in the arts and drama. Product-oriented teaching is, in general, the sole preoccupation of teachers and schools, thereby making training and its components of lesser importance. Furthermore, the speed at which shows are put together is astounding.

So we asked: what if the *process* is at the forefront and foregrounds the eventual product? Fast-paced experience habituates young minds, what if a slow-motion lens is added to the process? What can change? And what can processes achieve in fostering life skills and values in a young person long before the product is delivered? We likewise wondered if there is a way quality can be locked in at each step, enabling the product to be even more exceptional.

We believe they need to be asked because there is, first and foremost, the constant assumption that self esteem, self-confidence, collaboration, and motivation are the natural results of participating in a play. To what extent is this true, and can we begin to map this out instead of simply relying on anecdotes? Innumerable questions crowded our mind. The journey of the four *Bravo* cohorts from 2013 to 2020[9] was invaluable in finding answers (see chapter 5).

There were key process elements that we decided to traverse and which in time we relied on, one such being reflective practice as cardinal. In the process of the training, the ability to deeply reflect is a constant, so much so that it has been included as one of our organisation's eventual tools and skills.

Reflection is the time for the physical and mental selves to stop achieving the performance intention at breakneck speed and turn instead to the introspective self at a steadier pace. As we embarked on *Sm-ART Youth* and *Bravo*, it became evident

---

9. Cohort 4 from 2019 to 2020 was severely disrupted by the social unrest and COVID.

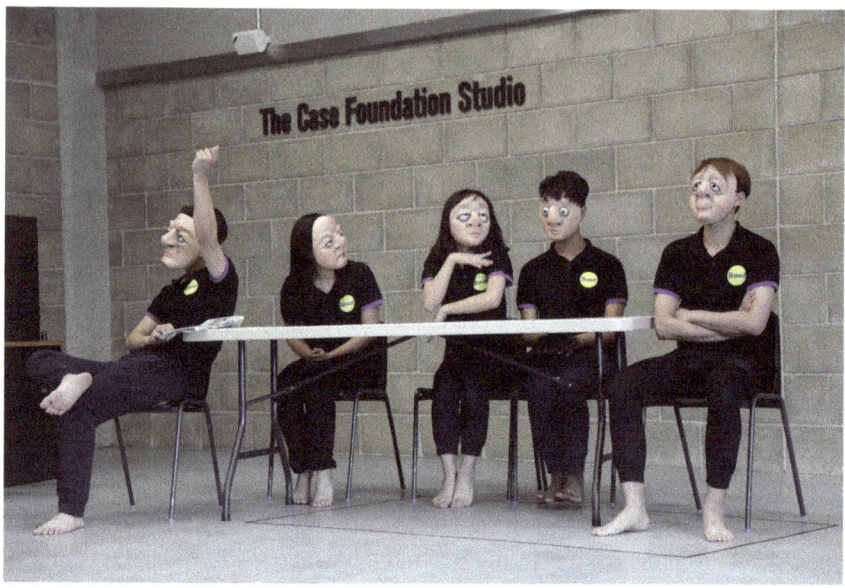

Figure 3.4: *Bravo! Hong Kong Youth Theatre Awards* at LAMDA, London. Photo by George Chao for AFTEC, 2018.

that formulating questions and then asking them out loud were in no way simple tasks. Consequently, we provided a series of questions to guide participants.

In *Bravo*, from auditions at the outset to full-day acting training over a few weeks, to rehearsals, the theatre production, and then overseas higher-level training (figure 3.4), reflective questions were scaffolded to encourage thinking. Additionally, the project was intentionally offered over eighteen months, to give much-needed time and space to digest the learning and to cognitively and mentally understand it.

As life skills and values were foundational, young actors admitted[10] to *Bravo* were given room to bridge training to their daily lives. Theatre is about life and living after all and should not be disengaged or disconnected from it.

The majority of young actors were from local schools, and like students in the *Sm-ART Youth* project, the actors were unused to reflection in general. Hong Kong's education system, in general, has always been one in which a one-way, top-down, high-stakes testing and teaching approach mattered. What if we could cultivate a habit of mind to think critically, regard matters from multiple perspectives, and give evidence-based reasoning outside of formal studies? Those from financially

---

10. Each cohort accepted a maximum of fifty young actors as a quality goal.

underprivileged backgrounds are at a disadvantage at the start, since their lives are of a lower quality all round, relatively speaking.

At the outset, after each week of workshops in April then August, reflections sent in were only a sentence or two from the underserved young actors. As time passed, particularly for those who made it overseas to LAMDA in London or Cloud Gate Dance School in Taipei, reflections became much deeper, and the length of writing increased, phenomenally for some. With richer experiences came more questions and with them, more reasons to think through matters and concerns. Put another way, the habit of mind to be able to think well independently is an indicator of success. Acting and performance are only the icing on the cake (again, see chapter 5).

One of the main factors why *Bravo* actors accomplished quite a lot and were motivated to do so in the programme emanated from a single phenomenon: working over a long period with other passionate young people.

Cohort after cohort, one major difference discerned by many of the young actors is the environment and ambiance from workshops to rehearsals to cultural outings. They were among those who wanted to act without having their desire diluted by others who were on stage as a result of a mandatory school show or competition. The deep desire to learn together as a collaborative meant the focus was total. And each step along the way in the process pointed to yet another discovery about the self, the skills, and the thinking.

Because we worked on the basis of challenging the actors, we brought out the very best in those who wanted to learn. Because of this, the upshot from time to time was the fact that we created gaps ourselves – there was attrition for those who were unable or unwilling to commit. Notwithstanding this attrition, instead of turning to those who had left and lost, we reframed our thinking to further encourage those who forged ahead with persistence. For this, we are immensely grateful to our strategic partner, Lee Hysan Foundation, which understood that scaling the mountain of quality is of greater importance than counting the climbers.

A third area for change comes in exposure to arts and cultural events. In Hong Kong, by far the most popular form of entertainment is the musical. From schools' own performances to professional public productions, more often than not, the audience will flock to musicals. For young people this is no exception. This experience sometimes includes the occasional foray into other art forms via school trips for pre-tertiary-level students. And here lies an issue: one-off visits may well fall short of cultivating a true interest in the arts.

Bravo's overseas learning is an attempt to counterbalance the situation to some extent. It is not that Hong Kong's cultural life is thin; far from it: the profusion of daily events speaks volumes of the enthusiasm locally. The challenge is that the hectic lives of young people both in school and outside seldom warrant enough head space and mindful focus to really understand and embrace the arts. That is why we opted to go abroad for weeks at a time.

Context matters.

In a day in Taipei or London, higher-level training is mixed with morning group get-togethers in the student hostel, onsite acting training, day-end group peer support, and reflections in journals. Regular cultural outings are interspersed and form part of the learning. Reviewing their thinking in their journals has been a great delight to us. Meagre sentences at the start of training in Hong Kong more than a year ago will, more often than not, give rise to long paragraphs, if not pages, of their day, their learning, their emotions, and their insights. Excerpts can be read in chapter 5.

Ironically, this away time gave them the luxury of time on their side and space to breathe and think. Many of these young actors blossomed. Imagine if actual schooling would permit this in the city: what transformations would students be capable of? Amazingly, many report to us that, years after graduating from *Bravo*, they still practise a reflective habit of mind in their studies and work lives. At the very least, this seed has been planted and will grow.

Cross-Sector Learning

Medical Humanities

Shortly before *Bravo* was discussed in 2011, our intention of capacity-building for young people through the arts was deliberated with our first cross-sector partner at the Li Ka Shing Faculty of Medicine at the University of Hong Kong. The performing arts module of the Medical Humanities (part of the Medical Ethics and Humanities Unit), a credit-bearing course, took off in the 2012 academic year with a first cohort of 200-plus Year 1 undergraduates.[11]

It has been a continuing fallacy that only those converted to the high altar of the arts will derive pleasure and knowledge from them and see their value. It is saddening that this has not been disproved. The Lascaux cave paintings in France, those in Dunhuang, Indian dance dramas, Grecian rituals, the ebullience of Chinese culture and all the folkloric music in the world must in some way prove that the arts are part of all our lives and not only those who earned a degree in theatre, passed a dance exam, or achieved a licentiate of music at the age of ten.

Apparently not.

We pondered which non-arts professions deal with being human and may appear to be the antithesis to the arts? Having had personal and vicarious knowledge

---

11. In the 2024 academic year, intake rose to approximately 300 students.

of the medical sector, thoughts naturally turned there. Could both ends of the spectrum – the arts and sciences – be entwined, or never would the twain meet? This bifurcation of the sciences and the arts in a world of accelerating complexity in the twenty-first century prompted us to take a leap of faith into the seemingly impossible.

Could medical students benefit from the humanities and the human perspectives of the arts? If doctors in waiting could have the benefit of a human-centred existence beyond textbook medical studies, would it motivate them to be more empathetic and enhance their medical professionalism? As medical students have some of the brightest minds for examinations, would the arts complement their learning, furthering the best of both worlds?

These and other curiosities drove and cemented what is perhaps one of the most fortuitous collaborations. In 2011, the discussion with the late Professor L. C. Chan, who headed the creation of the Medical Humanities for the faculty, was a meeting of true minds.

The aim of the entire Medical Humanities curriculum – of which the performing arts is one module – is to ensure that students are 'sensitised to the experiences of patients and are able to meet the expectations and demands of society, as well as being taught to the highest ethical and professional standards'.[12] The faculty saw the need to underpin the practice of medicine by underscoring the importance of human and humane aspects. We were able to extract the fundamental powers of the arts essentially rooted in what it means to be human and created the curriculum for the performing arts module. By doing so, we hope that the practice of medicine is strengthened.

Year 1 students were offered a choice in drama (figure 3.5) or music from 2012, experiential anatomy added for year 2 students the year after. Now moving into the fourteenth year, and chaired by Dr. Julie Chen as the convenor, Year 1 has seen music replaced by two programmes for drama, one in communications and the other in movement and relationships.

In the beginning, it was a culture shock to the undergraduates' science-trained minds. For many students, medical school has been the single goal all their lives, driven by parental nudging, or a calling, or both. Yet we saw for ourselves that many are actually accomplished musicians and keen amateur visual artists.

As we appeared in their classrooms, we could almost hear the silent incredulity. As workshops are interactive, all furniture is removed, and a gaping space is left to be filled by the participants themselves. That is discomfort zone number one. Growing up desk-bound has its drawbacks when the familiar is jettisoned.

---

12. 'Centre for the Humanities and Medicine', Centre for the Humanities and Medicine, The University of Hong Kong, accessed 2 July 2022, https://chm.hku.hk/medicalhum.html.

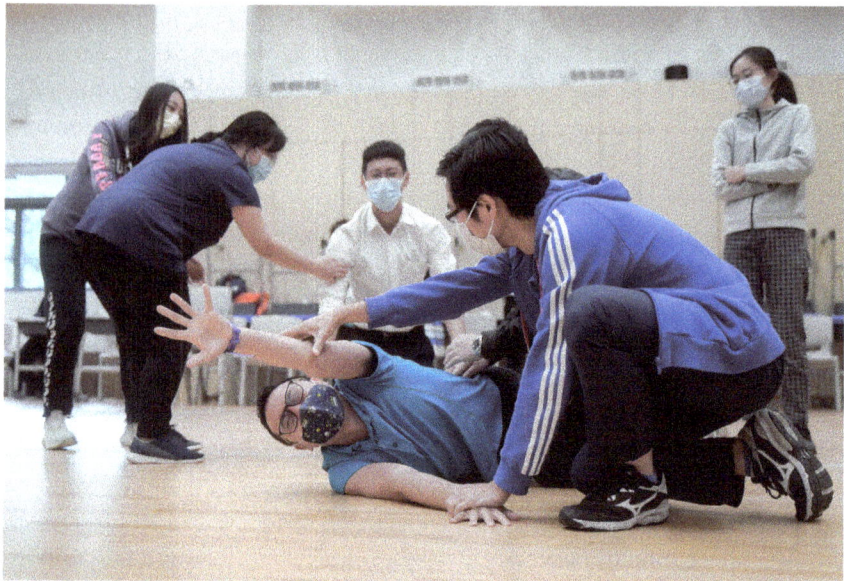

Figure 3.5: Medical Humanities Drama Workshop. Photo from AFTEC, 2022.

In the first two years or so, body language displayed by some students clearly showed a natural defensiveness and behind that, anxiety. If students felt out of place, we were likewise fish out of water. Working with scientists was new to us. The difference is that to us it was exciting, even as anxiety would grip us occasionally.

Some students, fortunately, are in their element, and these are generally returnees from overseas boarding schools or from international schools in Hong Kong. Year on year, with each new cohort, these privileged students could be identified within ten minutes of the workshop starting. They are much more proactive, willing to try, and will take risks. Local students are more passive, need much more prompting, and prefer to stay safe.

The second discomfort zone for participants was playing games and finding themselves having to physically and mentally adjust to a lack of detailed rules and the correct answers. The most indicative phenomenon is the simple walking activity as warm-up. Within the large space, inevitably they would walk in a circle in the same direction tightly bound together like a school of tuna offering safety in numbers. This is in no way to undermine these young people. In fact, that gap helped us to see where and how we needed to change to encourage them to explore themselves.

The pre-tasks completed, they were much relieved to be able to return to the normality of textual analysis. Without exception, they were very intelligent, so in the face of a short play script, an unconventional text, they rose to the occasion. The subsequent improvisation back in the surrounding space on their feet returned them into the realm of discomfort.

As the sole member from the arts sector on the committee that oversaw the Medical Humanities, I too was thrown into a semi-unknown world. Any initial trepidation though was replaced quickly by an adventurer's excitement. One by one, the doctors' generosity of spirit and accommodating mindsets meant I understood them much more, not purely as scientists but also as individuals who were accomplished pianists, and passionate film and literature aficionados. This brave new world was stimulating to say the least and led me to conclude yet again that siloes we have created artificially are a great disservice to human intelligence and sense of community.

In the early years, a few undergraduates tested the faculty's bottom line in the Medical Humanities and regarded the five modules as being akin to 'extra-curricular' activities. By not turning up for class and/or not handing in reflection assignments, they had to retake the course. The message could not be clearer: the faculty is as serious about the Medical Humanities as other subjects.

By accommodating the needs of each other and through growing a culture in the humanities, the performing arts module has gained ground with students understanding the values of the arts. In 2024, the module is ongoing.

Part III

Sustaining the Learning

Training the Trainers

By 2016, we had collected sufficient data and experience with the various signature projects to realise a considerable next step would be required. We realised that directly working with young people meant we could gain immediate and first-hand experience of the strengths and weaknesses of our programmes and be exhilarated by the resultant change. Yet we needed an additional strategy. Now that we were becoming progressively confident in deploying the arts in education, further impact could be explored if more trainers were available.

In hindsight in 2021, little did we know that a single thought and desire of calling for more professionals to come forward revealed a relative void in the system. Teaching artists who wanted to bridge the arts *and* education were rare and are scarce.

Many courses in Hong Kong are specifically tied to drama and theatre. A while back, at the Hong Kong Arts Centre, for quite a number of years, drama education was part of a taught programme in collaboration with the Royal Melbourne Institute of Technology. The programme has since ceased, and now at the Hong Kong Art School, a division of the arts centre, applied theatre is a customised course available as and when needed by clients.

Similarly, at the Hong Kong Academy for Performing Arts, since its inception in 1984, a diploma to foundation courses then degree courses is offered in training performers and backstage professionals.

Exploring theatre training, for example, at the undergraduate level, the drama-in-education module is part of the bachelor of fine arts in drama. At the postgraduate level, drama and theatre education is available in the master of fine arts programme. Recently, in 2021, a bachelor's degree in applied theatre was offered, and a master's degree in drama and theatre education was launched in 2008. Outside in the sector, quite a few theatre companies run drama workshops for teachers and other professionals interested in using drama in their work.

Some non-academy practising professionals generally have applied theatre backgrounds and most have theatre degrees. While some wanted to perform in the main and took on education as stop-gaps between productions, there is a lack of information on the actual numbers who pursued careers as arts educators.

Whether this is by choice or as a result of a lack of professional training is unknown since there is little research on the careers of arts educators. Schools that brought in artists mostly 'bought' service (see chapter 9) for competitions and festivals or year-end performances. Curriculum-based teaching through drama was at its height from early 2000 for about a decade, when Hong Kong's curriculum reform included the language arts, learning English through drama being one of four facets.[13]

We were looking for, and looking to, those who were committed to the arts-in-education and who would deploy the arts for change. We believe that different sectors of professionals need to collaborate closely to share expertise and experiences in order to effect change at young people's level. This, as it turned out, is an opportunity, one which can, in effect, create a subset of teaching artists as cross-disciplinary professionals.

A decade or so ago, we turned to faculties of education in local non-arts-based universities. That drew a blank, as both undergraduate and postgraduate degrees focused to a very large extent on language teaching, teaching science, liberal studies (now defunct), early childhood education, sports, mathematics, personal, social and humanities education, and so on. The shape of thinking at tertiary level appears to be firmly fixed on immediate demands.

It is therefore not surprising that except for the Education University of Hong Kong, the arts are not in any measure a core fundamental in other tertiary

---

13. Other language arts are poetry, short stories, and pop culture.

curriculum[14] in education. A personal experience went like this: on enquiring whether a local professor would be interested in being my supervisor for a Master of Education dissertation comparing the local and an international arts curriculum, the answer was simply, 'There is no market in the arts'. Despite a door slamming shut because of no interest and a lack of know-how, a seed appeared in my mind to redress the situation if an opportunity arose.

In order for the kind of projects we have to have further impact, training the trainers is a necessity to enable sustainable development and to pool experienced minds. Without further recourse to help, we took a deep breath and struck out on our own, equipped with a passion and what many would see as an act of sheer folly.

The Jockey Club Arts for Change Project

A decade on from my initial unsuccessful attempts in tertiary institutions, and by a sheer stroke of good luck, we embarked upon the *Jockey Club Arts for Change Project* in 2017–2021 as a one-track partner for the three-year *Jockey Club YouthCreate Series*.

The essence of the project was to enable social workers and artists to experiment with co-designing and co-creating programmes for young people from children and youth centres mainly based in and around public housing estates. We approached the project with much enthusiasm and, despite severe disruptions by the social unrest in 2019 and COVID in 2020, we gained a few years of invaluable and indispensable experience and insights into what succeeded and what did not.

The years were an uphill trek all the way from our opening naivete and inexperience in moving deeper into cross-sector training to understanding the complexities of social workers' mindsets and their spheres of influence. The commitment level of young participants was like a revolving door. Many were unable to keep to a schedule for a variety of reasons. Crevices and chasms appeared, yet still to this day, I regard the many pain points as manifestations of abundant learning moments that prepared us for a later and new three-year project, the *Jockey Club Arts-Based Cross Curriculum Creative Learning Project*, a pilot from 2021 to 2024 also funded by the Hong Kong Jockey Club Charities Trust.

---

14. The Education University of Hong Kong offers a bachelor's degree in creative arts and culture and includes arts management and cultural studies to complement discipline-based training in music and visual arts.

Figure 3.6: Training the Trainers in the *Jockey Club Arts-Based Cross Curriculum Creative Learning* Pilot Project. Photo from AFTEC, 2022.

The Jockey Club Arts-Based Cross Curriculum Creative Learning Project

The discussion of the *Creative Learning* pilot took two years to come to fruition, as discussions were extensive. Nevertheless, the project beginning in 2021 provided intense collaboration with twenty teachers and ten creative practitioners[15] in ten local primary schools. The yawning divide that arose in the previous project with social workers and artists paved the way for the improved bridging of teachers and practitioners here. In this *Creative Learning Project*, training teachers and creative practitioners together as an integrated whole was core (figure 3.6).

We now understand that it is of the utmost importance that we are able:

- to locate a project team that takes ownership of and affirms the values of the project understanding that process matters;
- to find the appropriate partners through a clear and thorough selection process as opposed to having ready-made ones at the doorstep on the basis of interest alone;

---

15. Creative practitioners include visual, performing artists, and those outside of the immediate arts sector who are engaged in creative work, which in this project is architecture.

- to ensure that there is strong buy-in from top management in schools and that teachers have the blessings and genuine support of the principal and not left to their own devices;
- to iterate and reiterate project fundamentals regularly, as professionals are enormously preoccupied with their immediate responsibilities and systemic pressures arising from their current institutions;
- to make no sweeping assumptions on abilities but to go back to basics and leave no learning stone unturned;
- to offer support at relatively close intervals to prevent mission drift; and
- to constantly assure stakeholders that they are on the right path and to reassure them that initial trepidations in the paradigm shift from traditional to creative classrooms is natural and part of the growth process.

On matters of sustainability, funders rightly ask where the longevity and return on investment are for their funded projects. Without their financial and strategic endorsement, little happens. However, they occasionally miss the details of the question.

It is not always prudent to expect longer-term continuity if the initial backing excludes a mechanism in the proposal for legacy, no matter how small. Trees do not bear fruit by being fertilised once. The quintessential action for sponsors to take is fewer projects but longer durational support. By definition, the inherent possibility of projects to extend their shelf life is a major criterion. For judgement of potential, knowledge is key.

Part IV

Aristotle is believed to have coined the phrase 'nature abhors a vacuum', and as fast as one appears, nature replenishes it with some form of life. The continuum provides a sequence, collection, and progression. Relinquishing the desire to become a producing theatre and instead seeking to understand, plan, and practise the arts in learning and for learning instead has meant we have travelled on the road less taken.

Gaps have always indicated prospect for action. Our attempts, small as they are, are just that. To make significant progress, however, much research and open dialogue is required within the arts and across sectors. Research in the arts, or the great lack, as is the case in Hong Kong, has constantly been an issue. This vacuum is a disservice to all stakeholders who plough in enormous resources, years of time, and great effort. Return on investment can be much higher if only there is data to illustrate, disseminate and, above all, to discover more gaps.

Not enough has been done and achieved in research since 1962, after the opening of the first performing arts premises, City Hall. To date, the focus in the arts has always been on delivering products, be these productions or exhibitions. What is immediately tangible is understood. Demand is slow (see chapter 9) in the cultivation for more of the arts and indeed arts-in-education if research is missing. The responsibility does not fall solely on any government's shoulders but on all of ours, government and civil society, arts organisations and individuals, educators and entrepreneurs alike.

4
Passivity to Engagement
Sm-ART Youth Case Study

Summary

This chapter focuses on AFTEC's initial sojourn in understanding key features for student-centred creative teaching and learning through diverse art forms.

Part I discusses the emerging pedagogy of early creative learning. Part II draws out three important aspects of a creative classroom environment. Part III investigates how parent-child relationships are managed. Part IV speaks of the important feature of cultural outings as part of integrated creative teaching, with part V listing challenges that we have encountered. The last section, part VI, concludes with working with possibilities.

Part I

The *Sm-ART Youth*[1] project spanned eight years from 2012 to 2020. There are three firsts to this project. It was the first non-theatre-based project mooted in late 2010 and implemented subsequently. It was the first long-term partnership project that saw us in partnership with a sponsor. It was the first project that benefitted economically disadvantaged children, working with them in-depth over time.

As a token of deep gratitude to the Jean C. K. Ho Family Foundation for its trust in us to innovate a project with no precedent, this chapter is dedicated to Jean Ho, the founder, and Dr Liliane Chan, the project director, for their generous support and magnanimity.

As a short overview, in addition to weekly classroom workshops, the project emphasised cultural outings, collaborating with parents/guardians, and working

---
1. Project description in the appendix.

with the same group of children over the years from Bronze to Gold levels.[2] Artists worked in the classrooms alongside an AFTEC administrator and volunteers. At this stage of our development, no teachers were involved in the project except as observers and for administrative purposes.

Pedagogy

In the early years, I developed the project and taught. With subsequent organisational development and its growth into other projects, my project collaborator, Dr Priscila Chu, a musician with a keen passion for education, became the leading light. Hong Kong's renowned classical pianist, Nancy Loo, for many years added much to the project through her deep experience in music, bolstered by her great insight into relationships with children.

As a newly established arts-in-education organisation in 2008, we were deeply curious as to how the arts in all their glorious splendour and permutations could support learning. *Sm-ART Youth* became the embryonic project that teased out the opulence of the arts for the purpose of creative teaching and learning. In this initial foray, we focused on:

- cultivating creative classrooms that would prioritise thinking, ways of seeing, and understanding;
- exploring and developing potential creative teaching and learning pedagogy through diverse art forms;
- deploying the intrinsic and extrinsic properties of the arts-in-education;
- offering inspiration and stimuli to students through multiple art forms and experiences inside and outside of school;
- understanding how the arts can support young people's general learning; and
- supporting young people in understanding and expressing themselves through various means.

In creating the pedagogy, we created a list of attributes for children aged nine to eleven. We believe children learn best if they are:

- lively and curious,
- adventurous,
- expressive,
- able to see things from multiple perspectives,

---

2. Levels denote passing years. Level 1 is Year 1 (Bronze), Level 2 is Year 2 (Silver), and Level 3 is Year 3 (Gold).

- able to ask questions; and are
- reflective.

As one can see, many on the list are familiar and natural to children. However, given the poverty of imagination (see chapter 2) we had observed, we decided to edge away from the traditional convergent approach to teaching to include an alternative way of more open and divergent directions. We began to explore this through *Sm-ART Youth*. Suffice it to say that we do not have all the answers, but the picture of some results is a steady one. Reflections taken directly from a few primary school students translated into English can be found in boxes throughout the chapter. Names have been changed to protect privacy.

> I believe this project can change us through self understanding. I am able to be a new me and not be stuck in the old me. I used to think I knew it all, but since this project, I know I don't have a deep enough understanding of the arts. *Sm-ART* is a platform for self transformation.
>
> NCC (2019–2020)

Being an organisation that deploys the powers of the arts-in-education, we coined the project name, *Sm-ART Youth*, to place the arts at the centre of the pedagogy for mindset change. In short, we were not looking to nurture the replication of factual knowledge or skills through rote-learning activities but to support young people in cultivating dispositions and habits of minds through engagement and experience. Because an infinitely expanding body of knowledge can never be taught, it was logical that the next step was to empower and give agency to children themselves to be increasingly adept at self-directed learning.

To achieve this, a larger premise had to be considered. Because of the narrow lives the children lived – moving from their housing estates or subdivided flats to school and back – exposure was, and still is, very limited in knowledge external to their environments, stimulation, and experiences. Exposure, however, needed to be redefined for better understanding other than simply what more the school could provide as a matter of routine. Consequently, the *Sm-ART* learning encounters were predicated and formulated on three Es:

- Exploration: self and others; multiple art forms, choice of materials and encouragement of ideas
- Engagement: in student-centred creative classrooms and connecting to

- Experience: including inspirational cognitive stimuli, other worlds, and senses plus actual cultural outings.

Decontextualised activities needed to give way to contextualised experiences. Cookie-cutter activities in which the standardised requirement of the teacher reigning as the sole source of information and students producing the same answers were replaced by authentic experiences that engaged the child's own experiences, thoughts, and feelings. Autonomy in being and thinking are important steps.

In the *Sm-ART* classroom, the pedagogy was explored with content across the arts. As a learning organisation with a base at the Sai Wan Ho Civic Centre, we were originally only regarded as a drama- or theatre-based education organisation. In reality, we offer a variety of art forms suitably situated into the classroom as appropriate. These include music, visual arts, drama, movement, and even films.

Content in *Sm-ART Youth* was not formulated on individual art forms because we were not inculcating specific artistic skills. We were looking to advance a creative habit of mind to complement school teaching where possible. The habit would include learning to ask questions, for example. Over specific modules, different kinds of arts would come together, and over a few lessons, children would investigate an artwork through questions. We have used stories, animation, and craft.

The origin of this thinking was twofold: that the power of different arts activities has similarities such as making connections, using the imagination, and promoting interaction, and therefore, they could be interconnected. Secondly, *Sm-ART* children from working-class backgrounds require stimulation. Finding an overarching thread or theme meant that students could be exposed at greater depth and breadth.

Needless to say, lesson plans took shape, but as we progressively understood the students, plans were adjusted from the learning opportunities that presented themselves to us during class. However, the first tangible change we felt necessary to adjust was the environment to teaching and learning.

Part II

Environment I: Physical Ambiance

The teaching environment is essential: children may either become completely withdrawn or engage actively. *Sm-ART Youth* has always championed classrooms that promote open discussions. We found that providing children with greater freedom of movement, space, and choices helped them feel more comfortable with learning once they adjusted to it.

By giving the opportunity for children not to be bound by desks and chairs, some were ecstatic while others were unsure, as they have been accustomed to a

Figure 4.1: *Sm-ART Youth* Classroom with Multiple Learning Styles. Photo from AFTEC, 2015.

norm. Not to be desk- and chair-bound was an unusual experience for them, as they have been conditioned to conform to one learning style only. At the start of each cohort, it would take three months and more for students to experiment with sitting on chairs with no desks in front of them, sitting on stools, or even sprawled on the floor (figure 4.1).

At some point, in each school, a startled discipline teacher would see the scene in the classroom as bordering on mayhem. Some would enter, trying to change the situation, and others would speak quietly to the principal, only to be informed that it was an exploration for the students. If any were unsettled in the beginning, many would eventually become supporters as they understood the purpose and saw the positive impact.

This way of setting up the physical environment did not mean that classroom management was unchallenging. Particularly with boys, freedom of movement meant their boundless energy was unleashed. Some would zip around the room like Formula 1 racers; others would just take to the floor. One boy pretended to be a rolled-up carpet for months, and class was spent like that. There were two requirements for their newfound liberation: that students did not harm themselves or others and that they participated in the class earnestly. The three-month wait was worth it in the end. Some settled back into chairs, while others preferred the floor. A very shy one would be curled up, sitting in an open cupboard[3] though this was an extreme case.

---

3. This student is now in tertiary education training to be a teacher.

Environment II: Mental State of Mind

Speaking Up

Restricted physical movement for students makes classroom management easier. However, without sufficient trust between regular artist educators like us and guests, an open, inquiry-based approach would not work if the mental and emotional ambiance remained closed. This is the more challenging game.

The students were very unused to speaking openly, giving their opinions, or even simply answering questions. They were orderly to the extreme at times, as in not answering questions unless called upon. We spent well over half a year explaining that they would learn better if they spoke, assuring them that even trying would score points, that it was not necessary to second-guess the teacher, that no answer was silly, and that if someone laughed at them, we would manage that person. This was the beginning of lowering the anxiety and enhancing trust.

Over time, iteration plus role-modelling by adults, the students came to see that we were true to our word. Their world changed in small steps. In the beginning and often in the first year, gaining trust with adults was the only goal. Then in the second term, some would venture to give answers truer to themselves; many would give brief replies, and they were appreciated.

Answers would vary from single words to statements such as 'Yes, I like this' without an explanation or evidence. Later, we started adding 'because' to their sentences to support exemplification. Very often, the few courageous souls would speak up and encourage others. More would join until, on occasion, a cacophony of voices would grow. The children would become energetic and talkative at times, at which point we would explain that it is good manners to give others a chance as well. However, by that time, noise was heaven to us instead of the normal silence.

In the first year, we needed to encourage students to open up to shed the fear associated with taking risks and the need for single correct answers. To achieve that, the already ingrained habit of not daring or wanting to give their opinions was reduced through constantly encouraging them to ask questions. This practice did cultivate in students a mindset that understands asking questions to share their thinking is important (figure 4.2) and that multiple answers were even more valuable to learning in a classroom.

> I believe my greatest change is to be brave in whatever I do. As I move up to secondary school, teachers will not necessarily teach you everything, and so one has to be courageous to learn by oneself and ask questions.
>
> YCY (2016–2017)

Figure 4.2: *Sm-ART* Pedagogy of Being Curious and Asking Questions. Photo from AFTEC, 2016.

Over three years, students who stayed with us learnt that, in the *Sm-ART* classroom, they were able to relax more and that expectations were different from those in the usual school classes. They learnt to adopt a flexible habit of mind and manage their behaviour appropriately, according to the environment.

In educational language, we advanced the constructivist model of teaching. We worked alongside children and from time to time, there were 'experts' among them who taught us in return. A case in point was Samuel, who lived with his cousin and his wife. He was a zoologist in training already at nine years old. He would not demonstrate much interest in the arts unless animals were permitted, whether two-, four-, or six-legged ones. Having a personal interest in the natural world myself, we would engage in discussions on exotic animals and challenge each other regularly. Samuel would beat me half the time. That was his entry point into thinking, and when he brought his crickets or lizards into the classroom, amazing things would happen.

By transforming the pedagogy from passive to participatory, standardised to the more personal, top-down didactic to shared learning and knowledge, the teacher's voice to a plurality of voices, we grew to see that children became cognitively present, motivated, and engaged adventurers instead. No joy was greater than the eureka moment when eyes lit up and voices tuned up.

Two Routines

Aside from health and safety in the classroom, two other practices were established in the classroom to support active learning: first of all, to desist from giving 'I don't know' as the regular answer when questions are asked, and secondly, to refrain from 'photocopying' behaviour. Rationale for the two practices was explained to students regularly to support their understanding of how personal growth could be better achieved.

For the first routine, 'I don't know' meant they were expecting spoon-fed answers or, worse, they were unable to think. The frequency and extent to which this phrase appeared was startling in the first few years. Questions as simple as 'What did you have for breakfast?', 'What might you be doing this weekend?', or 'What time does after-school tuition begin?' resulted in that same reply. While it is understandable that parents would be the main organisers of their lives, the phenomenon reflected the degree to which children were asked to follow orders without being involved in the conversation even in a superficial way of knowing their schedule.

One way of disrupting the pattern was to scaffold the key questions, enabling short answers to first appear; then as abilities surfaced, we modulated the questions to encourage students to answer in longer sentences. There came a time when we would not give answers but use guided questions instead as a way to facilitate further learning, thus empowering the children to step up. By Year 3, many were able to think better though some struggled still. Again, the home environment was the main cause when this came to light. The next section will deal with this.

As to the second routine, closely following or replicating the answer and work produced by another student was the norm in the local classrooms that we knew. We believe this stemmed from the standardised teaching that occurred, the expectation of single, correct answers from the textbook and the teacher, according to the set curriculum. As such, even in a creative classroom, the response was typical and predictable. If a comment was made on how nice the yellow flower was, it was almost certain that twenty other flowers of the same colour would appear in due course.

At the start of *Sm-ART* classes with each new cohort, there was almost no differentiation between and among children. It was sad to see this in young minds and children who should be naturally vivacious, curious, and inquisitive. It took a year or so to break the habit with positive reinforcement that multiple ideas and answers were appreciated. Acting like photocopying machines was greatly discouraged. In fact, once there was a breakthrough by a few and the kudos that came from us, the other children had peer modelling, resulting in a faster change in the habit of mind. It was exhilarating when this moment appeared. It was like a huge burst of sunshine in the classroom.

Environment III: Affective State of Mind

Emotional learning has seldom been part of school life[4] in Hong Kong. In classrooms generally, children have to behave properly by sitting up straight and keeping quiet. Sometimes we would see unhappy students in class whose behaviour might be misconstrued as difficult. In this project, we did not set out to manage their emotions. However, since the arts are vehicles for expressions, our needing to manage emotions naturally had to become part of the class.

In each *Sm-ART* school, one of the partnerships we formed with the agreement of the principal was that the in-school social worker was a professional we could call on and turn to for advice when the issue at hand was beyond us. This happened regularly in each school over the years.

Little did we know that most family backgrounds were truly complex. To give an idea, the following are real stories, the children's names changed to preserve anonymity.

Wing Yee was a shy ten-year-old whom we eventually realised felt very bad about her hair, to a degree that affected her self-confidence. She wanted long hair and a ponytail like her friends but was denied that by her mother, a wage worker, who found short hair much more manageable. She was small in stature and did not speak for an entire year. Wing Yee could not verbalise her feelings, as she did not know how to. Punitive measures her mother took when she showed signs of disobedience were to deprive her of having a bowl of rice.[5]

Jenny came to *Sm-ART Youth* on the recommendation of the school. She was very quiet, would smile when spoken to, and was given to extraordinary bursts of energy, dashing around the room. On one occasion, she decided to drag a boy by his neck. As the school provided a variety of extra-curricular activities, she enrolled in a few and was then summarily dismissed from them after a short while, or she left.

We were told by the teachers that this happened annually except for *Sm-ART* classes, where she stayed for all three years even though the first year was spent doing very little in class. Through interactions with Jenny, we then surmised that the environment of trust cultivated weekly and over time with a non-judgmental attitude from the adults around her in class helped her settle back to being a child without adult responsibilities.

This was her life.

She was of mixed parentage, and she had siblings with skin colour vastly different from hers. In this household, the children had two fathers, both absent. The

---

4. In recent years, positive education has become a practice in certain schools, giving social and emotional learning an opportunity to be cultivated as well.
5. We notified the school's social worker.

mother was expecting another child with a partner of yet a different culture and a third nationality, also never present. After giving birth to a boy, Jenny's mother ensured that the baby brother was fed formula milk by Jenny every four hours overnight. Jenny then attended school in the morning.

> I lacked self-confidence in the past. When I feel I am not understood, I would literally fight with others. Not anymore. I feel the arts have transformed me by helping me express myself.
>
> Jenny in *Sm-ART Youth*, 2017–2018

> I used to lose my temper easily in the past. Now I am able to better manage emotions. As a secondary school student, I am more persuasive when I speak, and teachers and students listen.
>
> Jenny as a teenage volunteer, 2021

In class, when different art forms and a selection of materials were introduced, the experiences connected to students' inner selves. Because there was quite a lot of choice as opposed to the same set of standardised materials, children were able to relate to each one differently. Choice encouraged individual thought. A collection of thoughts created a database in the minds of children who did not have much imagination at the start, as a result of the poverty of physical circumstances and exposure. From there, idea upon idea slowly took shape, and in time, ideas formed and grew to become part of the students' identities. Suddenly, many had things to offer for the first time.

Max would naturally and constantly gravitate towards some materials rather than others. During his learning journey, we conversed with him as with other students, to understand reasons behind their thinking and allowed them ownership. There was no right or wrong. We simply wanted to observe each child as growth happened. When trust was gained eventually, a child such as Max would increasingly find himself and reveal his thinking to us.

Max was from a single-parent household with a powerful father, tall, and muscular. Max turned out to be gay, and over the three years he was with us, he began to recognise this, accept it, and openly shared it with his classmates. They laughed at him for being effeminate, for choosing pink and scintillating objects above all else. At the end of the *Sm-ART* journey, his Gold-level project carried the same colours and shiny characteristics. The project theme, *Reshaping Me in My Mind's Eye: If I were*, was a huge humanoid figure with wings ready to fly.

Johnny was very bright, and he was constantly very observant. In class, he would be quick to respond and was one of the very first to give his own views. He also started asking questions early on after the ice was broken. His Gold-level project investigated painted masks and the relationship between colours and emotions.

Johnny's mother left the family when he was a toddler. His father worked in China and was very rarely in Hong Kong. He was looked after by his grandparents. His grandfather also depended on his wife for his daily needs. Johnny disliked learning English, refused to complete his homework, and did poorly in the subject. That was his weak point. His grandfather was visually impaired and his grandmother illiterate. When his father did return home, he bluntly told his son, 'You are not wanted'.

In each case, and these are only four examples, the arts gave us windows into the children's minds and hearts to see them as they were.

Part III

Parent–Child Collaboration

As adults, we are cognisant that we are all, to a greater or lesser degree, influenced by the environment where we grew up and shaped by the people around us, our parents to start.

One slim boy from a single-parent family who joined the *Sm-ART* classes had an adult vocabulary and tone of voice that constantly got him into verbal tugs-of-war with his friends in class. When we met his mother, whom he resembled physically, we understood. In the three years he was with us, they were like characters from a play.

The mother would blame the child, then nine years old, for her divorce. The role would then reverse, and the boy, in a similar vein and tone, would accuse the mother of forcing his father to desert them. It was actually a conversation between two adults locked in a Beckettian relationship of incessant and bitter recrimination. When he graduated, relations were slightly improved though the see-saw would continue.

Evidently, we are not social workers, but we realised that we could perhaps serve as a bridge for the project—if not directly for better communication between parent and child, then to extend the learning from class into the home, providing more continuity.

Consequently, one of the main features of the project was a protocol for a four-way dialogue between parents, their children, and us, alongside the foundation.

This ritual was also initiated because of one recurring incident in the first cohort of *Sm-ART Youth*, when parents attended introductory sessions to familiarise themselves with the project. To gauge parents' grasp of understanding their children beyond homework and grades, we showed drawings done by the nine to eleven age group that we had collected from other projects. We would show standard ones that were colouring by numbers on a template. 'Beautiful' was generally the reaction.

We also brought in much more intangible and free-form ones. One was done with crayons in bold, powerful strokes, and abstract (figure 4.3). We asked what parents thought. Almost without fail, some would quickly judge it as unaesthetic and commented that the child could not even draw within the given boundaries. They were considered 'poor' drawings. After some scaffolding, parents would then be guided to look longer and closer. Eventually, a mother or two in attendance would say, 'The child is very unhappy'. If children were merely walking report cards to us, would we not be undermining their innate potential to grow?

From this, we were even more determined that, annually, before the academic year, we would all meet individual families to set goals for the year. After a term, a second meeting would be held to review the previous few months, and a final meeting would take place at the end of the school year for a macro review.

Figure 4.3: Parents' Discussion: Beautiful or Poor? Image from AFTEC, 2013.

This was much more administrative work for colleagues, but they understood the importance of respecting and enacting this process of shared learning and understanding through the arts. As time went by, colleagues understood that the process was rewarding, even exhilarating, to see how families could break some barriers, grow together. Unsurprisingly, on occasions, in some cases, little would change.

In addition to regular meetings, we put in place a parent-child pledge for the year. How did this come about? I am sure many of us noticed that our parents would encourage us to make and keep promises as an incentive for more playtime or a favourite snack. The relationship was almost always one-sided. In other classrooms prior to AFTEC's establishment, we often witnessed how children felt they had to adhere to a promise unhappily and had no way of understanding the rationale or of expressing their frustration.

Behavioural issues sometimes became an issue in class, as seen from the cases in the section above. Because children's lives revolved around parents and guardians who took care of them, parent–child relationships would become the single positive or negative source of being for children in school on a daily basis. We realised it could inevitably turn into a vicious cycle.

In *Sm-ART Youth*, it was important to close some of the relationship gaps somewhat to find an entry point for conversations between parent and child and for the latter to regain some confidence.

> *Sm-ART* has helped me answer questions bravely. I have learnt there is no right or wrong in the arts and so I am more confident. I have also seen my strengths through this project.
>
> CPY (2019–2020)

The pledge went something like this: the child and the parent/guardian would undertake to improve one aspect of their lives that the other was not enamoured of. Within a term, both would try to commit to changing. Examples included a girl asking her father to give up smoking and she would clean up after herself; reducing video games if the mother would 'nag' less to give the child some breathing room; coming home slightly earlier, enabling parent and child to have some time together before bedtime, in exchange for better behaviour.

How many were willing to commit to their pledges? When schools recommended their students for the project and we met with parents, one of the criteria we adopted to ascertain suitability was whether the child would answer questions without the adults jumping in first or leading them. Adults who gave their children a chance indicated a willingness to listen. We felt we were unable to accomplish much for those who constantly answered everything on behalf of their child.

In the eight years of the project, improvements in cognitive, mental, and emotional development came from children and parents who worked with us both at home and in the school.

An intrinsic part of the meetings were appraisals based on three foci: continuous classroom formative assessment, a reflection notebook, and a reflection jar of coloured beads (see chapter 5).

Part IV

Cultural Outings

Without fail, at student assessment in all eight years of the project, parents/guardians and students would state unanimously that the highlight of each *Sm-ART Youth* year was the cultural events that took them beyond the classroom walls into the real world of the arts, culture, and heritage. In both interim and final evaluations, the trips were constantly the single most cited and desired aspects of their learning. Authentic experiences are truly the real thing.

Good arts and cultural events are entertaining, fun, and insightful. Crucially, if done well, cultural outings are inspirational. Inspiration should become an inextricable part of school life regularly.

The *Sm-ART Youth* project was the first to emphasise regular outings. Children whose routines consisted solely of traveling between school and home had fewer options in life. Our vision for cultural outings as a staple—rather than an addendum—to creative learning was to break down that binary and linear routine, reconstructing a multidimensional model of being that incorporated the outside world and ideas from the students.

To achieve a more divergent way of thinking meant that factual worksheets would not be sufficient for the experiences that we wanted for them, to empower the students' focus to shift away from pencil and paper as the sole learning tool, to performances and exhibitions outside of school. To borrow a theatre term, we were negotiating a sightline issue,[6] shifting the students' gaze dramatically from lowering their heads to worksheets, to raising their heads to gaze further afield, observing a stage or exhibitions or greenery and buildings.

As a result, their views of the world will be transformed from the school and home to new vistas, literally and figuratively. This is stimuli and much more; it is

---

6. Sightlines are imaginary lines starting from an actor's eyes to a particular object or area.

dismantling the encased poverty of the imagination extending to new possibilities not just for schooling but hopefully towards life itself.

Exposure

A cultural outing was an embodied experience, not just an activity (figure 4.4). Preparation would include collating learning to date in the classroom, seeking appropriate throughlines or connectors to the event, discussing with the artist on objectives, and workshopping volunteers a week in advance so that they too were grounded in the encounters to come.

Each year, these primary students were offered three cultural events. These would range from the performing to the visual arts and heritage visits. We were often asked whether the choice of outings was tailor-made for children of a particular age cohort. Our answer was no. Although we clearly avoided inappropriate adult materials for obvious reasons, we also avoided productions that were patronising and cute.

Over the years, we have seen that many students were actually interested in content that many deem to be challenging for them. Ironically, challenging materials when prepared and handled well actually animated and motivated students. There

Figure 4.4: Cultural Outing: Experiential Activity. Photo from AFTEC, 2018.

was always something that each child would connect to and grasp. Undermining children's abilities is counterintuitive to their innate potential.

Taking an easier example first. There would generally be attendance at a dance performance each year, as it was important to provide an array of expressive platforms to engage children who responded differently to just words and language. Almost none had seen ballet, for example. While some tended to fall asleep during the performance, the majority indicated that the experience was eye-opening. Many, too, quoted from these events long after the curtain came down, children, parents/guardians, and volunteers included.

The pre-show discussion was important. This was not simply an introduction to Hong Kong Ballet's *Sleeping Beauty* story; it was often preceded by an actual ballet class by a dancer. The workshop included dance exercises, learning basic ballet mime language with hand and arm gestures; sets, costumes, and the story of course. Basic etiquette was also taught to children to maximise their and other people's enjoyment.

The actual performance was then followed immediately by a tour or meet-the-artist session in which the students – and very often the teachers, parents, and volunteers – were free to ask questions. The session would be guided by an artist and attended by dancers as a post-show where questions were fielded by a facilitator, encouraging children to practise an healthy inquisitive habit of mind. Back in the classrooms, post-event discussions would be held, aligning ongoing *Sm-ART* lessons at hand.

Making Connections

A more complex outing was also achieved. In 2013, the Asia Society curated *No Country: Contemporary Art for South and Southeast Asia*, the inaugural touring exhibition of the Guggenheim Museum in New York. The exhibition featured the recent works of thirteen artists from the region, and *Sm-ART Youth* students were mesmerised by the range of voices in an upscale gallery. Using scaffolding questions, the teacher, the attending arts educator, and volunteers became facilitators.

Although there was Shilpa Gupta's own interpretation of her artwork[7] *1:14.9* (figure 4.5), the ball of string piqued students' curiosity the most and kick-started their critical thinking. We offered young people intelligent and generative artworks, and they did the rest.

In this exhibition, they moved away from the simple descriptive 'what' questions into a deep curiosity of 'how' and 'why'. They wondered about the ball of string

---

7. '1:14.9 (Thread Ball)', Shilpa Gupta, accessed 20 August 2024, https://shilpagupta.com/114-9-thread-ball/.

Figure 4.5: Reproduced by permission from Shilpa Gupta Studio. *1:14.9*. 2024.

and asked a profusion of questions. They understood that the artist was making an important statement that was clearly powerful.

Using their imagination, some students viewed the string as having been tied to many people's hands while others opted for fencing in people, and still others believed it to be an egg of sorts. There are many ways to see the world indeed. By comparing, connecting, and thinking of possibilities, students widened answers beyond what the artist interpreted. Learning became more meaningful as a result of a cornucopia of collective perspectives.

> I have learnt the possibilities of reflecting from different angles. But this year, I've realised you cannot simply do this either; things have to be seen in context. LSY (2016–2017)

The students in this visit realised that there could be many forms of communication and not simply language. While being accepted was important in relationships, they were excited about having different opinions as well. By pooling their thinking and working collaboratively, they began to manage their own learning, the material being the source of motivation.

The discussion of feelings is very much lacking in our education system. The arts support students to delve into their inner worlds for communicating complex emotions. The discovery that feelings are very much part of being human released children from the solely cognitive propositions and prescriptions that many schools focus on. While solutions to problems may not always be forthcoming, the sense of relief from being able to express oneself through diverse means offers a better sense of the self and well-being. It cannot be overstated how crucial the place and value of the arts is in schools and lives.

In the second year, these same students would explore learning in a deeper context, having been transported physically and imaginatively by cultural outings in Year 1. The inside of a professional theatre, a concert hall, and a space filled with sounds, lights, and magical representations of life would leave indelible impressions on young lives. Their world suddenly changed from monochrome to technicolour. The culturing outings stimulated their minds, hearts, and spirits to want to know more, and this rekindled innate curiosity so often demonstrated by children would light the fire to further and deeper creative learning.

By Year 3, with almost nine cultural outings under their belts, the majority of the students would be ready to undertake an individual project of their own choice or form a collaborative pair, not dictated by the artists or any adult, as long as the project was considered worthy of many months of time expended in research and investigation. Each would eventually complete three years of creative learning at Gold level which would draw together key learning from the past year.

The projects were as diverse thematically as the individuals themselves. Past projects included festivals from different lands, comparison of the Brazilian war dance and kung fu, a visual biography, a mood sculpture, creating scented candles, making an armchair from recycled cardboard, styling hair pieces for the public to try on, a new way of measuring one's height, a monologue on a boy who lost and found himself; the list goes on.

Part V

Challenges

The road along the *Sm-ART Youth* trajectory was very rewarding because of successes but more importantly, because of trials and tribulations during the process along the way. From these experiences, we gained first-hand understanding that proved to be the bedrock of what AFTEC is today. There were, of course, roadblocks along the way. I list three challenges here.

Attrition

The project intended the same children to move up sequentially from Bronze to Gold levels over three years, to introduce them to the arts-in-education and then on to deeper discussions and the final project where their learning was applied. This proved to be a long commitment for some parents and children, given that *Sm-ART* was an innovation in 2012.

If the project was a simple tuition approach for improved grades or an extra-curricular option for skills in an art form to add to the child's portfolio for application to secondary schools, staying power would have been easier. As a matter of fact, it was an interesting challenge to have to explain to parents firstly, why the arts should be taken seriously; secondly, to get across the more abstract yet important concepts of creativity, critical thinking, communication and collaboration, and finally, to persuade them that they were investing not in 'hedge funds' but 'blue-chip stocks' for their children.

Year on year, there was an attrition rate of under 20%. Students who dropped out would generally move to more tuition after school, more time for homework at home, and a preference for other non-arts activities. *Sm-ART Youth* as a project helped us understand that we should not be concerned with perceived failure (the attrition) but should instead focus on those who were very committed. After all, we have always prized quality first and foremost.

Mindset

On a larger scale it is a question of changing mindsets. When any school system has cultivated the mimetic learning at its heart as the routine habit of mind, grades being the only lens to intelligence, introducing a new concept could only be viewed as extra workload to be tolerated.

We learnt this in one unfortunate experience in a primary school whose principal seemed keen and who brought in teachers to the project. They came on board for one year, after which we thought it was best to discontinue. The issues were various but mainly pertained to a school culture that found it difficult to step out of its comfort zone. The schools that showed achievements were those with principals and teachers who cultivated an open mindset to give the idea a try and to patiently observe and chart progress.

A fixed mindset is a phenomenon we have continued to tackle in the past decade in other programmes. Early discernment at *Sm-ART Youth* saw to it that we became much more cautious in the choice of partners. Like prenuptials, the discussion process would be detailed, enabling both the school and us to truly gain a mutual understanding at a level other than project description and counting the benefits. In the end, details on processes were crucial to successful collaboration.

Training the Trainers

Shortly into the project, we saw that to support economically underprivileged children's learning, a larger pool of teaching artists truly committed to the arts-in-education would be needed. This was a matter of scalability. Although the project did not set out to train teachers or more artists, we were acutely aware of the fact that, sooner or later, that would be the subsequent path. That desire took another six years to materialise.

Part VI

Possibility Thinking

The *Sm-ART Youth* project is currently in hiatus, rudely interrupted by the sudden onslaught of the pandemic. Additionally, we thought it was a good opportunity to reappraise a project that has been running for eight years and seminal to our overall pedagogical development.

It has been a most purposeful and fulfilling journey with powerful and generous offerings from the foundation, artists, principals, teachers, volunteers, and administrators. Their hard work and enormous contributions have been integral to the quality of the project even though it was a new initiative with gaps that would require further thought and finer execution.

The *Sm-ART Youth* pedagogy that has developed in the intervening years became foundational to our programming. Elements of this embryonic concept have been transferred in varying degrees with modifications to enhance effectiveness and suit project appropriateness.

Cultural outings have become standard fare in many projects subsequently created and developed. It has come as no surprise that the degree of interactivity and discussions made available to participants beyond watching a show or visiting exhibitions are still the entry points to deep engagement for most age groups.

Engagement comes through the existence of a creative and flexible habit of mind. This is demonstrated through questioning and multi-perspectival understanding, fundamental to all signature projects, including *Bravo! Hong Kong Youth Theatre Awards*, the *Medical Humanities* (performing arts module), *Young Theatre Makers*, and three separate projects sponsored by the Hong Kong Jockey Club Charities Trust.

To achieve an open mindset, the environment of classrooms – in actual schools or as teaching spaces outside in our theatre or elsewhere – have all adopted an inquiry-based model. The physical, mental, and emotional space and trust have been incorporated into our learning philosophy, encompassing a progression of thoughts and ideas on pedagogy in an arts-based creative education.

The approach to redress the unquestioning and replication mentality in artistic endeavours operates throughout all programmes with the aim of rekindling innate curiosity and inquisitiveness. Craft calls this 'possibility thinking',[8] which carries the hypothetical opening of 'what if' as instrumental in opening up imaginative thinking.

Vygotsky's Zone of Proximal Development[9] speaks to our belief that learning is about raising the bar and not keeping it level for the sake of immediate accessibility and comprehension or, worse, making children think they are very clever. The balance between stimulation and challenge without proving to be a stumbling block is an intricate matter, one that has meant, and still means, that differentiation in the classroom is necessary.

While differentiation, or tailoring the teaching to meet the needs of diverse abilities, is a good approach, it is highly dependent on preparation and, to an even greater extent, on the abilities of teachers and teaching artists to think on their feet as learning opportunities arise. Training the trainers is consequently a major issue in our line of work.

While there are many dedicated teachers and artists in their respective professions, many are committed to either teaching the formal curriculum or their specific art forms. Artists' own training can often be skills-based. Some are tutored in art form education. It is unknown whether going into education is the original intent or part of using the downtime between performing and exhibiting.

As with *Sm-ART Youth*, our other programmes attempt to focus on 'less is more', hoping to cultivate quality and well-rounded individuals as opposed to scaling only for quantity. While this may be counterintuitive, we have tried to work on the quality principle as the prime directive while balancing numbers as best as the situation allows. Though conventional wisdom may suggest that funders understand quantity more than quality – because the latter's metrics of assessment prove inherently more elusive – this dichotomy is not one of superiority but merely of differentiation and value.

---

8. 'Examining possibility thinking in action in early years settings', ResearchGate, January 2007, https://www.researchgate.net/publication/42797985_Examining_possibility_thinking_in_action_in_early_years_settings.
9. This is the difference between what students can do on their own and what can be achieved with professional guidance.

5
Reflections as Assessment
Acknowledging Considered Thinking

Summary

Chapter 5 deals with a topic that is often overlooked and shunned in the arts circle: assessment and evaluation. Speaking from a personal perspective and discussing reflections as a platform for unmasking and identifying quality in creative teaching and learning, I have divided the chapter into six sections.

Part I reveals a quote on the impact that became the driving force at AFTEC and our initial journey in assessment and evaluation. Part II moves into attempts of organisational implementation of reflections as assessment and evaluation, and part III gives case studies as examples from the early years (2009–2012) from primary school to tertiary level.

Part IV takes a deep dive into one single project for teenagers during the middle years (2013–2018), giving both qualitative and quantitative data. Part V likewise examines one project in recent years (2019–2024) though the focus lies as much in students as in comparing schools and the professionals' abilities to engage young minds in reflections. Part VI lists concluding thoughts on reflections as an assessment tool.

Part I

In January 2008, the Department of Culture, Media and Sport in London published the McMaster review *Supporting Excellence in the Arts: From Measurement to Judgement*[1] to plan arts and culture in the UK. Six months before, it was James

---

1. Sir Brian McMaster, 'Supporting Excellence in the Arts: From Measurement to Judgement', *Cultural Trends Volume 17* (2008), https://doi.org/10.1080/09548960802362108.

Purnell, the then secretary of state for culture, who invited Sir Brian McMaster, former director of the Edinburgh International Festival, to undertake a review on the state of the arts. This landmark review involved artists, directors, curators, producers, and administrators from across the country and from diverse art forms. McMaster was supported by Nicola Thorold[2] and Arts Council England.

AFTEC was established in December of the same year, inspired by a sentence in the chapter of the review, Engaging Wider and Deeper Engagement with the Arts by Audiences: 'too many organisations, particularly in the performing arts, have been content to supply audiences with a superficial experience that provides immediate satisfaction but no lasting impact'. This eventually took on life as the guiding principle of what we would do and remains the inextinguishable beacon.

What impact were we aspiring to, and more importantly, why and how? Quantitative growth, such as audience attendance, is one undeniable aspect. Yet, armed with the understanding that we are not a producing theatre but one firmly grounded in the arts-in-education, the quality of programming, teaching, and learning was a high priority. In short, we were gunning for the qualitative because transformation through the arts lies in that direction. We had no idea how to even begin.

Many months of reading later, that engine had to be ignited, as experience is the only teacher. We began by adopting qualitative impact as the cornerstone in appropriate programming. In the strictest sense, one *assesses* individuals and *evaluates* projects although the two terms are used interchangeably nowadays. This chapter adopts both, and the context will differentiate them.

Assessment and evaluation, when done appropriately, support growth. We believe that assessment and evaluation are about storytelling, that through narratives, we can tell *how* we are doing *what* we are doing, thereby giving confirmation to *why* we should continue (or not) doing it. If you are a funder you may baulk at this thought of narratives. If you run an arts organisation, you may either nod if you believe assessment and evaluation to be necessary – not a necessary evil though – or join funders writhing in pain. Whatever you think, you are right. Whether you are believers or otherwise, let me begin with a story.

Before 2004, I was a firm non-believer in any kind of measurement in the arts. After all, how could the arts be calibrated, especially according to quantitative indicators? Above all, how can attendance be used to define success although yes, the world is essentially a bean-counting place based on capitalistic principles. A postgraduate degree in education in 2006 meant that I was put through a full module on assessment and evaluation even though the lens was firmly from the education

---

2. This chapter is dedicated to the late Nicola Thurold, my indefatigable and inspirational mentor at the Clore Leadership Programme 2010–2011. We communicated regularly until her untimely passing in 2016.

and not arts perspective. The discipline did not matter. In effect, there were then no postgraduate degrees in any of the arts that focused on measurement.

During the two years as a student in curriculum studies, my mind was stripped of innate prejudices (or enriched by another set, some might say) as I came to understand the rationale behind assessment and evaluation and the need for any of the hard work in the organisation to make sense to us and others, especially those who may not particularly understand the arts.

Three years later, in 2009, the ground-breaking publication of *The Qualities of Quality: Understanding Excellence in Arts Education*[3] sealed a keen interest in assessment and evaluation, this time from the qualitative side and specifically about the arts-in-education. Fortunately, 2009 was the same year that we became the venue partner at the government's Sai Wan Ho Civic Centre. Assessment and evaluation became increasingly part of the thinking though the route was experimental.

If assessment and evaluation are truly about narratives, then it leads to the question of why tell them, and whose tales do we tell? Do we tell them to please funders, or for us to be less risk-averse and find a path to communicate better, enabling sponsors to learn with us along the way? How is quality defined and by whose standards?

Barriers were manifold but generally revolved around managing expectations, our own, as we were comparatively new to thinking about and in playing the game. Additionally, sponsors in the arts were new at it, primarily focusing on the quantitative as easily comprehensible and a tangible recognition of success, in particular to those from the non-arts fields. To this day, many funders still rely solely on numbers although some of the progressive ones, who are more in tune with international trends, are going the extra mile to listen and read their grantees' qualitative evaluation of the sponsored programme.

Part II

Sitting Down Together

Assessment and evaluation have to do with accountability, and in this realm, it is easily understood. It does not mean, however, that we are held accountable only because we are given a part of the public or private purse. That thinking would be far too lopsided. Irrespective of whether we are subvented or subsidised, we are accountable. Even if an arts organisation is sponsored by an individual, accountability stands. Even internally within a company, where there is responsibility, accountability follows.

---

3. J. Hetland, E. Winner, S. V. Seidel, D. W. Tishman, and M. R. Palmer, *The Qualities of Quality: Understanding Excellence in Arts Education* (Harvard Education Press, 2009).

The word *assidere* is Latin for assessment, which literally means to 'sit beside'. Can funders and grantees achieve this? To what end? In Hong Kong, the trend of top-down evaluation of programmes generally rules. The piper calls the tune; the funder leads. Overall, there can be much more dialogue between grantors and grantees during (formative) or after the programme, unless it is on project completion (summative), and discussions are needed for project continuation.

Why do we need to measure or rate anyway? Evaluation of projects investigates the value behind the work for the purpose of being responsible, both to a grantor and to oneself (the company, colleagues, and beneficiaries). We tend to neglect the latter, as much sweat and steam is spent on programme operations, completion, and ensuring the sponsorship instalments come in at the end of the day for cash flow.

The *quality* of the programme is an area that we can fear to tread because if we are brutally honest, it can be painful. To be open about gaps and failures, as much as being overjoyed with achievements and successes, means a company needs to have very clear rationale for programmes at the foundational stage, reasons that go beyond merely producing a work on stage or getting subscriptions for economic benefits. In addition, grantees are uneasy about missteps, as grantors may view them as outright failures. Translated, this means that summative judgement may become the catalyst for the revocation of funding in the worst-case scenario.

Sixteen years on, I will be the first to admit that we still have some way to go in working out a structured and company-wide evaluation platform. As part of the quarterly routines, we follow funders' reporting requirements. However, there is already a culture of the need to be reflective of what we do in the organisation and who we are.

This did not happen instantly or immediately. At AFTEC's inception, we were crystal clear about making a deeper and longer impact. But detailed values created and applied as guiding principles only evolved over time with application, practice, and many crevices to fill. We could not turn to higher education for help as, very simply put, there is a tendency for each sector to work in silos, and thus, each sector functions within itself for its own purpose. In cooperation, occasional bridging occurs at project levels. Sustainable collaboration is a tune yet to be played.

It was paramount that we found our own way.

At a very simplistic level, for example, the first story we told was through the company's annual report, actual attendance/subscription figures as one indicator of self-assessment. This first report was published in 2013 for the previous triennium (2009–2012). Separately, we invited participants (audience and beneficiaries) to pen their thoughts (edited only for sense) on their experiences. The latter first featured programme evaluation as a reflective practice.

The report concept was not in place at the outset in 2009 but developed in hindsight. Subsequent to the first three-year-based publication, an annual report was published and still is.⁴ From 2014, the publication was divided into Engaging Participants and Creating Change, and reflections are sprinkled throughout. Other sections were added.

Internally, while annual staff appraisals are routine, this summative gesture is punctuated by regular in-house reflections – our own stories – as a matter of co-learning and charting the formative growth of individual members. A few avenues have been mapped out for reflection, led by senior team members and/or me.

A company-wide example is weekly company meetings, which in addition to sharing programme progress offer opportunities for insights during the week from colleagues of all levels and ages, including the clerical officer. While we do not ask for earth-shaking enlightening points, giving individual opinions was, and occasionally still is, challenging for many.

This is to redress a habit of mind which is generally passive and, in turn, is a result of age-old teaching practices that did not accommodate much interactivity and critical thinking as pedagogical tools. It has been very worthwhile spending time recalibrating this in in-house meetings through constant encouragement of colleagues to move thinking away from the descriptive, such as what happened in a programme or class, towards points of surprise or pain and new understanding. Modelling by more senior members is also a very useful tool. From ideas and insights, we naturally move to thinking about ourselves as the crucial factor in the success or problematic aspects of our work.

People do learn by example, and while funders seldom sit down beside us for deep or regular conversations, over the years, I have realised that supporting colleagues internally in self-reflection is the very first step towards the larger concentric circles of team-based, programme-based, company-based evaluation. The smallest and intangible space is within our inner selves. From there, we can all grow.

As evaluation is about values, what values do we have? These values have unfolded in the past decade as we put our beliefs into practice. Reflections have been ingrained in the company's DNA and are a very powerful tool.

This chapter will review examples and insights on assessment and evaluation through projects. Because of the very wide scope in assessment and evaluation, I will take reflections as the key thread for discussion. For one thing, they illustrate how the awareness and application of introspection (tiniest of space) is the source of self-knowing. Also, reflections contextualise their importance when individuals interact (the larger space) with each other with clearer starting points and thinking. In other words, from one's own stories to other people's stories.

---

4. See www.aftec.hk for digital versions. Pre-2019 versions are hard copies kept as archives.

The five selected key projects in table 5.1 represent a growing consciousness in assessment and evaluation and are divided into three chronological phases.

Table 5.1: AFTEC's Key Stages in Assessment and Evaluation Development. Image from AFTEC, 2023.

	Programme	Target	Level	Status	Tools
Early Years	*From Page to Stage*	12–16 year-olds	Level 1 Elementary	2009– ongoing	Teacher & Student Surveys + External Evaluation
	Sm-ART Youth	9–11 year-olds	Level 2 Intermediate	2012– 2020	Reflections & Others
	Medical Humanities (Performing Arts Module)	17–19 year-olds	Level 3 Advanced	2012– ongoing	Reflections, Rubrics & Others
Mid-Years	*Bravo! Hong Kong Youth Theatre Awards*	13–19 year-olds	Level 3 Advanced	2013– 2021	Reflections, KPIs + Social Impact Assessment
Recent Years	*Jockey Club Arts-based Cross Curriculum Creative Learning project*	9–11 year-olds + Teachers & Creative Practitioners	Level 3 Advanced	2021– 2024	Reflections (student & professionals), KPIs + External Evaluation

Part III

2009–2012: The Early Years

The year 2009 marked the start of the early years when assessment and evaluation began to take shape. This section covers the design and implementation of nascent ideas as defined by three projects.

From Page to Stage: The Basics

We invited Annabel Jackson Associates in the UK to carry out an evaluation of *From Page to Stage*[5] starting in 2010 (first year of production) and carried on for another six years as part of the funding from the Hong Kong Jockey Club Charitable Trust.[6] The programme continues today.

We aim to attract secondary school students learning English as a second language. The entry-point programme is also designed to address the issues faced by young people, such as underdeveloped reading habits, short attention spans, and a superficial approach to learning. Briefly, the programme has three key components:

- Pre- and Post-Show School Workshops
    - These are facilitated by artists engaged by us to engage with students, making it a point to ask open-ended questions to informally gauge students' comprehension of the play for that year.
- Education Packs
    - In these detailed packs, teachers are given the core parameters of the play along with class activities, which will be guided by open-ended questions based on themes. It is therefore the teachers' purview to address the answers from students.
- In the Theatre
    - Use of surtitles: We firmly believe that open-ended questions are core to kick-start students' critical thinking. Such questions are uploaded onto the theatre's electronic surtitles board when the house opens and are looped until the performance begins. These questions are then posed to students as part of post-show activities (figure 5.1).

The programme's assessment and evaluation came in the form of a tailor-made survey developed by Jackson and distributed to teachers and students. The return

---

5. Programme description is in the appendix.
6. The subsequent sponsor did not require evaluation although AFTEC continued with the survey, and this continues in 2024.

Figure 5.1: *From Page to Stage* Post-Show Interactive Activities. Photo by Hong Yin Pok for AFTEC, 2015.

rate in general was an average of 45%.[7] Questions were asked as part of the survey. At that point, learning how to create and implement reflective practices was at a very elementary stage for us.

Sm-ART Youth[8]: Inception of Reflectivity

Reflections as a core skill emerged with this project as we were able to focus on a cohort of twenty or more students as opposed to thousands[9] from *From Page to Stage*.

To see change, we experimented with a longer period of programming as a criterion, rendering one-off projects to a secondary position. The project ran from 2012 to 2020, when COVID brought it to an untimely end. The first cohort spanned three years, then subsequent ones two years.

As this project took off, it became apparent that a disjuncture appeared between the students' world and ours. Because of the poverty of imagination (see chapter 2) resulting from their disadvantaged circumstances, it was challenging to understand

---

7. At pre-COVID peak, there were over one hundred schools per year.
8. Project description is in the appendix.
9. By 2019, attendance stood at 12,000 annually.

them. It was a spatial and interconnection issue. Their lived experiences were few and far between; they were passive, and they did not know themselves. We knew that their learning environment had to change to instil more stimulation, yet irrespective of how willing we were to do this, the change had to be ignited first and foremost within the space of the inner self.

Attention for this after-school project focused primarily on developing cross-art form content from the performing and visual arts with the conceptual emergence of a creative classroom. Student-centred learning was the nucleus. This project is considered at level 2 with intermediate complexity. Three methods were created for assessment and evaluation. In each, reflection took on different meanings.

Mood beads bottle

Reflections meant we wanted to explore each child as an individual as opposed to using a generic questionnaire for all, as in *From Page to Stage*. We played with the idea of supporting children in articulating themselves beyond using a linguistic approach due to their relatively young age (nine to eleven) and difficulty in understanding and indicating their feelings in writing.

This obstacle was evident right from the start; they were unable to connect with their feelings, let alone write about them. A visual form proved to be the answer. The mood beads bottle concept was created (figure 5.2) and positioned as a step

Figure 5.2: *Sm-ART Youth* Mood Beads — Feelings Recollected by Children. Photo from AFTEC, 2018.

towards self-discovery and the expression of emotions. These two skills remained largely dormant, as schools did not have the resources to recognise socio-emotional displays.

The students were given a choice in decision-making. Each child was given a bottle in which coloured beads of their choice would visibly manifest their feelings for the day. Each class would discuss and determine how different coloured beads would represent diverse emotions. While some would select red for anger, others would prefer happiness as the signifier. White might be for being lost or unadulterated joy, while blue could be for peace or sleepiness, green for being perturbed or being calm, and yellow for excitement or deep anxiety.

This small gesture allowed every child to own their feelings, demonstrate their internal selves to us, and allow for the affirmation of their individuality. Furthermore, this summative assessment at the end of class gave us a glimpse into their sense of well-being and as an indication of how we needed to adjust our interaction with the students in learning in the next lessons.

While some were constantly happy, many others were not. To coax them gently into attuning to their inner selves, sometimes all that a few children needed was some quiet time, on their own and in a space of their choosing, being inactive in a corner, feeling safe under their desk, or putting their head down.

Gradually, we were able to decipher from these beads the students who were regularly down or vacant or disruptive. When the issues did not emanate from our creative classes, we sought assistance from the teacher and/or the social worker. More often than not, the beads revealed family relationships and/or school issues.

Throughout the years, the beads became a good and simple source of engagement and communication. At each parent–child meeting that we held in the year, the bottles would accompany the session. The child could choose to explain feelings in general, or we would take reference from the coloured beads to edify the parent/guardian on the child's performance.

Reflection journal

While mood beads provided visceral incentives for the students as a fun approach to their emotions, what would individual children say about themselves, we wondered? As part of a creative classroom habit of mind, the journals that each student was gifted with were used during class to write and sketch, colour or not, keep mementos etc., for activities that occurred. In the journal would be the individual's replies to scaffolded questions given by the artist in charge. This formative way of assessment during class also allowed them to review and keep track of their progress in the year, week after week.

For us, the reflective content demonstrated individual thinking, growth, and problems. The journals were always shared with us verbally by each child near the end of every class as one-on-one conversations to which others were not privy, thereby allowing for privacy. This built a large amount of trust between professionals and students.

It was of particular interest to witness students' thinking and change. Many drew familiar objects or wrote a few words. Some scrawled with a heavy hand in dark colours. Others illustrated their dreams whose subtexts revealed a recently deceased grandmother, to aspirations for their own bed. Others' huge Chinese characters sprawled over the pages were written as if in a storm. Many had no idea to start with and would often replicate others. Progressively, change would creep in imperceptibly, and the artists' keen eyes would sort out minute details.

Not having the resources at hand, what we were unable to determine was the extent to which their development was due to the project and our creative interventions that spurred their change, or to other factors at school. However, what was abundantly clear was that the project became a strong catalyst in opening up their worlds and ways of thinking, drawing out internal emptiness, anxieties, and giving space from the start to multi-perspective living.

Annual dialogues

The mood beads and the journal gave us privileged views into the inner workings of a young person. How would that data be effective in all-round care and growth? Would parents or guardians being part of a continued support network for the children make a difference? After all, we would only interact with the children weekly for a limited time. As a result, we were keen to see if some of the habits of mind we were cultivating in the very early days of a creative classroom could be practised at home as well.

In order to gauge this relationship between guardians and children, we instigated three dialogues a year per family unit: one before the academic year, one after the first term, and one before the summer break. Notes from both the interim and year-end discussions would be properly entered into assessment templates:

- Self-assessment

  We decided to turn the tables on top-down professional assessment of the child's performance as an extension of the mood beads. There seemed little sense in providing a choice of coloured beads, a choice of activities, a choice of expression, if we concluded with the standard practice of only the teacher grading students in the final performance. This turnabout was also how we were able to shift from the tiniest introspective space outwards to engage the child with others.

Instead, children would be invited to give themselves a score from zero to ten (ten being the highest, indicating maximum satisfaction). While normally the professional would agree or disagree and culminate with a final grade, we reshaped the routine. The twist was that the balance of points was what interested us the most. Why, we would ask, did you deduct, for example, three points from the total of ten? What were your thoughts? What did you think you missed? The conversations that ensued were sometimes powerfully meaningful, as the adults present understood the child from the child's own perspective instead of simply ours.

Unsurprisingly, many sat on the fence and answered with a five as a safe score. Those with more self-awareness and confidence and those with less were also able to seriously think before they gave a number. Quite a few scored themselves below four. Reasons for deductions were varied. Some resulted from extreme modesty; others had genuinely no idea about their own performance, and thus a lower mark would again be safe. In time, as a habit of mind was formed, scoring became more adventurous for many.

Overall, the scoring done this way provided an indication of how children perceived themselves and their abilities. During these early years, we slowly realised that formal evaluation by an external party to support our in-house efforts would be highly beneficial. This step was eventually taken up in the *Bravo! Hong Kong Youth Theatre Awards*.

- Parental dialogues

  By verbalising a score, we were able to connect to the guardian on the student's attitudes and behaviours at home. More often than not, because of age, ability, and absence due to work, guardians seldom see another facet of the child. Many times, the child's explanations were revelations to the guardians. These conversations provided a platform for them at least to be reacquainted with each other, for the child and guardian to speak their minds where possible and for us to plan the next steps forward.

  There were occasions when the child would not speak at all with the guardian present at the meetings, and from this, we would gauge family relationships. There were also days when the assessment template and pro forma had little to show for. In these instances, we noted this and moved on, looking forward to another year and progress.

  Would the year-end dialogue be summative? In the sense that it culminated the year, the answer is yes. Nevertheless, because the project ran for two to three years for each child, there was always a continuous window for better planning and hopeful change in the next school year. We did not see year-end as the final summation of who the child was but rather the gaps and possibilities ahead.

At the end of the academic year, the children would take the mood bead bottles home with their reflection journals. That token was always very well received, for in that bottle was the child's inner self personified. They almost always walked away with a smile.

As each gap presented challenges year on year, they became the platform to rethink what is to be done, why, and how. Learning from these assessment sessions fed back into our own growing reflective habit of mind and generated a virtuous cycle of thought and action. Suddenly, we understood that action research and/or practice as research formed the basis of our development in education and learning through the arts. Unknown to me at the time, I would grow to become a practitioner-researcher, in order to facilitate an integrated and whole perspective to our work.

Medical Humanities: Reflections as Formal Assessment

The performance module of the Medical Humanities allowed us to explore and push reflections further at tertiary level. The module was created due to an entirely coincidental communication. In 2011, we were casting our thinking towards cross-disciplinary teaching because we saw that the arts have the power to influence lives beyond those enamoured with them. A proposal was developed for the Medical Faculty at the University of Hong Kong. Concurrently, the faculty was taking steps towards a credit-bearing curriculum in the Medical Humanities. The performance module began life in 2012 and is still going strong.

There were two phases to our involvement in the teaching of years 1 and 2 MBBS (Bachelor of Medicine and Bachelor of Surgery) undergraduates as part of their academic learning. Phase 1 from 2012 to 2022 involved a choice of music or drama workshops. Phase 2 from 2022 until the present shifted to option 1, Drama for Communication Skills, or option 2, Movement and Dialogue in Relationships, as a result of feedback from students.

At level 3 complexity, and credit-bearing, the curriculum's overarching framework proposed was discussed with the clinicians in charge and a committee that oversaw the alignment of four other Medical Humanities modules taught by the faculty. The module's interactive three-hour classes are still taught by teaching artists who co-design and co-create lesson plans with us, in which regular assessment and evaluations are conducted. Student assessments are both formative (during class) and summative (at the end of class).

During class, undergrads are graded on their involvement and participation in activities, their response to questions, and how they relate to each other. At the close of the workshops, twenty minutes are accorded to written reflections where open-ended questions ascertained their understanding of the themes of Doctor and Patient Identities and Culture and Care.

Written reflections could not floor these medical students who had to be very high achievers to be awarded a place in the university's medical school. It was the activities that required them to be on their feet, to improvise, to express themselves verbally and physically during the intense workshops, areas the majority were unused to. Regardless, grades are allotted through a rubrics system. This became our entry point in articulating key performance indicators.

Part IV

2013–2018: The Middle Years

We have always had faith in Hong Kong's young people. What more, we pondered, could learning through the arts achieve for young people? Could the arts enrich lives further? Having a few years of experience in *From Page to Stage* for the masses tucked under our belts, it was evident by the end of the Venue Partnership Scheme's third year (2011) that we did not have the resources to go wide *and* deep simultaneously. Therefore, we made an intentional choice to go for depth and fewer numbers rather than the masses.

As such, thoughts on cultivating levels of increasingly higher capacity-building programmes surfaced. Hence, the idea for the Medical Humanities programme was seeded in 2011 as well. In addition to *Sm-ART Youth*, another project for young people began to crystallise for secondary school students, specifically for those with a passion for acting at levels 2 to 3.

How could the arts unlock the potential of secondary students? It was obvious that, due to the huge number of schools competing annually in the schools' speech and drama festivals, perhaps this appetite in drama could be leveraged by providing a platform for higher and deeper learning.

As the three early years programmes were ongoing, a prospective funder came into the picture with an interest in youth, arts, and education. We were very blessed with the Lee Hysan Foundation, which was also attuned to values that are similar to ours, particularly regarding depth and quality.

Bravo! Hong Kong Youth Theatre Awards: Reflections and Social Impact Assessment

In 2011, when the first meeting was set up with Lee Hysan, time was taken to explore an idea whereby young people in secondary schools could be awarded wider exposure in being trained in acting locally and overseas as part of their socio-emotional development in personal growth. Reviewing the need to encourage more young people who might wish to capacity-build, we knew that the earlier they were professionally trained over a longer duration, the better would be their chance of admission into tertiary education at the Hong Kong Academy for Performing Arts or equivalent institutions abroad.[10]

The first cohort of *Bravo!*[11] (for 13 to 19-year-olds) was launched in 2013 with subsequent intakes every other year on completion of each 1.5-year programme. Selected through rigorous auditions and interviews, beneficiaries were kept to a maximum of fifty.

Critical thinking was central to the training, and this is why the programme began at level 2 (locally), graduating to level 3 (overseas). From the very first local workshops over one week, six hours a day, written reflections would end the day with thirty minutes of quiet time, during which all young actors spent time reviewing the day with six recurring questions:

- What have you learnt today?
- What did you find easy?
- What did you find challenging?
- Do you think you have met expectations today? Why?
- In what aspects do you think you can do better in? How?
- Do you have any other thoughts?

The six questions were repeated daily for each workshop. This was both to familiarise actors with the thinking as part of self-assessment and to cultivate a habit of mind based on those enquiries. Actors were given the choice to write in either Chinese or English, thereby ensuring that the language they were most comfortable in supported their thinking without having to search for the next word. This also aligned with *Bravo*'s provision of two streams: the Physical Theatre stream and the Classic Theatre stream, facilitated in Cantonese and English entirely and respectively.

We have since completed four cohorts, the last of which was truncated because of the 2019 social rest and COVID in 2020. Regardless, one recurring pattern occurred from *Bravo* 1 to 3 (2013–2018). Almost inevitably, reflections from the

---

10. *Bravo* graduates have since been accepted for bachelor's and master's studies at the Hong Kong Academy for Performing Arts and Taipei National University of the Arts in acting in Asia. In London, they were trained further in London, at the East 15 Acting School, the Royal Academy of Dramatic Art, and the universities of Birmingham, Cambridge, Manchester, Nottingham, and Surrey, and in New York at PACE University. Some have become professional actors, and many others have turned to using their training in social work, law, etc.
11. Project description is in the appendix.

first round of workshops saw many staring into space, at a loss as to how to respond. Eventually they did with either single short sentences or for some, blanks (figure 5.3).

Moving into the second round of workshops, the situation would slowly improve for two reasons (figure 5.4). The mind became habituated as young actors needed to reconcile themselves to the fact that critical thinking is the modus operandi in *Bravo*. Secondly, in this ensuing phase, LAMDA artists from London joined us in Hong Kong, and they taught at tertiary level, fielding open-ended and probing questions at every turn. The actors had to respond to maximise such a rare opportunity.

In retrospect, most importantly, it is the degree of trust, the feeling of safety and camaraderie that was brought to bear in a *Bravo* theatre space. These three values were intentionally cultivated. From *Sm-ART Youth* to the Medical Humanities classrooms, it was evident that for participants to be open to their own thoughts and to communicate them to others, all answers were accepted without judgement, and no one person was made to feel less than another. The environment – physical, mental, and emotional – became a key facet in our philosophy in the years to come.

By the time rehearsals came around in the run-up to the theatre production a few months later, actors were reflecting more deeply, being accustomed to introspection (figure 5.5). And they could see that written reflections helped not only their own thinking but others as well, as they shared the goal of a collaborative endeavour.

Those who successfully auditioned for London training spent four weeks at LAMDA daily, as if they were in higher education (figure 5.6). Teaching reached level 3. In the mornings, actors warmed up their minds and bodies in groups at the hostel before breakfast. In the evenings, after the day's training, they gathered in study groups to review the day and reflect in journals. It was in London where their normal Hong Kong routines were disrupted, substituted with training and cultural outings as learning experiences. With this entire group of actors, reflections truly started to convert into a regular habit of mind.

They just wrote and wrote. From a few sentences on a page when *Bravo* started, to an abundance of words flowing at a pace of pages per day. Young actors generally became more meta-cognitive and were able to articulate their thoughts and feelings better, irrespective of their social-economic backgrounds. Their daily reflections are far too long to be replicated in this chapter. The following unedited excerpts are extracted from different cohorts.

Self-confidence

'I feel more comfortable being myself around people, having spent four weeks opening up to my *Bravo* mates. I got to better understand myself as an independent person in the circumstances, without the influence of my family. I also became more

Presented by 主辦 　　Strategic Partner 策略伙伴 　　Learning Partner 學習伙伴

AFTEC 　　利希慎基金
LEE HYSAN FOUNDATION 　　LAMDA
London Academy of Music & Dramatic Art

Bravo! Hong Kong Youth Theatre Awards 2013-14
Acting Workshop 1
Self-Reflection Form (English Stream)

Name: _____

Date: 3/04/2013

1. What have you learnt today?

- Tadashi Suzuki's way of training his actors.
- Discipline
- A.P.E
ARTICULATION. PROJECTION. EXPRESSION

2. What did you find easy?

& Nothing! I felt really challenged. I hurt my knee so I was pushing myself a lot!

3. What did you find challenging?

Figure 5.3: *Bravo* 1 (2013–2014) Workshop 1 Sample Reflections of Actor A. Image from AFTEC, 2014.

4. Do you think you have met the expectations of the workshop today? Why?

Yes, I was giving 100%. despite the pain in my knee.

5. In what aspects you think you can do better? How will you do it?

I needed to focus a lot more... I feel I broke concentration!

6. Any other thoughts?

Such a tiring session and fun!

Presented by 主辦
AFTEC 5th anniversary

Strategic Partner 策略伙伴
LEE HYSAN FOUNDATION 利希慎基金

Learning Partner 學習伙伴
LAMDA
London Academy of Music & Dramatic Art

Bravo! Hong Kong Youth Theatre Awards 2013-14
Acting Workshop 2
Self-Reflection Form (English Stream)

Name: _____

Date: 28/08/13

1. What have you learnt today?

I learnt about voice exercises and different ways to improve Physical memory.

2. What did you find easy?

I thought helping others was really easy, e.g. when MR. BAXTER asked me to "be in charge" of a group.

3. What did you find challenging?

Trying to give different tones to the governer's wife's voice.

Figure 5.4: *Bravo* 1 (2013–2014) Workshop 2 Sample Reflections by the Same Actor. Image from AFTEC, 2014.

Presented by 主辦   Strategic Partner 策略伙伴   Learning Partner 學習伙伴

      **LAMDA**
London Academy of Music & Dramatic Art

4. Do you think you have met the expectations of the workshop today? Why?

I think I was at a ~~%~~ 80%, I feel like there were times when I wasn't focusing.

5. In what aspects you think you can do better? How will you do it?

FOCUS, ~~and also~~

6. Any other thoughts?

I really enjoyed how we are repeatedly asked to repeat certain scenes. It really helps with remembering and improving the scene.

6. Is what you've done any different from your previous experiences in theatre? Why?

Yes, definitely. I've never done a theatre production like this before and everything was very amazing. Of course I had performed at school in front of audience but in the theatre everything is bigger and better! Like lights, backstage crew, cast, it was great having this experience, I've learnt a lot about what happens backstage, things I wouldn't have been exposed to if I wasn't part of this production.

On Drama & Theatre

7. How did the rehearsals change your perspective on "drama" and "acting"? Please illustrate with examples.

When you're part of a production, there are two key words that I learnt are very important. Dedication + communication. Dedicating your time fully into your character will show professionalism and you will find more ways to understand and portray your character. Communication amongst others to strengthen teamwork or create better relationship. For example, if Ivan and I didn't speak during rehearsals, our relationship on stage wouldn't have looked as natural.

8. To you, what is "team spirit"? What is its significance in a stage production?

Team spirit, I've learnt, doesn't only apply amongst actors but also with everyone involved in the production (stage hands, etc.) Without the stage hands we wouldn't have a smooth running backstage, without the make-up artiste and costume designer we wouldn't have such amazing visuals! Team spirit makes me think of the word "unity". This may sound cliche but, united, we can create a breathtaking performance.

9. During these rehearsals, are there any incidents that fully show the bonding between the actors? If not, how do you work out the team spirit in the remaining rehearsals?

Yes. It happened during our rehearsal, day before the dress. I had forgotten to put away my dressing gown the day before so as a result of that I was "punished" into being unable to go on stage with the correct attire. Being Beating myself up mentally I broke into tears backstage and the cast around me grasped the situation and comforted me. One even went into the adult room to take the dressing gown for me. Though I do not promote "stealing", it was touching that we had become so close that they were not afraid to get in trouble to take back the dressing gown.

On Personal Growth

10. In which aspects you have done well and which improvement is needed? (The answer is not limited to "acting skills".)

I felt I did quite well in motivating the other cast members, helping them when they felt they were in trouble. For example, a lot of the awardees worry about their english pronounciation and sometimes they're afraid to ask for help so I my my best to make them feel comfortable in asking me for help! I think I need to improve on not being hard on myself, self-loving!

11. Did this production bring changes to your personality? Please illustrate with example(s).

I honestly do think this production process has made me stronger. It has shown me how to work in the theatre and it has definitely shown me now to be more professional. If you make a mistake (this is an example referring to the dressing gown incident), rather than cry about it, accept the mistake and the punishment and learn and ensure that it doesn't happen again.

Figure 5.5: *Bravo* 1 (2013–2014) Rehearsal Reflections by the Same Actor. Image from AFTEC, 2014.

Figure 5.6: *Bravo* Young Actors (2015–2016) in LAMDA, London. Photo by George Chao for AFTEC, 2016.

confident in my own passion for theatre, I'm less worried about other peoples' opinions on my hopes to prove this path, and I've also let myself accept that this is where I want to be for my own happiness, disregarding the possible instability of such a career path. I've also loosened up my uptight mindset that I must get into acting school immediately. Though this is a goal, I've opened my mind to other possibilities and opportunities that may come my way.' (*Bravo* 2)

Overcoming challenges

'The second thing would be realising that I am the biggest challenge and obstacle for myself. During the training, I have sulked quite often because of interpersonal relationship problems, which obviously hindered my learning in the four-week training. Of course, afterwards I really regretted having ever done such a thing, but I realised that it was because of my ego and pride which partly caused me to isolate myself from learning. Therefore, I now believe that as long as I can overcome myself, I can overcome any challenge.

'Last but not least, I have learnt that the most efficient way to tackle a problem would be to face it directly and immediately... Sure, it might seem that this is a particular case, but I believe that this concept can be applied similarly to other scenarios such as when learning, it is best to ask about something you do not understand immediately.'

'In these brief four weeks . . . I have also learnt how to live as a person. I have learnt how to learn efficiently by asking and grasping every opportunity we can get – whether it is volunteering to perform in front of our peers, or as simple as asking a question, we should always go for these opportunities.' (*Bravo* 2)

Time management and commitment

'I remember that I was late for the airport assembly time by about three minutes. Well, a few minutes might not be that serious. But when everyone has this mind and collectively is late a few minutes, that will become a major problem. Therefore, I've never been late for the rest of the trip, including waking up and all the assembly times . . .'

'Being committed and devoted to the lessons and all the activities is also very critical. Having a proper attitude to attend every lesson could boost our energy as well as the efficiency of our learning progress. It is so important to stay energetic during lessons and outings to pursue as much knowledge as we can. I should keep this attitude when I go back to school. The public exam is coming, and I have to pay as much attention in lessons in the coming year.' (*Bravo* 3)

Being reflective and critically minded

'. . . were traits that I definitely obtained and worked on during my stay in London. For example, writing reflections required me to be thoughtful and critical of my day, picking apart what I had done, why I had done it, the effects it had on me, what I could do to improve.'

'The cultural trips we went on and the shows we watched also made us more critical of the information we were taking in; we weren't just blankly absorbing facts and reading museum plaques but actually thinking about how this information was relevant to us, what message certain pieces were trying to convey, and even wondering why these pieces were in museums. By doing this, being reflective and critical minded wasn't something that stayed on paper. It became a way of living, and I'm glad that I've picked up this habit.'

'We've also been encouraged to ask questions in *Bravo*, and I've found myself raising my hand more in class at school, or at least finding a teacher after class if I'm not sure about something. If I'm curious, I just ask! After London, I also feel like I've definitely become a lot more critical, being able to understand that things are not completely black and white, learning to appreciate shows while at the same time being able to identify parts that could have been improved. Through all of the cultural trips and shows we've gone to, I have been able to build up a database of information, becoming more aware of what's going on around me, encouraging me to be a world citizen instead of just a Hong Kong one.' (*Bravo* 3)

Social Impact Assessment

With the experiences of early year projects, a mixed-methodology concept began to emerge which spoke to the arts for transformative educational change. This began from the changes that we witnessed from *Bravo* 1 (2013–2014) in candidates that were able to advance their learning sequentially from local training (challenging) to international training at LAMDA in London (even more challenging). We realised that *Bravo* needed to reside in a macro framework along the lines of a theory of change. It was two cohorts later that this sequence for change appeared.

Reading from left to right, this is the building block (table 5.2):

Table 5.2: Arts Change Lives Theory of Change Concept. Image from AFTEC, 2023.

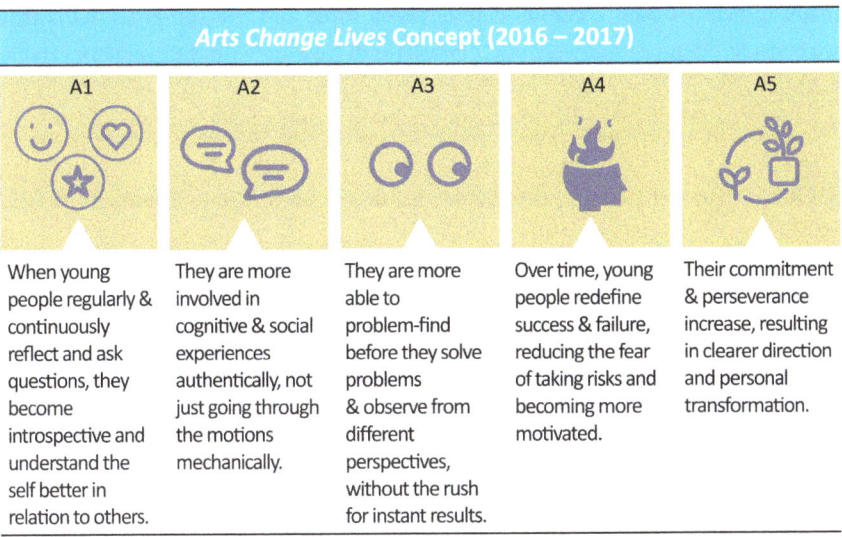

A1	A2	A3	A4	A5
When young people regularly & continuously reflect and ask questions, they become introspective and understand the self better in relation to others.	They are more involved in cognitive & social experiences authentically, not just going through the motions mechanically.	They are more able to problem-find before they solve problems & observe from different perspectives, without the rush for instant results.	Over time, young people redefine success & failure, reducing the fear of taking risks and becoming more motivated.	Their commitment & perseverance increase, resulting in clearer direction and personal transformation.

As we gained understanding from *Bravo* 1 and *Bravo* 2 (2013–2016), the concept was probed further and expanded. We saw the change, but others might contest that the anecdotes or qualitative data were inadequate. It is a fact of life that quantitative surveys with numbers mean 'reality' to many. Given this continuous buzz in the mind, we decided to take a leap of faith and experiment with the possibility of setting KPIs that would materialise as hard statistical data.

This was achieved as an internal venture at the outset, as we were unsure of the actual viability of quantifying learning this way. I am totally cognisant of the fact that the sample size is very small. Then again, the company is about working at depth, so it made sense for us to experiment anyway. As we did not have any expertise in this area, we reached out to our contacts, and in time, the evaluation duo at i4socialimpact, an NGO-friendly organisation, took up our cause at a low bono rate.

A social impact assessment was conducted for the 2017–2018 *Bravo* 3 cohort in addition to regular reflections. Throughout the *Bravo* programme, a series of four questionnaires via Google forms were given to the actors to assess important areas of youth development and empowerment such as growth in the self, communication skills, sociability, determination, and acting proficiencies.

The pre-test questionnaire was administered to students prior to their first workshop in March 2017 and from there three post-questionnaires (post 1 after the first workshop, post 2 after public performance, and post 3 after last workshop and auditions for LAMDA) tracked progress. Additionally, a questionnaire for parents and/or teachers was sent out the same time as the first post-questionnaire.

Two main blocks separate self-assessment and programme evaluation. Six major indicators each accommodate between three and five sub-goals. KPIs that we considered important were put forward for discussion with the evaluators (table 5.3).

Table 5.3: Key Performance Indicators for *Bravo* Cohort 3. Image from AFTEC, 2023.

BLOCK 1 Assessment					BLOCK 2 Evaluation
B1. Self	B2. Communication Competency	B3. Sociability	B4. Determination	B5. Acting Proficiency	Programme Evaluation
Esteem	Public Speaking	Personal Network	Discipline	Ambitions	Reaction
Confidence	Communication Skills	Socialness	Goal-setting	Knowledge	Engagement
Reflection	English Skills	Teamwork	Motivation	Acting Skills	Programme Evaluation
Open-mindedness			Risk-taking		Tutor Evaluation
Future			Problem-solving		

Table 5.4 demonstrates an emerging correlation between tables 5.2 and 5.3 except for the evaluation block which is not considered here, as it does not refer to personal transformation but the actors' rating of the *Bravo* programme. The connection is to be understood by reading between the two tables (5.2 and 5.3) in which A1 and B1, A2 and B2, and so on, are linked.

Table 5.4: Arts for Change and KPIs Correlation. Image from AFTEC, 2023.

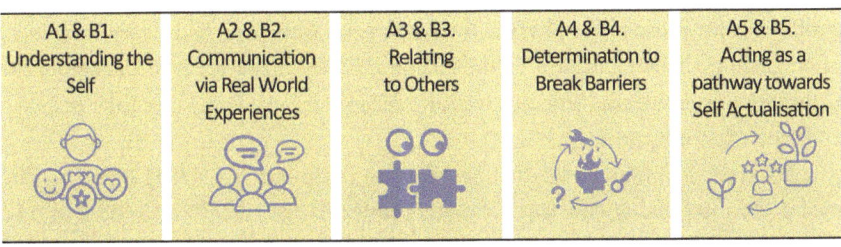

A1 & B1. Understanding the Self	A2 & B2. Communication via Real World Experiences	A3 & B3. Relating to Others	A4 & B4. Determination to Break Barriers	A5 & B5. Acting as a pathway towards Self Actualisation
Introspection emanates from the inner space of the self. As reflection is continuously habituated, self confidence is likely to slowly increase resulting in better self esteem. We hope to see that open-mindedness is enhanced and in time, actors will be more positive in their outlook.	Casual conversations are distinct from the ability to speak in public, as this has everything to do with the ability to know what to say and how to say it through organised thought. Through acting training, actors learn to communicate physically (body language) and verbally. For those from disadvantaged circumstances, the need to work in English with LAMDA tutors meant they can work on their language skills.	The inner self is a safe haven seeking to protect itself from external elements. As the self is increasingly aware and more secure of its identity through social interaction and teamwork in acting, we hope that actors can observe, listen and feel for others. By doing so, they are able to register opinions and viewpoints wider than themselves.	*Bravo!* provides a good platform for personal network development that specifically concentrates on acting as a strong communal passion. The resulting motivation of being in a peer group whose individuals share similar goals, means actors constantly encourage each other through highly disciplined training (including strict punctuality). Together, we anticipate they will create a community that will solve problems and take risks collectively, and where camaraderie outweighs success and failure.	Although *Bravo*'s training standard can prepare actors for careers in acting and the theatre, each actor's ambition to become professional is secondary. The knowledge, skills, values and attitudes of commitment & perseverance embedded in the programme empower young actors and give agency, if not the possibilities of future directions.

Research was carried out in phases with a pre-programme survey and three post-programme surveys over the eighteen months of training. While there was a general upward growth of individual KPIs for all actors, those with an asterisk indicated statistically significant ones (figure 5.7).

Acting Ambitions and Acting Knowledge[12] were statistically significant due to rich content, depth of learning planned in the programme, and the calibre of the professionals.

English language improvement was a surprise though in retrospect, it made good sense for those in the physical theatre stream. Almost all had a very basic level of English, primarily because of their economically disadvantaged backgrounds. Consequently, there was little motivation to learn and use English in their primary and secondary education.

We were delighted to see that Self-Esteem came out as a strong index, as this meant the interlinking constructs situated under A1/B1, A2/B2, A3/B3 and A4/B4 interrelated sufficiently to create a virtuous cycle, which in the end boosted self-esteem. From an Asian and Chinese context here in Hong Kong, this was noteworthy indeed.

In this quantitative research, we were also interested in the performance between two other groups of actors: those in systemic disadvantaged positions and those who had no financial issues.[13]

Figure 5.8 reviews progress for those who did not need financial assistance. These young actors tended to come from more middle-class backgrounds and were more academically inclined. These are attitudinal changes. As seen from the figure, the group of financially able students experienced statistically significant changes in their Acting Ambitions, Acting Knowledge, Self-Esteem, and Teamwork.

The group of financially underprivileged students (figure 5.9) experienced statistically significant changes in their Acting Ambitions, Acting Knowledge, English, and Public Speaking skills. On average, the financially underprivileged group rated themselves lower than their financially able counterparts did. As with *Sm-ART Youth* children also from underserved areas, a lack of exposure and routine living without much stimulation at home and in school also meant a higher degree of passivity and a tendency to be less forthcoming.

---

12. Acting Knowledge includes acting skills.
13. *Bravo* prioritised the selection of actors from economically underprivileged backgrounds, and free training was offered abroad. Those who could manage the overseas trip were asked to do so at cost, to subsidise their less able counterparts.

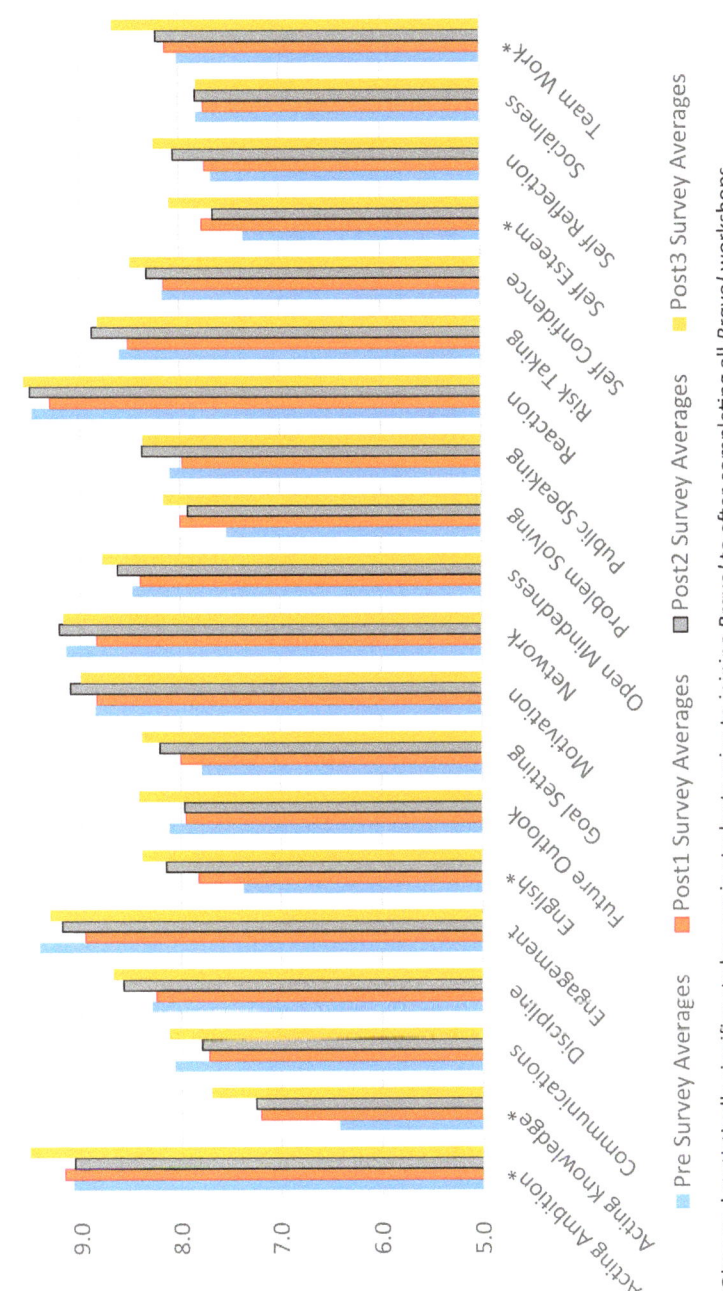

Figure 5.7: KPIs for All Actors from Both Classic and Physical Theatre Streams. Image from i4socialimpact for AFTEC, 2017.

*Observed statistically significant changes in students prior to joining Bravo! to after completing all Bravo! workshops.

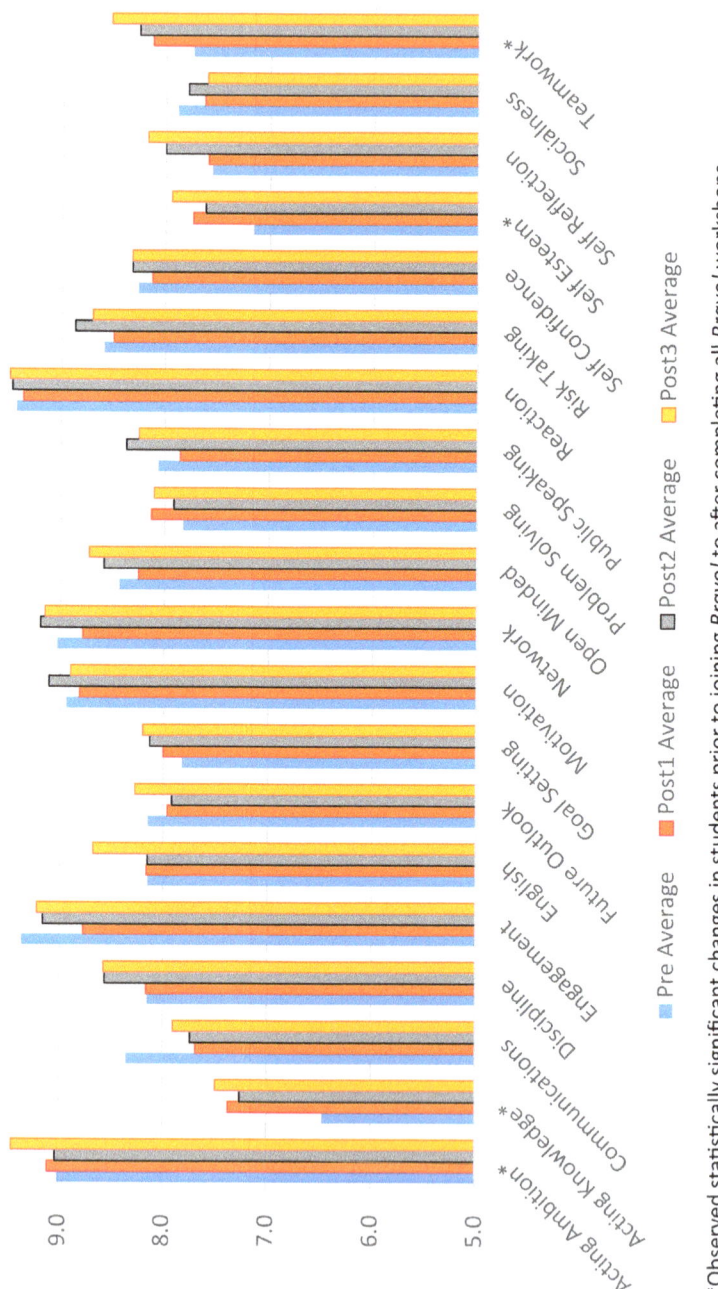

Figure 5.8: KPIs for Financially Able Group across Both Streams. Image from i4socialimpact for AFTEC, 2017.

*Observed statistically significant changes in students prior to joining *Bravo!* to after completing all *Bravo!* workshops.

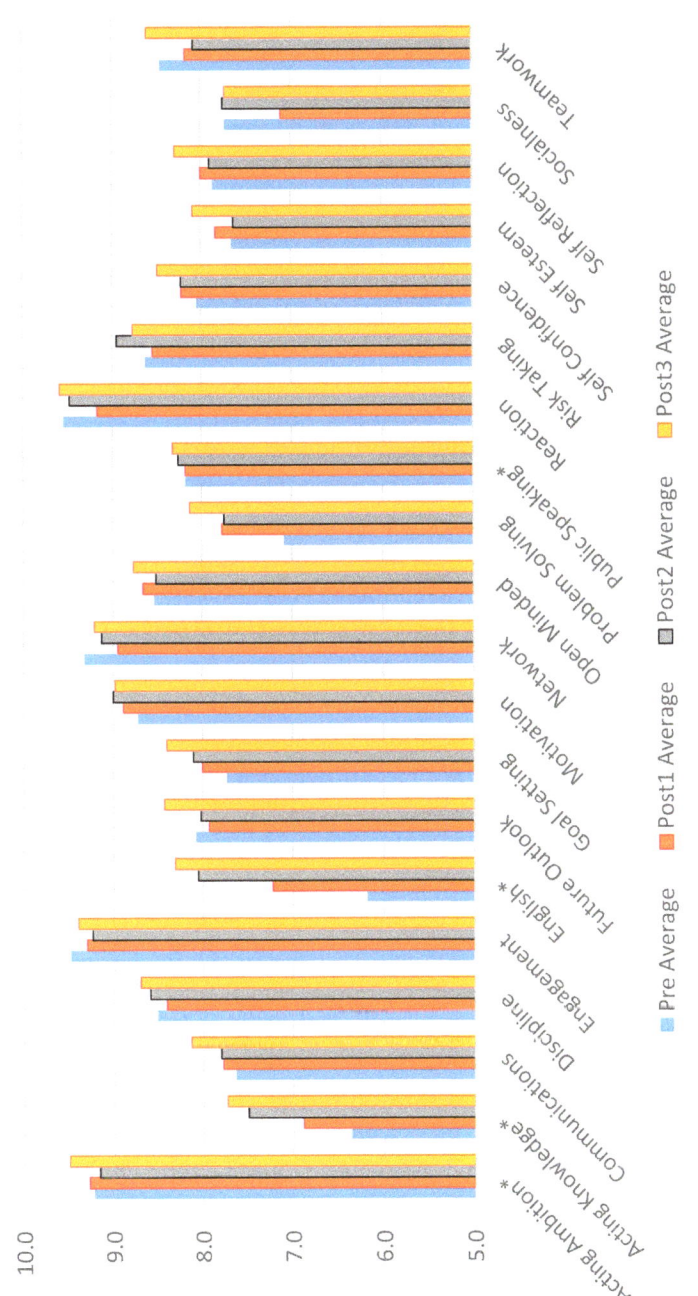

*Observed statistically significant changes in students prior to joining *Bravo!* to after completing all *Bravo!* workshops.

Figure 5.9: KPIs for Financially Disadvantaged Group across Both Streams. Image from i4socialimpact for AFTEC, 2017.

Behavioural Changes

Data from figures 5.7 to 5.9 revealed attitudinal shifts. To understand whether accompanying behavioural changes were also present, we expressly requested the evaluators to investigate this as well. Results are documented in figure 5.10.

Behavioural changes are shown in post 1 to 3 averages. While Goal-Setting and Socialness topped the KPIs in actual transfer, other data were equally interesting.

Acting Ambition was highest in post 2 data because of the theatre production that occurred just before the survey. In post 3 data, this dropped, as there was only one production, and although a mini showcase was produced at LAMDA at the end of the month-long training, it was for LAMDA staff only in a rehearsal and not a professional theatre space.

Similarly, for Communications, Discipline, and Risk-Taking, actors in a theatre production facing an audience were full of adrenaline to achieve a good production. This is generally where peak performance occurs. One noteworthy point with Risk-Taking at post 3 was that it was only slightly lower than at post 2. The reason was that, at LAMDA, where training was raised to higher-education level, teenage actors were pushed to step out of their comfort zones even further.

By then, the rare opportunity of being in LAMDA trained by global experts of the highest calibre became a strong motivating factor to keep on breaking barriers. Another point on Discipline, which was lower in post 3, was probably the result of the now routine habit of having to be highly disciplined daily at LAMDA.

It is exciting to note that Self-Esteem remained on a high, illustrating that changes in attitudes have transformed into action. Clearly shown in figure 5.10 are data recognition that Self-Confidence has improved as well. Reflection came down in ranking possibly because of it being a habit already ingrained into the mindset and daily activities. This was evident from the earlier discussions and extracts from actors' journals. Similarly, Problem Solving remained on the high right to programme completion, also as a result of LAMDA training, where lecturers constantly posed questions through activities for individual and group engagement.

Motivation and Ambitions indicators broke the scale at nine points, whereas the other KPIs did not because *Bravo* was developed to be very motivational even at the outset. To rephrase this, those who completed the London segment were extremely inspired and stimulated. Those who dropped out even before the end of the Hong Kong training did so because of an inability to keep up or because of the demands of schoolwork.

From the early years to *Bravo* as a middle-year case study, it was programme intention and insistence on quality with embedded assessment and evaluation that effected systemic change. In turn, this brought positive change and impact to artistic

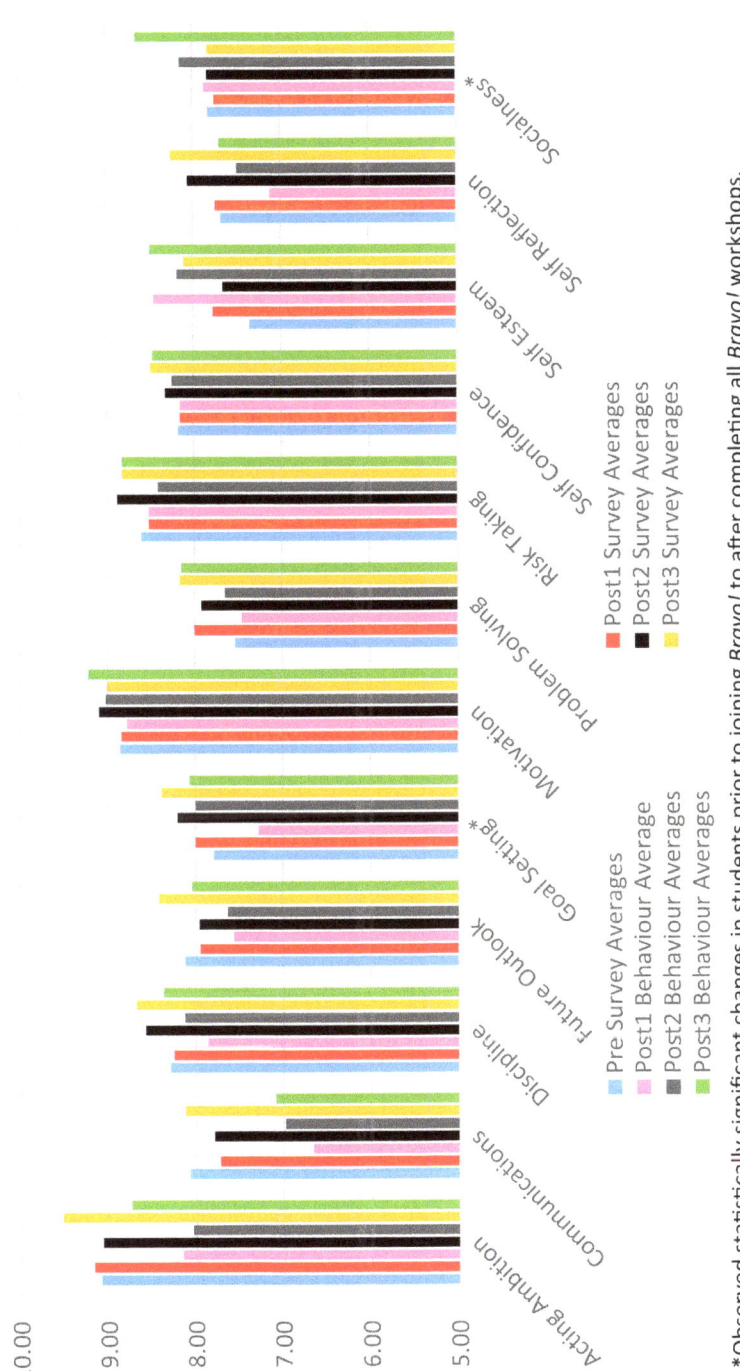

Figure 5.10: Attitudinal to Behavioural Change for All Actors from Both Streams. Image from i4socialimpact for AFTEC, 2017.

*Observed statistically significant changes in students prior to joining *Bravo!* to after completing all *Bravo!* workshops.

and personal development. This appears to be crucial above all else, more than growing a greater number of programmes for a larger number of beneficiaries.

For schools with huge numbers coming to the annual theatre productions, *From Page to Stage* level 1 programme worked as a means of initial access for young people and professionals who may not have encountered learning *through* the arts, as opposed to learning *in* the arts. For schools then and now, the main intent is language learning through drama, not youth development.

Part V

2019–2024: Recent Years

Jockey Club Arts-Based Cross Curriculum Creative Learning Year 2 (2022–2023)

Assessment and evaluation focus accountability. Crucially, though, they also assist an organisation that desires to review the past, track the present, and aim to do better in the future. Assessment of individuals is a running mate to the evaluation of organisational purpose.

The questionnaires for *From Page to Stage* students and teachers were at a basic level with broad questions. Journals for students in *Sm-ART Youth* provided scaffolding over a wide range of art forms. The Medical Humanities performance module assessment was specifically designed for medical undergraduates' understanding of the workshops on their path to becoming doctors. The vigorous and rigorous plunge into critical thinking for *Bravo* young actors elicited thoughts that few have attempted to investigate, let alone express.

In review, effort and time had primarily been accorded to students and mindset growth. It was apparent that an area worthy of attention is the development of adult professionals, such as teachers and artists, who are a force to contend with, given that their collective impact can be formidable.

This *Jockey Club Arts-Based Cross Curriculum Creative Learning* project was a three-year pilot completed in mid-2024. This project for creative teaching and learning through the arts involved ten primary schools, ten principals, over fifty-nine teachers,[14] and seventeen creative practitioners by project end.

A core premise of the project was to cultivate a local creative thinking pedagogy. This required a purposeful shift from traditional teaching methods to a more creative approach. As demonstrated by our ongoing work, one type of classroom learning does not overshadow another; a harmonious balance must be maintained.

---

14. Originally only twenty teachers, two per school, were intended, but word of mouth and evidence of student change caught the attention of more teachers, who signed up.

A creative habit of mind had to be nurtured by professionals before students could effectively engage in thoughtful expression. The professionals involved in this project comprise teachers and creative practitioners, who worked as peers, learning and influencing one another.

Influential educator Donald Schon's 'reflection on action' and 'reflection in action'[15] played a huge role here. His prescient understanding of the ways professionals act foregrounds open-ended questions as an approach to facilitate critical thinking. Open-ended questions prevent single empirical answers and opt for diverse ones. It is through this strategy that students not only learn how to think on their own, facilitated by follow-up questions, but more particularly, to become active learners through self-motivation. It is amazing that, when professionals take time to genuinely listen, as opposed to looking for the intended answers, children become increasingly driven to want to learn (figure 5.11).

Students in this pilot project undertaken within formal curriculum hours were asked to reflect as a matter of routine in class and during cultural outings, on paper,

Figure 5.11: Collective Reflection Sparks Thinking and Prompts Ownership. Photo from AFTEC, 2024.

---

15. Donald A. Schön, *The Reflective Practitioner: How Professionals Think in Action* (Basic Books, 1983).

a padlet, or on the learning management system created for the project. As schools were usually less used to open-ended questions as a key strategy in thinking, the professionals had to be comfortable asking them in the first place before this habit could extend into the classroom. This was cultivated in full-day training workshops throughout the year. By the end of the second year, a majority of professionals in year 2 schools were able to achieve this to varying degrees.

In March 2023, as the team prepared for the annual year-end Knowledge Exchange Forum, a conversation on how professionals were conducting reflections in those schools concluded in a decision to take a straw poll among the team, ranking the ten schools according to the quality of reflection methods and nature of answers that students gave. For confidentiality, school names are not revealed. The teams' votes, based on their weekly observations in class, are listed in table 5.5.

Schools 8 to 10 had yet to manage reflections in class, though they were in the minority. A few reasons could be attributed to this: they were still adjusting, shifting from a traditional mindset to a creative one; school leadership had not yet become actively supportive, and teachers and creative practitioners were still working on understanding how creative classrooms differ from traditional ones.

Classified as middle-performing schools, schools 5 to 7 revealed that reflections were becoming a regular in-class feature. In these classrooms, professionals were quite comfortable fielding open-ended questions though follow-up was still lacking. The main difference between the struggling schools and this middle group was that students in the latter schools were able to provide descriptive answers about what they have done in class.

Top-ranking schools (1 to 4) had a strong professional team of teachers and creative practitioners who consistently embedded reflections into their facilitation throughout the teaching process, rather than using reflections solely as an assessment tool. Likewise, they stimulated students to go beyond descriptive responses, encouraging them to provide evidence for their comments, personal opinions, and ideas, even at the primary school level. We often underestimate children's thinking; as some teachers have noted, they have seen students open up and come alive. Only when adult professionals undergo transformation themselves can they empower children further.

Table 5.6 records a rubric created from the informal reflections ranking in creative classrooms for professionals based on our overall experience in the past two years. This six-point rubric may be helpful for those who seek an overview and a platform for further thinking.

Table 5.5: Informal School Rankings for Reflections Facilitation. Image from AFTEC, 2023.

School Ranking (1 = Best)	Reasons
1	- Professionals facilitate reflection weekly through open-ended questions, from individuals to groups sharing. - Students are encouraged to respond to each other's work and answers. - Reflections are done through different formats (padlet, reflection corners, journals). - Student give evidence-based answers.
2	- Professionals facilitate reflections weekly through open-ended questions. - Professionals discuss good examples in class illustrating those that gave reasons and evidence to their answers. - Debriefing in class with students verbally explaining their feelings & insights, then padlet written reflections to be done at home.
3	- Professionals facilitate class wrap-up & reflections with open-ended questions. - Students complete padlet reflections after class. Answers are in-depth. - Professionals discuss good examples in class and preview the next class in response to students' present queries.
4	- Professionals facilitate reflections mostly during class. - Recap class content and draw out students' insights including feelings. - Written reflection in class with professionals sitting with each group. - Discussions among students to reflect their learning.
5	- Professionals facilitate reflections weekly through open-ended questions. - Students reflect in journals after class with professional feedback and good examples.
6	- Professionals facilitate reflections weekly through open-ended questions. - Students generally complete padlet reflections after class with around 20% completion rate. - Mostly descriptive reflections of what was done in class.
7	- Teachers facilitate verbal reflections in small groups. - On an index card, students complete drawings which reflect their expressions. - Provide some words for special need students to express themselves. - Provide emotion stickers for students.
8	- Reflections happen occasionally. - One teacher broke ground at one cultural outing with good open-ended reflection questions. - Students' answers are descriptive of what was done in class.
9	- Simple verbal reflections achieved requiring immense effort from professionals. - Padlet reflections are descriptive. - Professionals' realisation of the importance of reflections from Term 2.
10	- Professionals attempting simple reflections in class. - Verbal reflections in the main.

Table 5.6: Possible Reflection Rubrics for Professionals in Creative Classrooms. Image from AFTEC, 2023.

Very Good	Coming Along	Not Yet
1. Reduction of teachers' workload and provision of structured time from top management for teachers & CPs to review, reflect & plan. Top management is actively interested and involved.	Provision of structured time from top management for teachers & CPs to review, reflect & plan.	No provision of structured time from top management for teachers & CPs to review, reflect & plan.
2. Reflection is firmly embedded as part of the integrated lesson plans.	Reflection is a regular routine.	Reflection is barely done.
3. Questions are open-ended and follow-ups are directed from the single student outwards.	Questions are open-ended and follow ups happen for the individual student.	Questions are close-ended.
4. Highly aware of the impact of reflections and will occasionally stop the classroom to pursue learning opportunities relevant to the whole class.	Aware of the impact from reflections.	Unaware of the the power of reflections and/or unable to include reflections as yet.
5. Students are excited about giving their evidence-based viewpoints regularly with or without scaffolding from professionals. Feelings are part of the answers.	Students answering with their own viewpoints. Mainly giving descriptive replies ("what"). Giving evidence to viewpoints occasionally. Able to explain their feelings as well.	Students not engaged in critical thinking.
6. Professional collaboration amongst teachers and CPs are at a level in which they follow on from one another and the energy is three-way: teachers, CPs and students as class happens.	Getting and giving feedback from professionals and among students are part of the main energy in the classroom aside from hands-on activities.	Main energy in the classroom is hand-on activities.

Part VI

Assessment and evaluation represent not only a review (looking back) but more a preview (looking forward) through missed opportunities, new discoveries, and teaching occasions to come. Reflecting on assessment and evaluation origins once more, we realise that our company culture may indeed have contributed to it. While I would not presume that internal company meetings, where colleagues routinely share updates and contribute to collective learning, directly inspire our programme pedagogies, I would suggest that we have deliberately cultivated a culture of lifelong learning as an adopter of Peter Senge's 'learning organizations' philosophy.[16]

Based on reflections woven throughout this chapter's exploration of assessment and evaluation approaches across five case studies, the following are concluding thoughts on their efficacy and why they should be endorsed by both education-focused arts organisations and institutions, regardless of the learners' ages.

1. Reflection is exploratory. It is process- and not product-driven in the sense that the goal for reflecting occurs at each phase of the activity. The flow is such that each phase is in and of itself a culmination of thinking, each adding to the next.
2. It moves in concentric circles from the inner self outwards, connecting within and beyond to others. It is a privileged encounter with others' deeper selves.
3. It has a dance movement of backwards, forwards, twisting, and turning around, starting again. Pausing every now and then continuously to take stock is the key to good pacing. The thinking is considered, not rushed.
4. Reflection needs time and needs intentionally structured time with the blessings of top management.
5. Reflection is framed by the values that one believes in that underpin the fabric and quality of the programme. It adds value to the creative classroom with the possibility of extending the same values to become a school culture.
6. It is understanding, problem-finding, and problem-solving. It is about challenging oneself with support from others.
7. Reflection is encountering alternative experiences.
8. It is communication, accountability, and setting standards.

In this organisation, the discomfort of missed steps dissolved long ago into better planning, more tweaking, and even more reflections. As an arts-in-education

---

16. Peter M. Senge, *The Fifth Discipline: The Art & Practice of The Learning Organization* (Doubleday, 1990).

organisation, we believe that, in bringing our aspirations and passions to the forefront (soft powers), we additionally foster the rational habit of mind to analyse data (hard powers).

Over the years, I have come to understand that assessment and evaluation are ongoing processes, never ending and thus, imperfect. Indeed, we have sometimes, in our ardent endeavour to explore, perhaps fallen prey to over-zealous programming. This challenge arises partly from the difficulty of distancing oneself from daily routines to consistently cultivate a mindset that embraces assessment and evaluation, partly from a lack of expertise within the organisation and beyond, and finally, because arts evaluation is inherently complex.

Nevertheless, challenging though it may be, there is little excuse to discontinue. To do so is akin to blindly assuming that all is always well, that we are healthy, we are constantly at peak performance, and the ills of body and mind belong elsewhere. That would be far too escapist.

All in all, the reason for a lack of support in undertaking more qualitative evaluation and results acceptance lies in the difference between anecdotal evidence and empirical data. We need a different language and approach that speaks to the arts. This necessitates the collaboration between the arts (including the humanities) and social sciences, which excel in research methodologies.

6

Those COVID Days

The Arts and Well-Being

Summary

Few saw COVID-19 coming, and none believed the routine of daily life would be restricted in a major way for the three years of lockdown. This is the context of the chapter in which the implications of the pandemic are analysed through organisational change and development.

Part I contextualises the affective aspect of being human. Part II trains a lens on how AFTEC coped with those work-from-home years and our programming. Part III is the main discussion on two case studies demonstrating the effect of the arts on young people who are in special schools that manage social–emotional learning and other examples of arts and well-being work done by others in the city.

Part I

Reflections on Emotions

Why do we seldom deal with feelings in school? Arts lessons could, though from experience, the feelings are more likely the painter's, the character's, and the composer's.

Talking about feelings is definitely challenging, particularly in comparatively conservative Asian societies and families, as it involves working through raw emotions brought on by the body's rising sensations and then having to organise and articulate them. That takes work and it is messy. In too many of our workshops when we attempt to encourage participants to enter into another's consciousness – animate or inanimate – and feel, little trickles through.

This chapter is about feelings, processed raw emotions. Feelings and emotions were not subjects of open discussion during my days in school decades ago. They are now part of the curriculum guideline, as holistic development is the educational tune. How much they are connected to classroom teaching and learning is unknown beyond a teacher having to deal with a sleeping student, an ill-mannered one, or one in tears.

COVID has changed this somewhat, I believe. Far beyond just a family or a classroom issue, COVID has forced open the affective door to collective acknowledgment and recognition that, as a city, we saw overwhelming disruption and displacement, we felt the pain and suffering of loved ones, and we empathised with sick and dying strangers.

It took a global pandemic to start this conversation. COVID is the sixth C, the unwanted one, after the 5Cs: creativity, critical thinking, communication, collaboration, and contribution. This chapter is also about COVID and its impact on life from 2020 until January 2023, when pandemic restrictions were finally lifted in Hong Kong.

Finally, this chapter channels feelings and discoveries during and after COVID to well-being, a topic that is involving the arts sector increasingly and which now advances cross-sectorial advocacy to champion the arts for well-being.

The COVID Backstory

During the COVID years, we were blessed with strong team leaders and individual colleagues who voluntarily stepped up and took all things digital and logistical in good stride. It is important that we acknowledge their endurance, perseverance, and commitment. It is even more crucial that their thinking and feelings are recognised as the human faces that saw the organisation through those challenging years. In this chapter, all boxes with a full name are actual reflections and anecdotes from some of our colleagues. They present embodied experiences during those years.

> COVID was a test for everyone, as you would never know how strong you are until you have stepped outside the comfort zone. For so many years, we have been well trained to follow the safest routines within the standard model answers.
>
> With the unexpected and unforeseeable impact that COVID brought, there was no answer to anything. However, a problem without a solution may not be something negative. Indeed, it is a challenge,

it is a chance, it is an opportunity. When there is no precedent, it is time for us to create one. I seized it as a chance to create and experiment every possible way together with others, irrespective of whether it worked or not.

When it came to online teaching and learning, we went through a lot of trial and error. It was very rewarding and frustrating at the same time. Apart from finding the best for students during difficult times, it was indeed good training for our mentality. The practice of constant reflection and evaluation was to prepare for a better me. Failure was inevitable, so I learnt not only to focus on the items that didn't work but to learn from mistakes. As long as we devote ourselves, we will naturally grow and gain.

Ebona Yeung

Part II

The COVID Impact

It was 29 January 2020, just past the Chinese New Year holidays, when the first pandemic wave hit Hong Kong. On top of multiple cautionary and preventative measures being undertaken in the office, we decided to work from home once cases reached the 1,000 mark. Having experienced SARS in 2003, in which 8,098 individuals[1] were infected and 774 patients died, Hong Kong citizens were vigilant and very quickly practised social distancing and mask-wearing. Once bitten, definitely twice shy and extremely wary.

From February 2020 until February 2022, the government launched multiple rounds of fiscal measures to support affected industries and the public. In total, some HK$348 billion[2] (nearly US$44.6 billion) was spent during the period. As all performing arts venues were shuttered, the arts came to a standstill. As schools closed, life as we knew it came to a halt as well. AFTEC's main preoccupation both in the theatre and in educational institutions remained in limbo. The knee-jerk reaction was attempts at salvaging what could be done online. As colleagues frantically

---

1. G. M. Leung, L. M. Ho, T. H. Lam and A. J. Hedley, 'Epidemiology of SARS in the 2003 Hong Kong epidemic', *Hong Kong Medical Journal* 15 (2009): No 6 Supplement 9.
2. 'Anti-epidemic Fund', COVID-19 Thematic Website, The Government of the Hong Kong Special Administrative Region, accessed 2 February 2024, https://www.coronavirus.gov.hk/eng/anti-epidemic-fund.html#:~:text=The%20%24120%20billion%20relief%20package,Council%20on%2018%20April%202020.

rearranged schedules with teachers and arts professionals, the year of living disruptively loomed large. Suddenly, we were thrown into the virtual world.

Here are some statistics to give a picture of the 2020–2021 season.

By the end of the 2020–2021 season, we experienced THREE lockdowns, in which we stayed away from the office.

- We spent a total of SEVEN months working from home as a result.
- Our workload jumped at least 100% salvaging programmes, at online meetings and contingency planning regularly, team heads undertaking multiple group meetings before weekly company ones.
- The team proactively took over FIFTY online courses.
- We researched over 1,000 sites locally and internationally to gauge the arts world in the pandemic and coping strategies.
- Only 33% of our live theatre productions were rescued.
- Together, the team managed to save 80% of classes/workshops using a hybrid blended learning mode of basic online AND live workshops when conditions allowed.
- The words branded firmly into our psyche and DNA-ed into us were COVID, masks, disinfectant, pandemic, change, and Zoom fatigue.

Emotionally, I had self-doubt even before COVID, but the first two years of the COVID period were the worst for me. I kept doubting myself, not sure if I was really capable of the work I was doing, afraid to disappoint my team.

I think COVID actually helped me improve both personally and professionally because it had put me in an uncomfortable situation where I was forced to get out of my comfort zone after some failures and unsatisfactory performance in work.

I lacked the confidence to make decisions or to step up to lead the digiAFTEC team that wasn't working effectively and efficiently. But through this experience I've learnt to take responsibility for the work I did, not just to follow someone's order or wait for others to make decisions. I also further understood the importance of being an independent administrator who could quickly adjust to constant changes in situations. This is part of my personal growth, because being more proactive in work also helped me build better relationships with the people around me.

Eleanor Lam

Individuals and organisations came together to help the sick, poor, and vulnerable. As an arts organisation, we were likewise supported. In diverse ways, donors and institutions came forward, often unsought and unasked. We were blessed, but we knew we could not simply depend on the kindness of strangers, as they too have their own circumstances to deal with. The leg-up in cash and in kind was already a substantial gift.

Once, we were used to routines. Being upended by the pandemic was a rude wake-up call. Once, we were cosseted by a relative order of things. Disorder tested our collective resilience. By February 2020, we knew COVID was much larger than SARS. There was no silver lining on the horizon, and it could not be a matter of waiting it out. Instead, we were inspired by the opening lines of T. S Eliot's *Burnt Norton*, shared in regular team learning sessions among other matters.

> Time present and time past
> Are both perhaps present in time future,
> And time future contained in time past.
> If all time is eternally present
> All time is unredeemable.[3]

COVID squashed all time into an immediate moment. How we would use those moments mattered. This meant that the traditional ways of doing things had to be radically altered, not for the next few days but for an unforeseeable future. Since the pandemic threw us a curve ball and ironically gave us time, we decided to stop and reflect, a fundamental tenet in our organisational culture, and desist from plunging too deep into the usual firefighting mentality.

The entire team began to work from home in late January 2020. From 3 February, we kicked into overdrive. We became introspective and proceeded to audit our work at weekly company virtual meetings.

Rekindling Processes

How could we start? Colleagues clearly needed time to reflect on themselves as individuals and in the face of unrelenting masked days. Vicki Ooi, the artistic director, and I, also needed to catch our breath to plan forward, whatever that meant in the face of enormous uncertainties. If the external world is chaotic, let us ground ourselves first and foremost. We needed to stay positive. We believed the first step was to centre our being and align the self to learning, thereby fuelling personal advancement as the core defence for a crumbling external world. As a learning organisation,

---

3. T. S. Eliot, 'Burnt Norton', in *Four Quartets* (Harcourt, 1943), lines 1–5.

learning was and is for all, irrespective of age, ability, experience, and role in the company.

Step one.

In mixed teams, we investigated the T-shaped learner (figure 6.1) to discuss breadth and depth of being, each colleague deciding the degree in which the path will be taken.

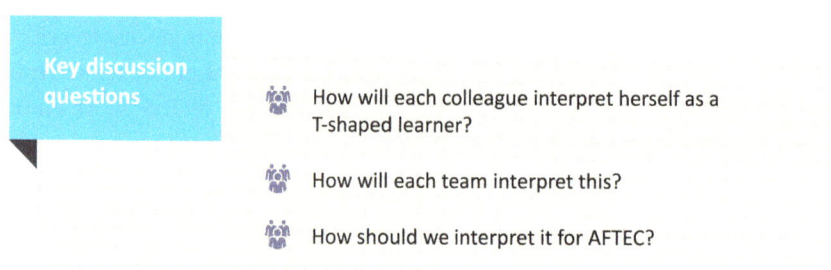

Figure 6.1: Internal Meeting Slide 6 (3 February 2020). Image from AFTEC, 2020.

Step two.

Another week we embarked on a YouTube video journey with psychologist Professor Carol Dweck on her theory of fixed and growth mindsets. Colleagues, again in mixed teams, read and analysed extracts from her book *Mindset: Changing the Way You Think to Fulfil Your Potential* (2017). As T-shaped learners, a growth mindset (figure 6.2) was taken on board to face the many challenges ahead.

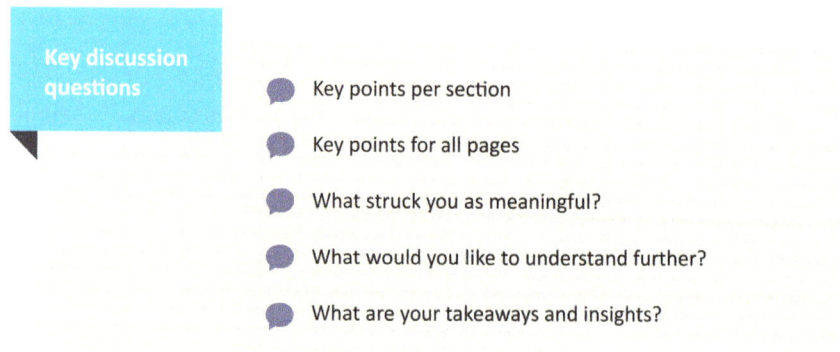

Figure 6.2: PowerPoint Slide 23 (24 February 2020). Image from AFTEC, 2020.

If we could ground ourselves in a growth mindset, we believed we could tackle the pandemic through recognising inner fears, the opportunities to learn and grow. The team leaders, Calvin Co, Natalie Ting, and Ebona Yeung, were superb listeners and proactive leaders. Without them, the struggle would have been far greater.

> What mindset should we adopt in the face of these new changes? I think this is the most important question for me. Actually, I felt discouraged at first, but with each change, my adaptability and problem-solving abilities gradually improved. I found myself gaining new experience and growing every time.
>
> With a growth mindset, I started to face each change positively and saw it as a challenge and an opportunity to improve. Therefore, this change in my mindset also led to changes in my actions.
>
> ———
>
> Many students were underprivileged; we spent a lot of time providing support for them. For one girl who lived with her mum in a protected house with no-Wi-Fi, I prepared a portable Wi-Fi egg and tablet for her for class. To assist her in joining online classes, I guided her through the process step by step.
>
> The arts have the power to inspire, unite, and transform individuals. They can provide a way for people to express themselves, communicate their ideas and feelings, and connect with others. Social interaction does not just benefit beneficiaries but our team as well.
>
> Quoting the *Jockey Club Arts & Action* students as an example, we witnessed their process from being introverted to expressing themselves gradually through colours and lines. With an artistic way to connect themselves with others, they opened up their world and communicated. They even started to cooperate with others in the end.
>
> Christie Yam

Inter-team learning and online learning also became a staple of the organisation that first year. The team proactively took over fifty online courses[4] from tracking

---

4. From self-directed research to sponsored LinkedIn learning licences, courtesy of the Hong Kong Jockey Club Charities Trust.

how the arts field was coping with the pandemic globally to personal interests in museums and theatre to more practical courses in resilience, digital marketing, and coding.

Survival Is Not Enough

By March 2020, and heavily in lockdown at home, the pandemic picture was not looking good. Living in uncertainties warranted a stronger and more structured approach. Led by Vicki Ooi, the company-wide *Survival is Not Enough* think tank was established to galvanise everyone. Adapted from the Borg character Seven of Nine's line, 'Survival is insufficient', in the *Star Trek: Voyager* series, the think tank reviewed and projected pre- and post-COVID work. Various geological ages were included, to emphasise the role of human development and our impact on the world as an aide-memoire (figure 6.3).

> On a personal level, I'm fatalistic, so I accepted the possibility of getting COVID and dealing with it if I were unfortunate enough to be infected. My modus operandi had to change from face-to-face discussions with my team to telephone or Zoom discussions.
>
> I guess this is a mental strain, as I'm not good with the computer and with tech, and my eyes are not good with screen use. But everything is now online and I have to teach myself to be at least adequate with it even if I dislike it. Nevertheless, the use of Zoom instead of face to face is still a change of mindset. I deal with it every day to keep up with my colleagues, from their twenties to thirties all the way to the seventies.
>
> Professionally, COVID has affected me most by having to change my productions from stage to videos. This was tough at first because I don't have much practice with or knowledge about videos. But I have always found challenges by challenging myself to learn faster to solve new problems. In my personal life, dealing with COVID meant being able to improvise with small jobs like safe travel.
>
> COVID has taught me that in life and work we need constant alertness to the changes around us. This is a mindset that I have to live with. And the emotional satisfaction comes with my ability to work with my younger colleagues on their level.
>
> Vicki Ooi

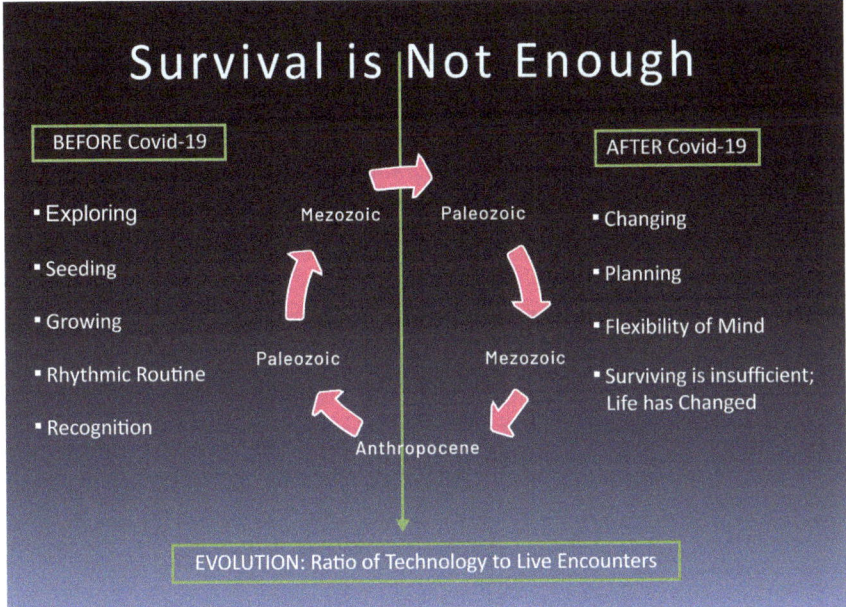

Figure 6.3: Survival Is Not Enough Think Tank Internal Slide 3 (3 March 2020). Image by author.

There was a time when managing an arts organisation meant a three-year plan could be worked on and would pan out more or less as anticipated in iterative cycles. There was a time when the world, or so we thought, would chug along as a matter of routine. Looking back at pre-2019, those were halcyon days indeed. With the brave new world that we were entering, it was important that the think tank discussed the current complex present and an uncertain future.

Assessing our current portfolio and its continuation, we asked ourselves 'What does it look like now? What is appropriate and what is no longer?' It did not take us long to arrive at the answer: the time of bountifulness is over. Let us streamline projects and programming. The way we created projects mattered. How was it done previously? What grounds did it cover? Armed with those questions, we laid out the parameters for intra- and inter-team exploration investigating.

- The partners we choose and the duration
- The sites where we produce projects
- The space we offer to participants
- The format in which we present products
- The approach we use
- The commitments to be made

- The quality of the team
- The nature of financing and marketing

From April 2020, the company regularly met to research, discuss, and debate findings. This resulted in everyone embarking on the creation and development of digiAFTEC, our first-ever digital online learning platform.[5] There was no precedent, and we forged ahead with nothing more than a fierce determination to do so, learning as we went, to collectively gain ground inch by inch.

Although the truncation of life was major, we had, in retrospect, been psychologically preparing for a government-planned change even before 2020. The Sai Wan Ho Civic Centre, the venue where we have been a partner since 2009, was finally given the green light for major renovation. As a result, from 2022, we would be itinerant in other venues for a few years. COVID simply precipitated the pace and magnitude of change two years early.

> In view of the restrictions and difficulties, it would be easy to simply cancel the programmes. Yet, we have developed our resilience and flexibility since the social unrest. We were already used to developing contingency plans and adapting according to the circumstances. However, the pandemic lasted much longer than we first expected. At the beginning of the pandemic, it felt like a getaway from routine work because the pace of work was adjusted and we spent more time with our families. But as the pandemic continued, the frustration grew, as it seemed to be an endless wait. While the support of family and friends was very important, I was also glad that we continued with our programmes while making new and groundbreaking endeavours, as it gave me a lot of energy and motivation.
>
> Meanwhile, COVID also imposed many challenges on schools. Teachers had to conduct classes on Zoom, and it was much more difficult for them to engage students. It was very hard to collect responses and feedback from students, as they would easily lose focus because there were so many distractions online and at home. For students, it also meant they lost face-to-face interaction with teachers and students. Their relationship with peers and their social skills diminished. It was even more challenging for the underprivileged, who might lack

---

5. 'digiAFTEC for Schools', The Absolutely Fabulous Theatre Connection, accessed 3 January 2024, https://www.aftec.hk/digiaftec-for-schools/.

the technical support to join online classes and have less support from families who were not able to work from home to make a living.

But the most impact COVID had on me was it reinforced my belief and eagerness to stay in Hong Kong to contribute to the arts and education sector.

Calvin Co

Part III

Being Human, the Arts, and Health

Feelings of stress and frustration, as of elation and breakthrough, are what makes us sentient beings. Although sometimes dismissed in expedient and instrumental societies, feelings exist in full force every day, grating as they may be. Yet with COVID, it was the passion and the indomitable human spirit of individuals and supporters whom we were fortunate enough to know and work with who buoyed the organisation to focus on its mission and drive projects forward past those unrelenting years.

Because of our colleagues and like-minded associates, the burden and misery of other lives were lifted, even if momentarily. Perhaps, therefore, the action to be taken post-pandemic is not to deny that emotions and feelings exist but to seriously probe and examine the ways in which they can be channelled to living a better quality of life, physically, mentally, and affectively.

These individuals' positive mindsets have a clear connection to the arts as they work at and/or support us. We are fortunate as a result, but it is important to know that the arts are actually innately linked to our minds and bodies, as the rising trend in neuroscience research in the twenty-first century is revealing. In the rest of the chapter, I put forward a few highly informative publications that have the arts and well-being as central to living well. Linking these international studies are narratives of beneficiaries in our programmes to connect theory with practice and reality.

One of the latest research studies – Susan Magsamen and Ivy Ross's *Your Brain on Art: How the Arts Transform Us* (2023) – clearly reveals this, proving the arts' generative impact and dispelling unfounded ideas that the arts are only for leisure and discardable.

Collaborators in inter-sectorial fields, the neurologist Magsamen from the International Arts + Minds Lab at Johns Hopkins University and the designer Ivy Ross at the helm of Google's hardware design, have been breaking new ground with neuro-aesthetics or neuroarts. Neuroarts reveal that the abilities of experiences in

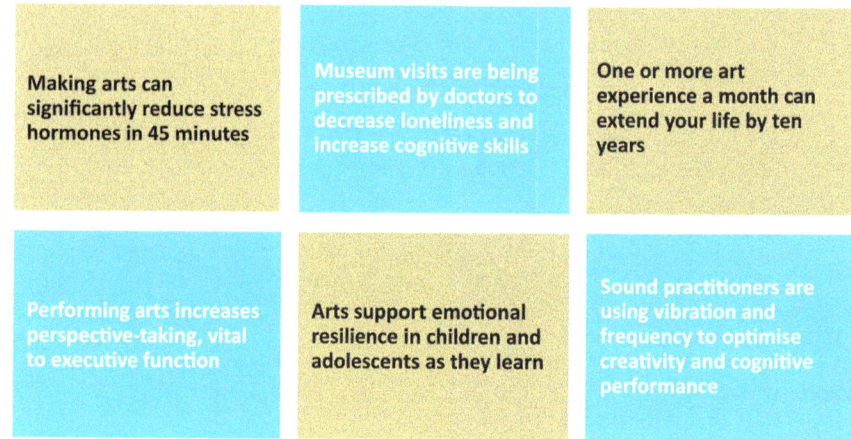

Figure 6.4: Neuroscience Data on Arts and Well-Being. Data courtesy of *Your Brain on Art: How the Arts Transform Us*, 2023.

the arts can change our body, brain, and behaviour and how this precipitates health and well-being. Some of their headline evidence makes for intriguing reading[6] (figure 6.4).

Health Perspective on the Arts

> COVID enabled me to rediscover the possibility of arts and reflect on human relationships, mental health, and the relationship between technology and our lives. I learnt to be flexible to cope with the quick development of the pandemic and its impact on our daily lives and work. I became more aware of my health and planning for solutions to cope with many possible scenarios.
>
> We changed the working environment and mode of communication in work, leisure, and social life. Many things could be done online, and I became more open to the virtual world and technology. However, the more I relied on technology for daily communications, the more I valued the human touch.
>
> Natalie Ting

---

6. 'What is NeuroArts', *Your Brain on Art*, accessed 26 March 2024, https://www.yourbrainonart.com/what-is-neuroarts.

During the first full post-pandemic year of 2023, the World Health Organisation (WHO) and the Jameel Arts and Health Lab announced a forthcoming Lancet Global Series on the health benefits of the arts. This initiative was the result of a pre-COVID scoping review completed by the WHO to understand the evidence on the role of the arts in improving health and well-being. In the WHO's 2019 study, a logic model[7] sets out the Components in arts experiences, various human Responses and possible Outcomes (figure 6.5).

Translating this global logic model to a more manageable scale was the *Jockey Club Arts & Action Project* from 2019 to 2021.[8] The project was a forty-four-month project for two schools with students who have special education needs, offering them year-round in-school classes deploying the efficacy of the arts for well-being. These students were referred to these schools for social development by social workers, because of their temporary incapacity to deal with socio-emotional development issues in routine schooling.

The schools supported them in reframing their attitudes and behaviours. Together with the school, our team also planned a black box theatre for teaching purposes year round (figure 6.6).

The narrative[9] on Ah Keung[10] (case 1) demonstrates how participation in the arts in this all boys' school informed and changed his mental well-being. As Special Educational Needs (SEN) students are not fond of writing, Ah Keung's development was told to us below by our colleagues and his teacher.

> **Case 1: Drama**
>
> Ah Keung (Form 2 in 2020–2021) used expletives as a matter of habit. During *Arts & Action Project* drama classes, he had to play the role of a gentle person (gentleman) and realised that if profanity was included, the character would be odd as a result. In rehearsals and performance, he decided to pay attention to his choice of words and tone of voice. After a lot of hard work, he took on a character who was diametrically opposite to himself.
>
> From then, he took careful note of the tones and attitudes of others and discovered that the artists/teachers were always polite and made

---

7. Daisy Fancourt and Saoirse Finn, *What is the Evidence on the Role of the Arts in Improving Health and Well-Being? A Scoping Review* (World Health Organization, Regional Office for Europe, 2019)
8. Due to COVID, the final showcase only happened in August 2022.
9. All quotations in the chapter are translated from the original Chinese.
10. Pseudonyms are used in the rest of the chapter to protect the privacy of individuals.

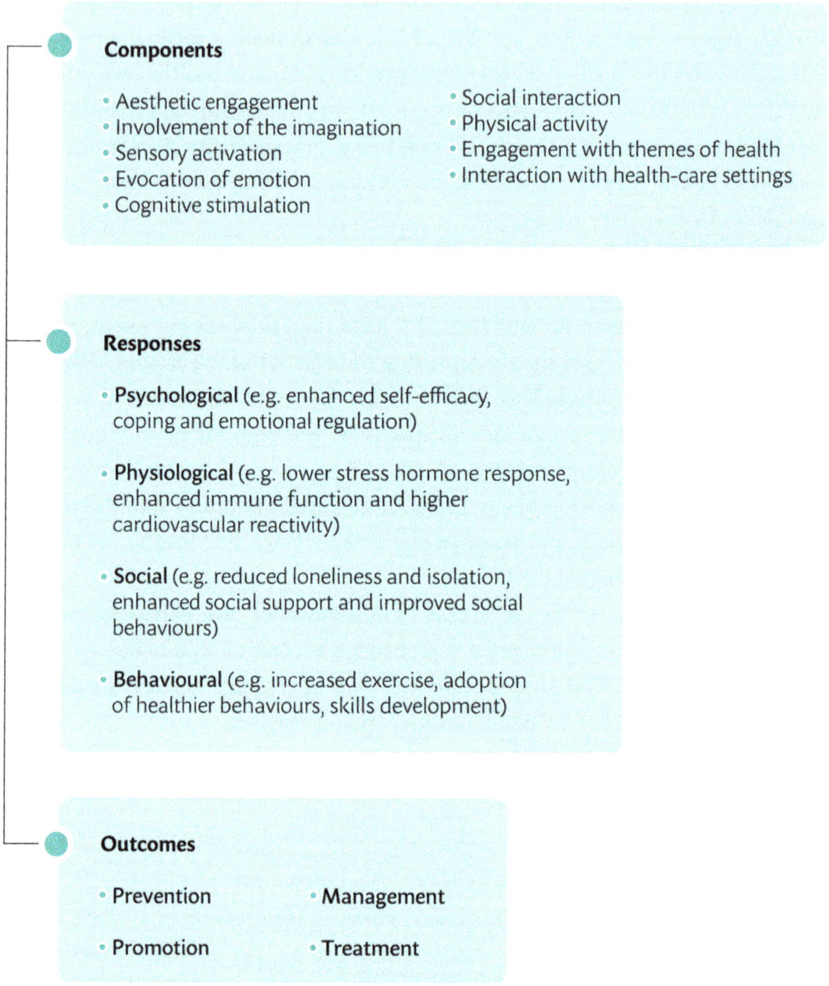

Components

- Aesthetic engagement
- Involvement of the imagination
- Sensory activation
- Evocation of emotion
- Cognitive stimulation
- Social interaction
- Physical activity
- Engagement with themes of health
- Interaction with health-care settings

Responses

- **Psychological** (e.g. enhanced self-efficacy, coping and emotional regulation)
- **Physiological** (e.g. lower stress hormone response, enhanced immune function and higher cardiovascular reactivity)
- **Social** (e.g. reduced loneliness and isolation, enhanced social support and improved social behaviours)
- **Behavioural** (e.g. increased exercise, adoption of healthier behaviours, skills development)

Outcomes

- Prevention
- Management
- Promotion
- Treatment

Figure 6.5: Logic Model Linking the Arts with Health. Image courtesy of Fancourt and Finn and the World Health Organization, 2019.

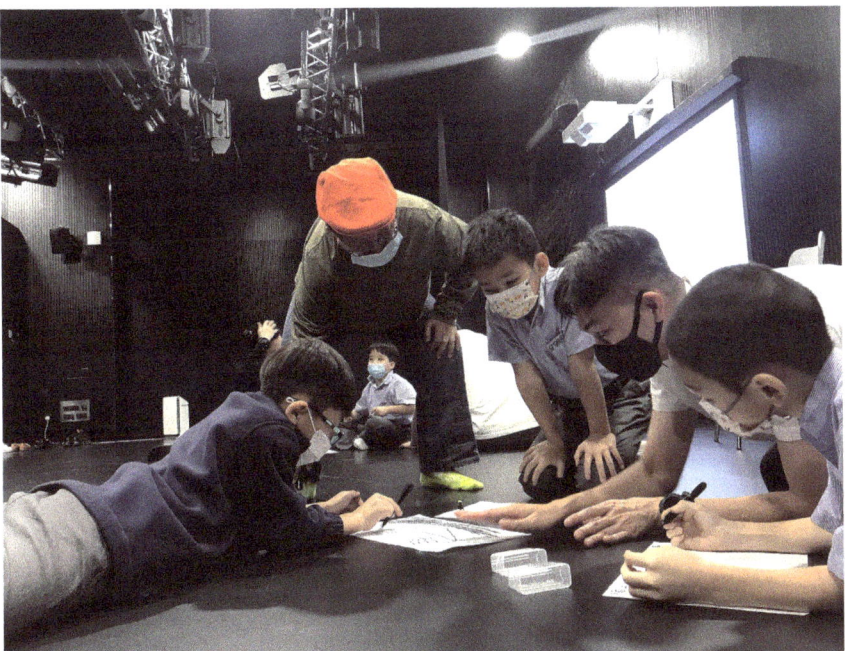

Figure 6.6: Vicki Ooi at Work in the Black Box Teaching Theatre. Photo from AFTEC, 2021.

everyone feel good. He therefore took the initiative to shed expletives from his routine and began paying attention to how other people felt. His friends were pleasantly surprised by his change into a polite student.

It was a matter of practice that students needed to clean up after themselves. As Ah Keung took on this practice over time, he realised that perhaps at home he should also help out with domestic chores and be responsible. He did, and his relationship with the family improved.

His wish now is to transform his own friends into empathetic and responsible young people.

Drama is an art form that often speaks of transformation. Of Fancourt and Finn's nine components associated with the arts in table 6.1, eight (left-hand column) explain drama features as Catalysts (middle column), and the right-hand

Table 6.1: A Narrative of Change Through Drama. Image from AFTEC, 2024.

Case 1

Components from Arts Engagement Activities	Drama Features as Catalysts	Triggering Responses (Psychological, Physiological, Social and Behavioural)
Aesthetic Engagement	Drama is an art form and Ah Keung was involved aesthetically as an actor.	Gives space for emotional expression, emotion regulation and stress reduction managing our mental health.
Physical Activity	Drama requires actors to move around in rehearsals and on stage.	Reduces sedentary behaviours, which are associated with health conditions such as chronic pain and depression.
Social Interaction	Ah Keung works with other student actors to create the play on stage and the director, designers, stage crew backstage.	Reduces loneliness and increases opportunities of social support. Different groups of people can enhance social capital by lowering discrimination, the latter being linked with mental illness and a range of other health conditions.
Involvement of the Imagination	Ah Keung becomes a character who is very different from himself. He needs to imagine what a gentle non-foul-mouthed man is like and how he behaves. He works with other student actors in the same imaginative realm to imagine different scenarios or situations that the play offers.	
Sensory Activation	When Ah Keung plays the part of a gentleman, various senses are called into play. He has to be <u>visually alert</u> to see what is happening around him which causes him to move at the right time in the right place. He has to be <u>aurally aware</u> all the time, listening to the director or his fellow actors in order to speak his lines at an appropriate time. If he has to <u>touch</u> a prickly object, he needs to imagine how it might hurt him in order to recoil his hand. If the scene includes a fire from next door, he has to be able to imaginatively smell the fire. If there is a lunch episode, Ah Keung needs to conjure up his sense of <u>taste</u>.	

Table 6.1: (continued)

Cognitive Stimulation	With the above components and drama catalysts. Ah Keung's mind is constantly stimulated to think out of his usual routine first by the script and the character he plays, and then by the non-routine habits of mind drama immersed him into.	This offers opportunities for learning and skills development, and is interrelated with mental illness such as depression.
Evocation of Emotion	When Ah Keung becomes another person (the gentleman), he has to feel and express the character's emotions as he encounters different occurrences in the character's life in the play.	
Engagement with Themes of Health	As a SEN student in a special school, Ah Keung is accommodated into a setting in which all professionals collaborate to explore his socio-emotional issues.	Emotion regulation is intrinsic to how we manage our mental health, while stress is a well-known risk factor for the onset and/or progression of a range of health conditions including cardiovascular disease.

column lists whole-person Responses, also from Fancourt and Finn, where available. Reading from left to right, we are able to see how the arts can affect health positively.

At the bottom of figure 6.5 again, four Outcomes are introduced: Prevention and Promotion, Management and Treatment. These are the areas in which arts application can affect individuals' health and by extension, the health care system. Figure 6.7 takes a closer look at each Outcome. Upon closer scrutiny, we see that the arts can play significant roles in enhancing physical and mental health.

In Prevention and Promotion, the arts can

- affect the social determinants of health,
- support child development,
- encourage health-promoting behaviours,
- help to prevent ill health, and
- contribute to care-giving.

Within the Management and Treatment theme, the arts are able to

- assist those with mental illness,
- support care for those with acute conditions,
- aid those with neuro-developmental and neurological issues,
- be of service to the management of non-communicable diseases, and
- help end-of-life care.

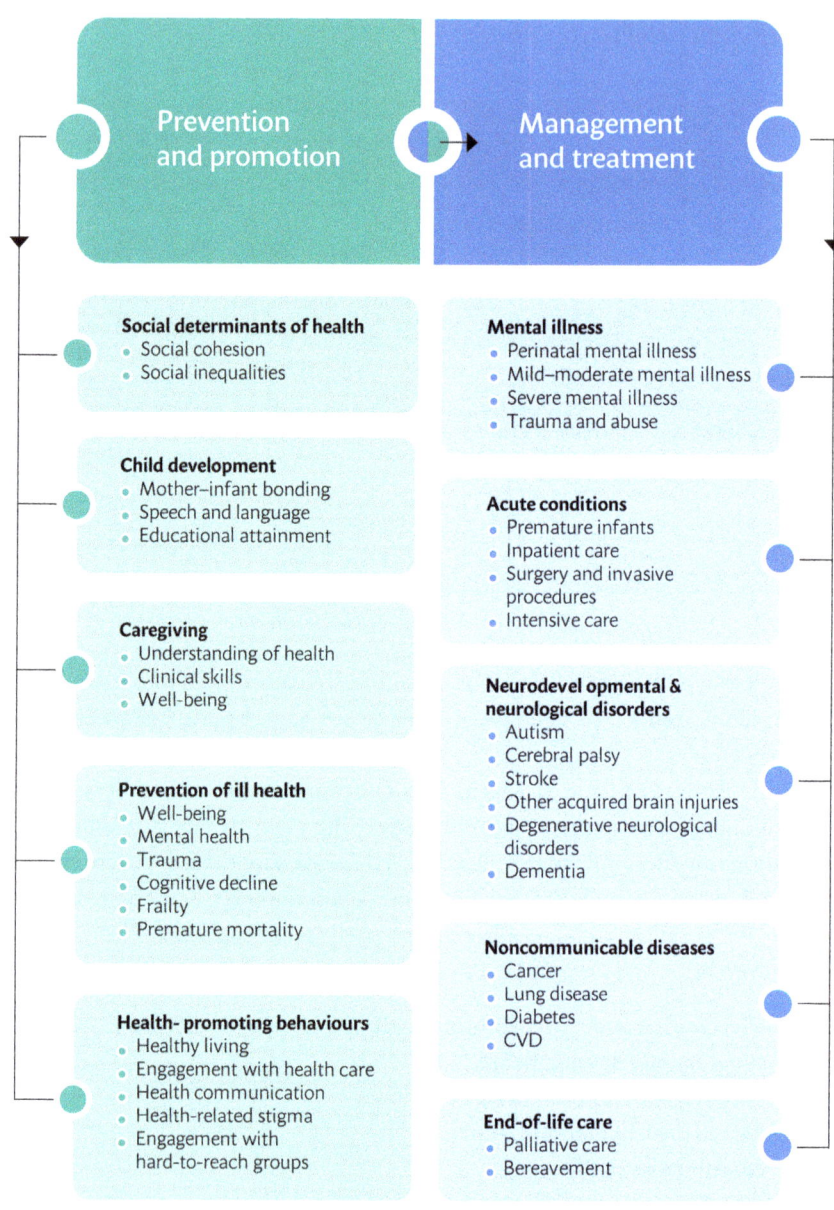

Figure 6.7: Thematic Content for Prevention and Promotion and Management and Treatment. Image courtesy of Fancourt and Finn and the World Health Organization, 2019.

While it is beyond the purview of this discussion to delve into the contributions of the arts to the health care system as a whole, two cases from the second school for social development, a girls' school, exhibit some of the Outcomes. Unlike case 1, where drama was the focus throughout the school, the girls were offered multiple hands-on arts choices with strong vocational learning. They chose costume design and making (case 2, figures 6.8 and 6.9) and stage make-up (case 3, figure 6.10).

Although the study springs from the health sector and the schools belong to the education sector, a correlation can be deduced. Two overarching outcomes from figure 6.8 apply to both cases 2 and 3.

- Health-related stigma (Fancourt and Finn 2019, 19): students referred by social workers to the special schools have socio-emotional issues. In regular schools, they may have been labelled as non-conformist, if not unmanageable. The arts in the WHO review are seen to be used to lower stigma aligned

Figure 6.8: Creative Work Through Costume-Making. Photo from AFTEC, 2024.

Case 2

Costume Design & Making

Lily (Form 4, 2021-22) was the big sister in class as she believed her recommendations were the most expedient and simplest although others were maybe more comprehensive and detailed. Throughout JCAA's [costume design & making] classes, she began to relinquish the blind desire to be boss as she slowly discovered that by listening to others, she would understand how they think. She has changed to accept other viewpoints and as a result, has won over many friends.

Over time, Lily has learnt to proactively ask questions and seek assistance voluntarily. Because of the teaching artist's continuous stories of life in the arts world, Lily has decided to pursue her dream as a tattoo artist and has since signed up for an external course.

Lily's case demonstrated how the arts supported the development of prosocial behaviour. As students constantly worked in groups from designing to actually making costumes from the drawing board to taking turns on sewing machines, they nurtured collective achievements through the process of creation, solving problems together and motivating each other on.

Of course, tears, arguments and failures were part of the learning as well. By collaborating, the girls built social cohesion and group identity by ironing out personality and ability issues. On a personal level, as they needed to communicate as a collective, they began to empathise with each other and slowly trust grew among them giving them a group identity.

In many arts programmes, participation supports increasing self esteem and confidence leading to self worth. All these are corroborated in various research papers in the WHO report where preventative healthcare measures reduce and forestall further decline in mental health issues.

Figure 6.9: Tracking Change Through Costume Classes. Image from AFTEC, 2024.

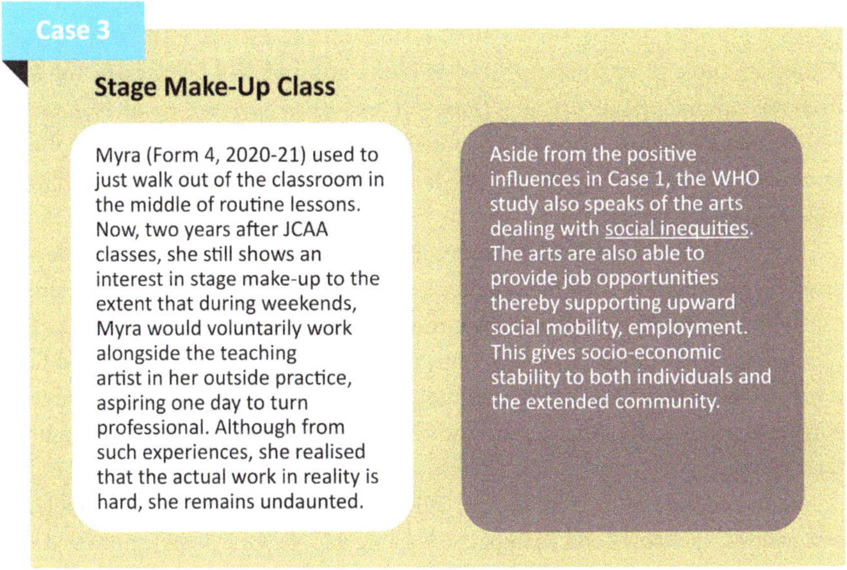

> **Case 3**
>
> **Stage Make-Up Class**
>
> Myra (Form 4, 2020-21) used to just walk out of the classroom in the middle of routine lessons. Now, two years after JCAA classes, she still shows an interest in stage make-up to the extent that during weekends, Myra would voluntarily work alongside the teaching artist in her outside practice, aspiring one day to turn professional. Although from such experiences, she realised that the actual work in reality is hard, she remains undaunted.
>
> Aside from the positive influences in Case 1, the WHO study also speaks of the arts dealing with social inequities. The arts are also able to provide job opportunities thereby supporting upward social mobility, employment. This gives socio-economic stability to both individuals and the extended community.

Figure 6.10: Tracking Change Through Make-Up Classes. Image from AFTEC, 2024.

with certain health conditions. In the research, arts activities in schools have been used to improve mental health, empathy,[11] and inclusion.[12]

- Engaging marginalised or hard-to-reach groups (Fancourt and Finn, 2019, 20): These girls are likely to have been ostracised in their regular schools. In *Arts & Action Project* classes, our first port of call is always to build trust between students and professionals which, together with the pedagogy, can lead to enhancements in the children's self-esteem, resilience, skills development, empowerment, and social support networks.[13]

---

11. L. Campos, P. Dias, A. Duarte, E. Veiga, C. C. Dias, and F. Palha, 'Is it possible to "find space for mental health" in young people? Effectiveness of a School-Based Mental Health Literacy Promotion Program', *International Journal of Environmental Research and Public Health* 15, no. 7 (2018): 1426, https://doi.org/10.3390/ijerph15071426.
12. Monika Twardzicki, 'Challenging Stigma around Mental Illness and Promoting Social Inclusion Using the Performing Arts', *Journal of the Royal Society for the Promotion of Health* 128, no. 2 (2008): 68–72, https://doi.org/10.1177/1466424007087.
13. B. Kelly and L. Doherty, 'A Historical Overview of Art and Music-Based Activities in Social Work with Groups: Non-deliberate Practice and Engaging Young People's Strengths', *Social Work with Groups* 40, no. 3 (2017): 187–201, https://doi.org/10.1080/01609513.2015.1091700.

Arts' View on Well-Being

A third example of international studies in the arts and well-being takes the lens from the cultural perspective. The *Durham Commission on Creativity and Education* (2019 report), a joint research collaboration between Arts Council England and Durham University, was undertaken to look at the role that creativity could play in educating young people.

Of the various aspects that the commission addressed was mental health and creative thinking, investigating how arts programmes are valuable in transforming capabilities and behavioural attributes resulting in contributions to happiness and well-being. In education terms this time, evidence from the report suggested that, through creative activities, the arts promote self-realisation, support physical fitness, encourage emotional resilience, and contribute to young people's needs throughout their lifetime.

In its second report, published in 2021, the commission focused on the UK's first national lockdown and its impact on young people. One main feature that the organisation experienced aligned with our COVID attempts in blended learning and showed how crucial social interactions through the arts were. The commission shared this as well but took one extra step and recommended that the arts and creativity should become part of everyday school life as a matter of routine to ensure health and well-being, given that cultural experiences are foundational to school culture and, by extension, to young people's lives.

As a result of the study, the Arts Council established an action research project that networked schools in teaching for creativity in October 2021, around the same time that we embarked on the *Jockey Club Arts-Based Cross-Curriculum Creative Learning Project* pilot (2021–2024) also with artists in schools.

The final evaluations (see chapter 8) of the pilot project have shown promising results for arts and creative learning. Albeit in different parts of the world, this coincidence in the launching of both projects points towards a conscious decision of the need to explore how creative competencies can be part of an education system that builds the capacity of students and professionals alike.

UK Parliament Research

The Durham report echoed the call a few years earlier by the All-Party Parliamentary Group on Arts, Health and Wellbeing, formed in 2014 to improve awareness of the benefits that the arts can bring to health and well-being.

From 2015 to 2017, the group conducted an inquiry into practice and research in the arts in health and social care, and subsequently made recommendations to improve policy and practice. *Creative Health: The Arts for Health and Wellbeing*[14] published the findings of two years of research, evidence gathering, and discussions with a host of stakeholders including academics, artists, health and care professionals, government officials, other policymakers, and parliamentarians from both Houses of Parliament.

Of particular interest is the *Arts on Prescription* project, a UK initiative across the arts and health care sector that has been positively influencing lives for over two decades through prevention and reduction of symptoms in non-communicable diseases such as loneliness and social isolation.

Via 'link workers', patients would become participants in community arts activities and actively engage in such programmes instead of being medicalised and thus drawing on tight health care spending. The evaluations from *Arts on Prescription* have shown benefits for mental health, chronic pain, long-term conditions, social support, and general well-being.

Economically, the scheme has also demonstrated a return on investment – an average £2.30 for every £1 expended – creating cost-savings in the health care system through reductions in expenses.[15] Such cross-sector effort from the health care system and the arts sector is also one of three recommendations put forward by the WHO for policy considerations, one which Hong Kong should seriously consider.

While there is concerted effort abroad, is drawing the arts and health care together as a matter of policy possible in Hong Kong? There are diverse discrete attempts at this but no overall policy to interconnect different sectors currently exists.

As seen from chapters 3 and 5, we have been working with medical students at the University of Hong Kong as part of their innovative Medical Humanities programme.

The Movement and Dialogue in Relationships workshops, for example, adopt the Doctor and Patient Identities theme from the Medical Humanities curriculum exploring three core facets. First is that of the undergraduates as individuals across the spectrum of medical qualification and their diversity of experiences, influences, and dilemmas. Next is their relationship with patients and their families in a medical context that shapes the way they see, interact with, and trust their health

---

14. 'Creative Health: The Arts for Health and Wellbeing' All-Party Parliamentary Group on Arts, Health and Wellbeing Inquiry Report, July 2017, https://www.culturehealthandwellbeing.org.uk/appg-inquiry/Publications/Creative_Health_Inquiry_Report_2017_-_Second_Edition.pdf.
15. 'A Review of the Evidence Assessing Impact of Social Prescribing on Healthcare Demand and Cost Implications', University of Westminster, London, June 2017, https://www.socialprescribing-network.com/media/attachments/2022/02/22/review-of-evidence-assessing-impact-of-social-prescribing-1.pdf.

care providers. Finally, the theme examines interacting roles when a doctor becomes a patient and vice-versa.

In the workshop, students are encouraged to engage the body, mind, and emotions to explore the body as a primal resource in understanding the internal self to connect with others, and the relationship between doctor and patient through body language and wellness or caring for the self as a clinician.

Activities created embed discussions on the physical, psychological, cognitive, and relational aspects of the individual as a holistic being. Foremost is the interplay of body language for building empathy, trust, and rapport with patients. The process-oriented collaboration between the teaching artist and students includes self-care techniques for stress relief and management. As one undergraduate put it, 'I felt like it [the movement] brought out my creativity and allowed me to understand how to understand other people's feelings and communicate with others.'

The 2022–2023 student evaluation[16] of the workshops (table 6.2) was positive, making the question of the possibility of arts integration into well-being at university level a probability.

Table 6.2: Performance Workshop Student Evaluation Summary. Image from AFTEC, 2024.

KPI	Group A Drama	Group B Movement
Q1: I achieved the stated learning outcomes of the workshop.	8.86/10	8.66/10
Q2: The workshop learning activities were effective in helping me to learn.	8.9/10	8.5/10
Q3: The teacher(s) was effective in helping me to learn.	9.16/10	9.03/10
Q4: Overall, the workshop was effective.	8.96/10	8.68/10
Q5: This workshop was relevant to my development as a doctor.	8.96/10	8.45/10

More Local Efforts

Aside from our own effort, there are arts organisations, individuals, and charitable foundations that deploy the arts for connecting health and well-being in a range of settings and age groups. These are not arts therapy programmes but initiatives that engage with aspects of being human.

---

16. Total Year 1 student intake was 299, half each selecting the movement and the drama module.

Central to Grace Cheng's *Art in Hospital*, founded in 1994, is collective art-making with artists, medical professionals, and volunteers to bring comfort and cheer those who are hospitalised. *Arts with the Disabled* (1996), also a long-time non-profit in which Grace is a board member, is an inclusive arts company dedicated to providing nurture and support in the artistic development of people with disabilities.

Since 2002, veteran concert pianist and music educator Nancy Loo has been working with offenders under the age of twenty-one and life sentence inmates at various correctional institutions and prisons almost daily across the territory except during the enforced hiatus during the COVID years. To this day, she is there though now concentrating on those serving life sentences in Shek Pik and Stanley prisons.

Another veteran, James Mark, in the drama field this time, has spent a large amount of time since 2011 in Category A prisons working with inmates who are incarcerated for life or seen to be the hardest criminals. He is still an active driver of the arts for well-being. The arts do indeed benefit the 88-year-old artist as much as the beneficiaries.

The Ho Cheung Shuk Yuen Charitable Foundation, likewise inaugurated in 2011, aims to enrich the lives of older adults by enhancing their psycho-social well-being and improving their cognitive functions, to facilitate ageing with respect and dignity. Their programmes vary from Cantonese opera to music/movement interventions to the Chinese culture's Six Arts[17] for brain health.

More recently since 2022, and at university level, is the *Jockey Club Dance Well Project*, a three-year initiative adopted from Italy by Professor Anna C. Y. Chan, dean of dance at the Hong Kong Academy for Performing Arts. The project is a creative movement programme designed to include those with Parkinson's disease and people of different ages and abilities through regular dance classes and activities in a diverse range of artistic spaces.

As with the WHO and the Durham Commission, much more cross-sector collaboration needs to happen to sustain health and well-being locally. The arts are very deserving and meaningful vehicles though as yet unrecognised at policy beyond performances and exhibitions.

Arts and Life

One comparatively urgent problem that may well call upon the arts for support is the marked increase of youth suicide in 2023. This has worried Professor Paul Yip, director of the Hong Kong Jockey Club Centre for Suicide Research and Prevention at the University of Hong Kong. Professor Yip has called for early diagnosis and

---

17. Rites, music, archery, charioteering, literacy, and numeracy.

treatment, noting that multiple causes coexist, including the long periods of COVID social distancing. Perhaps we could recommend that the Arts on Prescription approach become the pre-medical or early preventative strategy across schools as part of primary health care.

Undeniably, the arts are not a panacea, but as evidenced in this chapter and related data from global research, being human means that emotions and feelings need attending to, preferably through preventative health care, as in the discovery, dilution, and dissipation of problems at the early stage, before the need for actual medical attention. Time is required for effectiveness of the arts and their power permeate an individual's system, nudging the person towards being well.

In Hong Kong, perhaps some young people with suicidal tendencies are the product of this city's clamour for immediate and unflagging success at all times, in school, at work, and in life. In the end, time-poor actions may only be palliative, not curative. And these really do cost lives.

What warms the heart and bathes the whole being in feelings of genuine happiness is that all the effort during and post pandemic has been very worthwhile. Perhaps Mr Chan, who works in one of the two Schools for Social Development, should have the last word. This is his reflection after completing a full-day's continuous professional development workshop.

> As a son, husband, father, boss, colleague, and social worker, my life has always been full of responsibilities. My daily routine is dull and lacklustre, just rushing to finish one task after another handed down to me. It is as if completing a task successfully is my reward. The workshop made me realise that the arts, which I seldom explored in the past, lit up this dark cavern within me and brightened up my unimaginative life. I do hope that the arts will, in future, become a set of keys for the rest of my life!
>
> May 2019

Part C: Bearing

7

Creative Mindsets, Creative City
OECD PISA Creative Thinking Test

Summary

Chapter 7 provides an overview of the results from the ground-breaking OECD PISA Creative Thinking assessment conducted in 2022. Hong Kong's performance on the global stage is viewed through comparative analysis with neighbouring economies. The chapter offers insights and suggestions regarding Hong Kong's results on this innovative assessment.

Part I contextualises the city's desire to be creative and innovative. It also sets the scene for the PISA Creative Thinking test for the next section. Part II gives the city's results and focuses on several aspects pertaining to creative domains and test criteria. Part III illustrates the test with an actual example revealing how students are graded. Part IV sums up gender and socio-economic status data.

Part V moves into the way teaching pedagogies and in-school activities may have affected student outcomes, and the final section, part VI takes reference from economies that have achieved better outcomes than Hong Kong.

Part I

Three Questions

In this book, numerous terms beginning with 'C' appear. In the city as well, creativity and its attendant associations pepper official documents, both within the arts and outside. A quick research by the team in the upper layers of government websites and diverse documents produced the following data.

Unsurprisingly, the 'C' words present themselves quite often first and foremost in the Education Bureau and the Culture, Sports and Tourism Bureau. Under the latter ministry, 'creativity' is used often by the Hong Kong Arts Development Council and the Leisure and Cultural Services Department. Happily, the 'C' word also makes appearances in the bureaux for Commerce and Economic Development, Home and Youth Affairs, and the Constitutional and Mainland Affairs.

Creativity drives innovation, and this term plus its adjective, 'innovative', appear eleven times for the Leisure and Cultural Services Department and at a hefty 232 times in the website for the Innovation, Technology and Industry Bureau, 'creative' surfacing twice. Even in the Financial Services and the Treasury, the Security Bureau, and the Environment and Ecology Bureau, 'innovative' surfaces once.

Given this ardent desire to be creative and innovative, three thoughts emerge.

- As a city, do we wish to further enhance our competitiveness regionally and internationally?
- As a city fascinated by creativity in its many spheres of influence, how do we actually go about developing that capacity all round?
- How content are we currently with our creative thinking[1] as a fundamental building block in creativity?

No jurisdiction would in any mental mode refuse to gain ground competitively, especially in a world that is so fissured and fractured. The answer to the first question is a definite 'yes'.

As to the reply for the second question, it begins to be less unequivocal.

Aside from the arts and education sector, at the time of writing, I am unaware of creativity and creative thinking per se being nurtured strategically, consistently, and progressively elsewhere in Hong Kong outside of a few institutions. Beyond academia, how is a professional's creativity in the technology industry, for example, being developed? Or in economics, how does one grow mindsets that can create new financial instruments that will catapult the city as being innovative? I am confident there are such initiatives out there although I am ignorant of them.

The third question is enigmatic because it is likely no research has ever been carried out. Nevertheless, it is important to ask since the level of satisfaction is an indication of how far we, as a city, wish to develop as an economy that prides itself on being cosmopolitan and global. If we are indeed to be the East-West Centre for International Cultural Exchange (see chapter 10), then the degree of contentment, or complacency, should be a driving force.

To be desirous of becoming creative and innovative asks the basic question of how creative we are currently. Do we think creatively, as this propels creativity? How are we doing this and where?

---

1. Researched websites and documents did not contain 'creative thinking'.

The innate creativity of children is an undeniable truth, readily observed in the unbridled joy of their play. While the wellspring of creative thinking lies at the heart of human potential, research from luminaries such as George Land[2] and the late Ken Robinson[3] reveal a lamentable decline in creative capacities and divergent thinking as children progress through the stages of development. Findings of the recent ground-breaking OECD PISA Creative Thinking assessment (2022) illuminate further details on young minds.

As this book delves into the arts, teaching, and learning mainly at school level, this chapter's discussion will start there. This chapter is not a critique of the test but a review of Hong Kong's first performance and the path down our collective creative futures.

OECD PISA Creative Thinking Assessment

PISA, the Programme for International Student Assessment, is a triennial global survey of 15-year-old students. It assesses the extent to which these young people have gained important knowledge and skills that are essential for full participation in social and economic life. PISA assessments do not just ascertain whether students, some of whom are near the end of their compulsory education, can *reproduce* what they have learnt. They also investigate how well students can *extrapolate* from what they have learnt and apply their knowledge in unfamiliar settings, both in and outside of school.[4]

Results for the seminal creative thinking test were released in mid-June 2024. In 2022, a total of sixty-four participating countries and economies fielded their 15-year-olds for this test.

It is important at this juncture to establish what the PISA Creative Thinking test is and is not. First of all, creative thinking is defined as the 'students' ability to engage productively in the generation, evaluation and improvement of ideas that can result in original and effective solutions, advances in knowledge and impactful expressions of imagination'.[5]

How this relates to economies is obvious. Due to increasing complexities in many walks of life (daily operations to climate change to mass immigration and health to geopolitics), effective ideas and solutions need to be at the forefront of

---

2. George Land and Beth Jarman, *Breakpoint and Beyond: Mastering the Future Today* (Harper Business, 1992).
3. 'Changing Education Paradigms', ESA Animate, 14 October 2010, RSA, YouTube, 0:09:11, https://youtu.be/zDZFcDGpL4U?si=pGDDq90DJMRfUCdL.
4. 'PISA 2022 Results (Volume III) Creative Minds, Creative Schools', OECD iLibrary, accessed 18 June 2024, https://www.oecd-ilibrary.org/education/pisa-2022-results-volume-iii_765ee8c2-en.
5. PISA 2022 Results, 42.

many jurisdictions. This is creativity at its optimum, where the population is conscious of their innate abilities and the city is proactively supportive of developing creative mindsets.

The creative thinking test has, as a focal point, ideation processes that can be embedded into different learning and problem-solving contexts that call the imagination and expression into play. This test requires students to undertake creative writing or the visual in addition to the questions that require the generation and improvement of ideas via investigating problems or designing innovative solutions.

Creativity, creative thinking, and innovation are amongst important competencies for this century, as we have seen in chapter 1. By virtue of this, the creative thinking test is not about measuring artistic talent, often confused with being creative. Stated another way, students are assessed neither for a story's quality of writing nor a visual image's aesthetic attractiveness. It calibrates whether students can make original and diverse idea associations and the capacity to 'think outside the box' given diverse situations, another axiom heard very often, at least in the arts and learning circles.

The *PISA 2022 Results Creative Minds, Creative Schools Volume III* is an intense and immensely detailed report of some 300 pages. A copious amount of data meant I had to be selective. This chapter scans Hong Kong's creative thinking performance against the global backdrop while regularly referencing Singapore as a comparison, both being of high GDP and similar in its internationalism where Chinese, English, and other languages are part of our cosmopolitan lives.

The spotlight is on analyses that directly cite Hong Kong (China)[6] and those that are relevant to understanding contextual and creative thinking issues. Other lenses to be explored here include students' performance in creative thinking, students' beliefs and attitudes, the school environment, and glimpses on variations in gender differences and socio-economic levels. Where appropriate, interspersed in the discussion will be our work in creative learning over the years as a specimen of the possibilities and probabilities in creative learning. The concluding discussion will look at system-level examples of how creative thinking is being integrated into creative schools.

---

6. For ease of reference to the *PISA Report*, names of participating jurisdictions used replicate those in the report: Hong Kong (China), Macao (China), and Chinese Taipei.

Part II

Creative Thinking Results

The top five jurisdictions in Creative Thinking, in descending order, are Singapore (scoring 41), South Korea (38), Canada (38), Australia (37) and New Zealand (36). As an indicator, the OECD PISA global average is 33.[7]

Table 7.1 is an amalgamation of data from the *PISA Report*. The table offers an at-a-glance perspective of Hong Kong's performance in the three core domains of mathematics, science, and reading plus its maiden voyage in creative thinking.

Table 7.1: Hong Kong (China) and Singapore PISA 2022 Ranking. Data courtesy of OECD PISA Report Volume III, 2024.

	Hong Kong (China) 2022	Compared with 2018	Singapore 2022	Compared with 2018
Mathematics	4th (above OECD average)	-11	1st (above OECD average)	+6
Science	7th (above OECD average)	+4	1st (above OECD average)	+10
Reading	11th (above OECD average)	-25	1st (above OECD average)	-7
Creative Thinking	22nd: 32 pts (below OECD average of 33 pts)	NA	1st: 41 pts (above OECD average)	NA
Socio-economic Status Equity in Creative Thinking	High Performance High SES Equity Quadrant	NA	High Performance Low SES Equity Quadrant	NA

Source: PISA Report Volume III, 2024

Internationally, our performance has always been highly commendable in the three core subjects. In creative thinking, Hong Kong (China) performed one point below the OECD average of 33. The exception is in socio-economic equity, where the city is a global leader.

Nevertheless, in creative thinking, this first attempt is a good gauge of not just our positioning but where we are lacking. A gap is an opportunity, and this is the sentiment and attitude taken in the chapter. Curiosity to improve in the light of

---

7. Because schools were closed in 2022 as a result of COVID-19, the provinces/municipalities of Beijing, Shanghai, Jiangsu, and Zhejiang that represent China, and ranked first in PISA 2018, did not participate in 2022.

Singapore's top marks should propel us to want to understand our mediocre performance. 'Why' and 'how' form the mental mode in this discussion in addition to 'what' can be done in the call to action.

Students' Performance in Creative Thinking

In creative thinking, a large gap can be evidenced. Extracted data from figure 7.1 show the OECD average, Hong Kong (China) and Singapore outcomes.

The 2022 assessment calls for three ideation processes to assess the abilities of students to

- generate diverse ideas: students' capacity to think flexibly by generating ideas that are different from each other;
- generate creative ideas: originality is measured in relation to the responses of other students who complete the same task. The fewer the students who create the same ideas, the more the responses are seen as original; and
- evaluate and improve on ideas: students' capacity to evaluate limitations in ideas and improve their originality. (*PISA Report*, 2024, 48)

The test is also implemented across four domains: written expression, visual expression, social problem solving, and scientific problem solving, the definitions of which will be explained.

Our 15-year-olds are 5.8% below the OECD values average in their ability to Generate Diverse Ideas. This is narrowed for generating creative ideas: OECD at 44.1% and Hong Kong, 40%. The better performance lies in evaluating and improving ideas: OECD at 34.2% and Hong Kong, 33.5%. As shall be discussed, the discrepancies are not exactly surprising.

In creative thinking, the city showed a 'moderate overall relative weakness' (*PISA Report*, 2024, 88).[8] How does this translate into distribution levels for further understanding? Level 3 equates with baseline proficiency for creative thinking. Levels 2, 1, and below mean that competency has not been achieved. Levels 4 and above show increasingly higher abilities, Level 6 at the zenith. Figure 7.2 gives a comparative snapshot.

As the PISA report explains, in most countries and economies, the largest proportion of students performed at Level 3 or Level 4. In Singapore, more than 88% of students are proficient at Level 3 or above, indicating that these students are able to create appropriate ideas for a range of tasks and likewise begin to put forward original ideas for familiar problems (OECD average 78%).

---

8. Macao (China) achieved 32 points like Hong Kong, and Chinese Taipei, 33.

- Countries/economies with values **above** the OECD average
- Countries/economies with values **not significantly different** from the OECD average
- Countries/economies with values **below** the OECD average

Success in the creative thinking test (percentage of full credit)

	Across ideation processes			Across domain contexts							
	Generate diverse ideas (12 items)	Generate creative ideas (11 items)	Evaluate and improve ideas (9 items)	Written expression (12 items)		Visual expression (4 items)		Social problem solving (10 items)		Scientific problem solving (6 items)	
				All students	Gender gap[1]	All students	Gender gap	All students	Gender gap	All students	Gender gap
	%	%	%	%	%	%	%	%	%	%	%
OECD average	42.9	44.1	34.2	50.3	-6.3	32.2	-7.6	39.0	-4.3	32.2	-1.6
Singapore	61.0	57.6	44.5	66.2	-3.3	34.1	-6.4	58.1	-2.4	42.6	-1.9
Hong Kong (China)*	37.1	40.0	33.5	47.6	-4.9	25.7	-12.4	38.3	-7.8	25.9	-2.5

Figure 7.1: Snapshot of Performance Across Ideation Processes and Context Domains. (Data from *OECD PISA Report Volume III*, 2024.) Adapted from Table III.4.

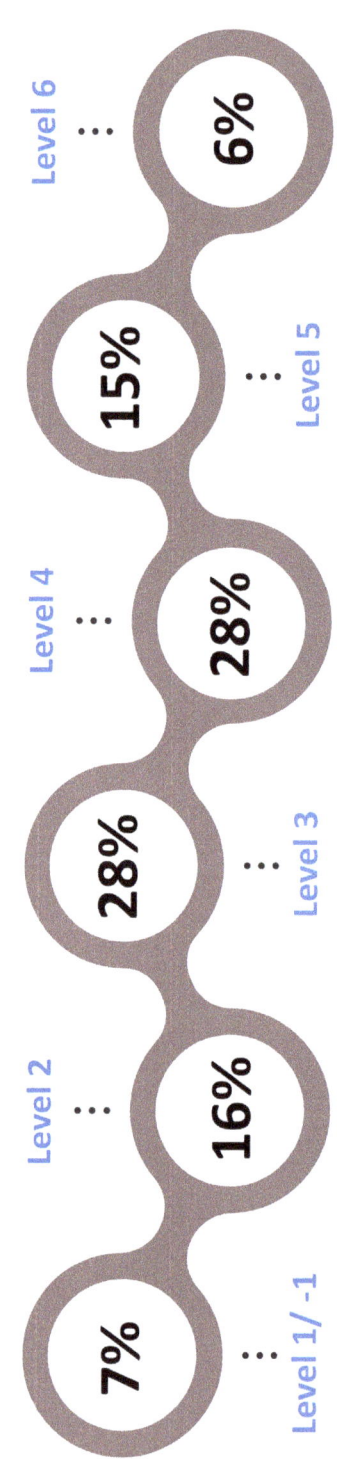

Figure 7.2: Hong Kong's Multilevel Creative Thinking Results. (Data from *OECD PISA Report Volume III*, 2024.) Adapted from Table III.4.

At Levels 2 and below, Hong Kong stood at 23%; the OECD average is 22%. Singapore's most basic scorers were at 6%.

Table 7.2, the numbers rounded off, extrapolates *PISA Report* data according to the different levels of proficiency at baseline and above. Hong Kong has a solid middle ground percentage of students inclining towards a higher Level 4 as in most economies, whereas Singapore is much stronger, having a greater proportion of top performers.

Table 7.2: Comparison of Proficiency Levels for Creative Thinking. Data courtesy of *OECD PISA Report Volume III*, 2024.

	Level 3	Level 4	Level 5	Level 6	Cumulative
Singapore	13%	24%	30%	28%	95%
Korea	17%	27%	28%	18%	90%
OECD Average	25%	27%	18%	9%	79%
Hong Kong	28%	28%	15%	6%	77%

Source: PISA Report Volume III, 2024

Top performers are those who demonstrate the ability to generate, evaluate, and improve creative ideas in diverse and complex tasks, including abstract design tasks or more constrained/unfamiliar scientific and social problem-solving scenarios (PISA Report, 2024, 93). At Level 5, Singapore's 30% doubles ours, and at Level 6, they outstrip Hong Kong by 4.5 times.

Therefore, if we are to take a visual panorama of Hong Kong's performance vis-à-vis the OECD average and the two top-scoring economies, it will resemble figure 7.3 (*PISA Report*, 2024, 92). Again, numbers are rounded off.

The city's results show the normal bell curve. In Singapore, the distribution departs from this and is positively skewed. A further comparison with Korea, which came in second in creative thinking, displays a similar top-performing pattern.

The crucial point here is not who wins and who loses. It is whether Hong Kong will be able to grasp the importance of creative learning and its implications for its development. If so, we will then need to encourage and find systematic ways and approaches to cultivate better creative thinking for this group of 15-year-olds. If left well alone, they may otherwise continue along a similarly average trajectory relatively speaking and eventually lead the city as average professionals.

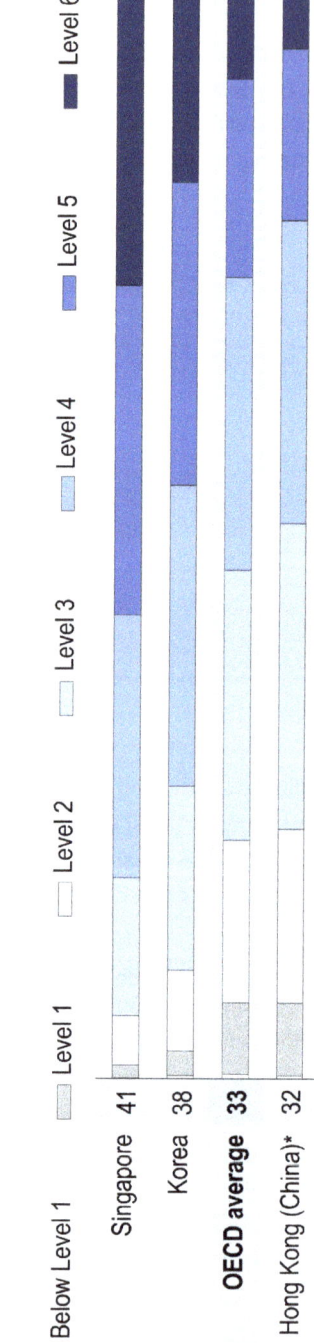

Figure 7.3: Students' Proficiency Level in Creative Thinking, by Country/Economy (Data from *OECD PISA Report Volume III*, 2024.) Adapted from Table III.4.

In theory, this means that if creative thinking systems become common in education systems globally, and in Hong Kong, then in the real-world context of human-generated problems, a proliferation of original thinkers will be able to create more effective solutions and innovative ideas, for economic development, climate change, mass migration, and more.

Part III

Visual Expression Component

Our students' values are lower than the OECD average in two out of three ideation processes: in the values for the generation of diverse ideas and in the generation of creative ideas. In evaluating and improvement of ideas, we are not significantly different from the global average.

Of the four domains investigated, Hong Kong was under the OECD par in written expression (47.6%), visual expression (25.7%), and scientific problem solving (25.9%). In social problem solving (38.3%), students were not significantly different from the OECD average of 39%.

What may be the issue here? Taking visual expression as an example where the OECD average, Singapore, and Hong Kong had the lowest values as a common denominator in the four domains, the Science Fair unit offers some answers.

The Science Fair Example

In the Science Fair unit, with the help of a graphic tool, students are asked to create a simple design. The tool enables them to use lines and shapes, change colours, and fill in, in addition to using stickers from a tool library that is provided.

PISA reports that difficulties across the board can have resulted from students' unfamiliarity with using a graphic design tool and/or using it in a formal assessment for visual expression as an output. Those who obtained only partial credits did so because their answers remained within what was being provided. This is in spite of the test explicitly stating that the poster should be original 'in the sense that not many people would think to represent the theme in this way'[9] in the Generate Diverse/Creative Ideas segment. The same was made clear for the ideation process of evaluating and improving ideas.

Revisiting figure 7.1, of the four assessed domains, Hong Kong students' social problem-solving expressions at 38% of full credit almost reached the OECD average of 39%. In written expression, we were 2.7% under the OECD average of 50.3% of

---

9. PISA 2022 Results, 129.

full-credit results. In scientific problem solving, we missed the global average by 6.3%, achieving 25.9% of full-credit receipt. In visual expression, we were below par by 6.5% (OECD average 32.2% of full credit). This last statistic is unsettling, since the most obvious vehicle for visual literacy, the visual arts, has been a long-time curriculum subject in Hong Kong. Perhaps the ensuing discussion can help shed some light on this.

Definitions of the four test domains will also illuminate the issues.

- Written expression: communicating ideas and imagination through written language
- Visual expression: communicating ideas and imagination through a range of different media
- Social problem solving: understanding different perspectives, addressing the needs of others, and finding innovative and functional solutions for the parties involved
- Scientific problem solving: generating new ideas, designing experiments to probe hypotheses, and developing new methods or inventions to solve problems

The need for the imagination to generate new ideas and multiple perspectives for problem solving cuts across all four areas. And we fell short of the OECD average in all but one. A view into this can be delineated by thinking in the abstract (intangible) and thinking with a given (tangible). Of the domains, social problems emanate in our societies daily. They are reported and discussed in the media. They are tangible in that sense.

It is safe to work with given material; after all, you cannot go wrong with it. However, the consequence of this approach is that students who resort to copying and pasting only receive partial credit. While this may be less significant for a single test, the long-term impact on cognitive development is concerning. Such habits undermine the ability to think creatively and outside the box. Solutions derived from limited thinking tend to be predictable and unoriginal, restricting the advancement of knowledge and wasting the potential of imagination. Chapter 2 of this book addresses not only economic deprivation but also a deeper issue related to mental capacity.

Partial and Full Credits

The examples in figure 7.4 demonstrate 'in-the-box thinking' (*PISA Report*, 2024, 129) because the elements are not applied in meaningful or imaginative ways that go beyond the visually relevant and which connected the Life in Deep Space theme.

Creative Mindsets, Creative City 169

Figure 7.4: Visual Expression Domain Examples of Partial Credit Responses. Courtesy of *OECD PISA Report Volume III*, 2024.

The answers are the usual ideas of space (example A), mechanically copying and pasting stickers without much thought (examples B and C).

In our work, we can attest to similar situations. From projects over the years, using what is tangible, palpable, and instantly in front of students has always been the most expedient method. This is human.

As we gained experience over the years, we have observed several issues that may explain this phenomenon: many students exhibit habitual passivity, having been nurtured in classroom environments that are prescriptive rather than exploratory. This passivity often results in a lack of self-confidence and a hesitancy to engage with material beyond what is presented in textbooks, compounded by a pervasive fear of making mistakes.

In quite a few signature projects that we have rolled out in the past decade, the pattern recurs. The good news is that the root of the problem can be addressed through setting up trusting relationships in the classroom, role-modelling by teachers and artists, and iterative practices that balance traditional teaching and learning with exploratory and creative thinking. Change does occur and evidence exemplifies this, the most recent being the *Jockey Club Arts-Based Cross Curriculum Creative Learning Project* 2021–2024.

Students who earned full credit in PISA's visual expression test (figure 7.5) did so because they gave free rein to their imagination yet it was thematically aligned (*PISA Report*, 2024, 130). Deploying the graphic tool's ability to create shapes, colours, and lines, these students worked more creatively and at greater depth, adding characters, objects, and symbols that meaningfully engaged with Life in Deep Space.

Figure 7.5: Visual Expression Domain Examples of Full Credit Responses. Courtesy of *OECD PISA Report Volume III*, 2024.

In the arts, this is the start to having a 'concept' instead of simply doing activity after activity. 'Learning by doing' is a highly valued classroom pedagogy in Hong Kong. What if it is enriched by a creative mindset that puts reflections at its core as well? The ideas from the 15-year-olds who achieved full credits are a case in point. Example A seems to be representing some of earth's continents (the Americas) using stickers and a drawing tool on a blue surface. After all, the earth is nested within space.

In example B, this student took a view from a planet possibly inhabited by humans (buildings and nature) but which has a view of a sun, a planet with a ring around it, and spacecrafts in the atmosphere. Perhaps example C, with the most original concept, to me at least, is as it is nuanced true and effective and thus provides possibilities. Is it an outline of space mountains or lights light years away? Or could it be the student portraying irregular heartbeats as they are at the same time excited and terrified at the thought of being in deep space?

Translating words and images into something new takes the relational inwards. One needs to be able to be introspective and grow a habit of mind that is comfortable with playing with ideas. Even in scientific problem solving, it takes a leap of the imagination to think laterally to arrive at novel thinking. To what extent do we cultivate a convergent-divergent-convergent thinking pattern in our young people? In providing students with questions that require them to understand landscape, objects, text, or phenomena, do they have basic cognitive tools to handle them? Do we offer the much-needed tools and skills for students to go beyond the obvious, palpable, and instant replies?

Perhaps because we work predominantly with the underserved we see a lack of teaching and learning that excites and propels students further than the textbooks.

However, in our other experiences, it is not always true that those who are privileged are able to be creative. This can be witnessed in the *Bravo! Hong Kong Youth Theatre Awards project*, where teenagers from diverse socio-economic backgrounds are intentionally mixed for peer learning. At an outing to the Tate Modern in London as part of the International programme, a sculpture that two young people stood in front of perplexed both of them. One teenager was from an elite school and has travelled much, and the other, a new immigrant from China who is on welfare. The arts are formidable social equalisers.

We need to vastly improve on values for the three ideation processes not for the sake of the PISA Creative Thinking assessment alone but vitally, for the quality of minds Hong Kong desires. By giving credence to creative learning, we will do better in coming up with creative ideas that are diverse.

Part IV

Gender and Social Economic Status

In all three ideation processes, globally girls generally fared better than boys. Though it is stereotypical, boys performed better in scientific problem-solving tasks, and girls were at their weakest. As in the majority of jurisdictions, girls outshone boys in visual expression tasks, Hong Kong being one city in which the largest gender gap is witnessed (*PISA Report*, 2024, 207).

Overall, students with higher socio-economic status did better in creative thinking. Compared with boys, girls performed better in written expression tasks and those requiring them to build on others' ideas. Socio-economic differences accounted for the largest performance difference in the written expression domain. Again for the *PISA Report*'s data, we saw that, in socio-equity, Hong Kong did very well, meaning that students who are economically disadvantaged are cared for as much as those who are advantaged. This is made evident in table 7.3, where the city has the narrowest gap.

The research indicates that beliefs, attitudes, and dispositions towards creative thinking influence performance. In other words, the mindset is equally important in performance.

Seven out of ten students believe that creativity is not exclusive to the arts across OECD countries and economies, whereas eight out of ten believe that it is possible to be creative in nearly any subject. This optimistic mindset has resulted in scores that are around three points higher than those of their peers on the creative thinking scale on average.

Despite the above, however, only about 50% of students think that they are able to do something about their creativity. When they are given prompts to think

Table 7.3: Socio-economic Differences in Performance. Data courtesy of *PISA Report Volume III*, 2024.

	Disadvantaged Students' Mean Score	Advantaged Students' Mean Score
OECD	28	38
Singapore	36	45
Hong Kong	29	35

Source: PISA Report Volume III, 2024.

about solving broad, real-life problems, rather than when working on school tasks, then they become more able to think creatively. Although the report does not state the reason, our own work in schools reveals that, while this is true and prompts are effective, it is also a matter of confidence and of being regularly exposed to an environment that supports a creative habit of mind.

These habits of mind encompass different attitudes or dispositions. These include the 'imagination and the sense of being adventurous, an openness to intellect, openness to arts and experience, and creative self-efficacy'.[10] Social-emotional characteristics such as curiosity, perspective taking and persistence are also identified as part and parcel of being creative thinkers. These are the dispositions that are based on creativity research by Lucas, Spencer, and Claxton[11] trialled in eleven countries prior to the OECD welcoming it on board as part of PISA's creative thinking test.

Reviewing gender and performance, in a large majority of participating countries and economies, girls' beliefs and attitudes were stated as being more favourable in creative thinking than boys' were. Overall, students who are socio-economically advantaged, as well as students in socio-economically advantaged schools, consistently reported more positive dispositions towards creative thinking.

In Hong Kong, local schools subvented by the government are by and large well funded although some school premises and facilities are dated. I would venture to say that even schools in areas serving grass-roots students are relatively well

---

10. PISA 2022 Results, 25.
11. Bill Lucas, 'A Five-Dimensional Model of Creativity and its Assessment in Schools', *Applied Measurement in Education* 29, no. 4 (2016): 278–90, https://doi.org/10.1080/08957347.2016.1209206.

resourced, as evidenced from the schools that we collaborate with. Consequently, this is one likely reason why we have done well in socio-economic equity. Since this is the case, it does seem apparent that we have an advantage even over top-performing Singapore. How can we capitalise on this?

Part V

Teaching Pedagogies

Teachers are fundamental to creative thinking development, and classroom pedagogies can make a difference. Across OECD countries, between 60% and 70% of students reported that their teachers value their creativity, that they encourage them to come up with original answers, and that they are given a chance to express their ideas in school (*PISA Report*, 2024, 195).

PISA corroborates the fact that the use of classroom pedagogies which encourage creative thinking plus the opportunities to participate in activities related to creativity are conducive to good creative thinking. In the report, about two-thirds of students reported that their teachers encourage them to come up with original answers (63%) or creative solutions on assignments (64%).[12]

Figure 7.6 (*PISA Report*, 2024, 188) charts the views from principals and students on teachers' use of creative pedagogies. The upper-left quadrant illustrates above-average students' perception of creative thinking pedagogies with below-average principals' perception of creative thinking pedagogies in class. The lower-left quadrant explains below-average students' perception of creative thinking pedagogies with below-average principals' perception of creative thinking pedagogies in class.

In the upper right, we see above average students' perception of creative thinking pedagogies with above-average principals' perception of creative thinking pedagogies in class. At the lower right, data are given on below-average students' perception of creative thinking pedagogies with above-average principals' perception of creative thinking pedagogies in class.

At the very top of the figure, in small print, is the critical description 'Jurisdictions where "developing students' creativity" formally features in teachers initial training'. The legend reads Yes (diamond shape), No (square), and Missing Information (circle). This visual data are where the change needs to happen, in the training of pre-service teachers. Our brains are wired to be creative (see chapter 6, *Your Brain on Art: How the Arts Transform Us?*), but to develop and sustain it requires practice and commitment.

---

12. Figure III.6.3 in *PISA Report*.

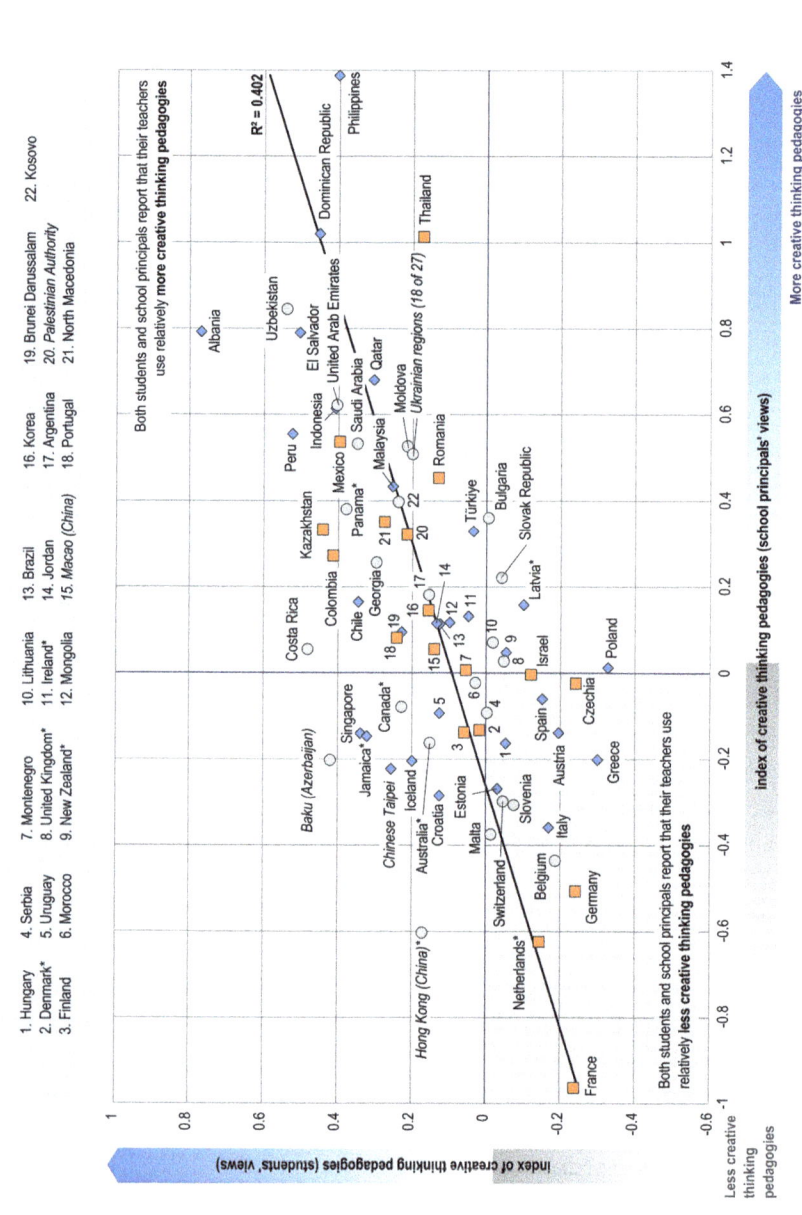

Figure 7.6: Views from Principals and Students: Teachers' Use of Pedagogies Encouraging Creative Thinking. Courtesy of *OECD PISA Report Volume III, 2024*.

While we understand that this illustration deals only with perceptions, a few points of interest are noteworthy:

- Singapore students' views of the use of creative thinking pedagogies by their teachers are higher than that of their counterparts in Hong Kong.
- In leadership perspectives, when compared to Singapore, Hong Kong principals believe that teachers are not using many creative thinking strategies.
- Top-scorer Singapore indicated its inclusion of teacher training in creative thinking in their system. In Hong Kong there is an absence of any data.

I am curious about the missing information on initial teacher training. In chapter 9 (figure 9.3), there was a similar response. Hong Kong ticked the 'Not Applicable' box in answer to the question of progress in system-level teacher qualifications and training requirements related to creativity. Given the missing information in the PISA test as well, one begins to wonder whether Hong Kong actually has no data because they are still being worked on, or it is unimportant to ascertain, or of far greater concern, whether there is no intention to cultivate creativity and creative thinking in the school system beyond statement policies in curriculum guides.

Compared with our Chinese-speaking neighbours, Chinese Taipei came between Singapore and Hong Kong (China). Surprisingly, Macao (China) is in the segment that shows relatively more creative thinking pedagogies are applied in schools. Korea is in this category as well and higher placed than Macao.

Of the other four top-ranking economies' performance in creative thinking, only Korea seems to have fared better in students' and principals' perspectives. The real revelation, however, is in the top right: that comparatively low-performing economies in the creative thinking test have much higher ratings in teaching creatively. Added to this is the fact that developing students' creativity is formally integrated into initial teacher training in those jurisdictions.

The natural query is thus the apparent discrepancy in the comparative underperformance in the creative thinking test in those economies *in spite of* teacher training for teaching creatively. There are, of course, many reasons, economic, social, and political. One insight may suffice to advance possibilities of major sea changes. Decades ago, when China opened up, non-Chinese could only use Foreign Exchange Certificates as currency. They were taken only to Friendship Stores, and the yuan was lower than the Hong Kong dollar was. China's economic development since has been nothing short of astounding, and the yuan has been higher than the Hong Kong dollar for a while now. With the right conditions, many countries can rise.

Data from figure 7.6 offer much food for thought. They do testify to the novelty of a creative thinking test and its early recognition, the introduction, and permeation of creativity into the formal education system, and teaching in creative thinking being less easy to pin down than in reading, science, and mathematics. Fortunately, it also shows that there is growing global awareness and discussion on creative thinking. The PISA test is indeed pioneering and necessary, and 2022 was a good starting point to tackle capacity-building issues.

PISA continues to suggest that groundwork is essential. It is not sufficient for students to simply perceive that their teachers' increased attempts to encourage creative thinking are the end of the story. Educators need to be supported by training.

In previous projects, and particularly in the most recent 2021–2024 *Creative Learning Project*, many schools gave one common application reason for a coveted spot. Although creativity and critical thinking are key generic skills concepts in curriculum documents, principals and teachers say they require actual training that is applied, interactive, and practical. We very much hope that the pilot's extension in the *AFTEC Jockey Club Creative Futures Project* from 2024 to 2028 will continue to fill this need and fuel creative teaching and learning locally.

In-school Activities

Good research data permit cognitive adventures. The *PISA Report* is definitely one. Continuing from figure 7.6, while Hong Kong students do not seem to believe that their teachers' pedagogies bolster their creative thinking, figure 7.7 gives a somewhat different perspective (*PISA Report*, 2024, 36–37).

On the left, the segment 'Pedagogies encouraging creative thinking' shares details of teachers' support to students in creative thinking. Hong Kong's percentage of students who agree to the four points outperformed the OECD average by quite a margin.

Compared with Singapore, the gaps are not that large either, the narrowest being 80.6% for Singapore's students believing that 'At school, I am given a chance to express my ideas', and 80.3% for Hong Kong's students.

On the right, statistics reveal 'Weekly participation in classes/activities at school', offering a correlation to the left-hand segment. Distilling from an assortment of activities to four categories, it is clear that Hong Kong is on par with OECD countries but significantly higher than Singapore in arts, music, computing though the percentage for creative writing is more equalised. A closer comparison between OECD and Singapore in fact shows that the latter is below the global percentage.

The data indicate that there may be only a limited correlation between school activities and students' perceptions of teaching pedagogies. For instance, achieving top results in creative tests does not necessarily correlate with participation in numerous classes or activities, as seen in the case of Singapore. Additionally, involvement in many classes or activities does not guarantee strong performance in creative thinking tests.

Countries/economies with values **above** the OECD average
Countries/economies with values **not significantly different** from the OECD average
Countries/economies with values **below** the OECD average

	Pedagogies encouraging creative thinking				Weekly participation in classes/activities at school			
	Percentage of students who agreed:				Percentage of students who reported weekly participation in:			
	My teachers encourage me to come up with original answers	My teachers give me enough time to come up with creative solutions on assignements	My teachers value student creativity	At school, I am given a chance to express my ideas	Art (e.g. painting, drawing)	Music (e.g. choir, band)	Computer programming	Creative writing
	%	%	%	%	%	%	%	%
OECD average	63.7	62.5	70.1	69.3	27.4	21.7	17.2	16.3
Singapore	79.6	76.5	79.9	80.6	14.9	18.0	11.9	15.4
Hong Kong (China)*	74.3	74.5	77.9	80.3	29.2	32.7	15.6	16.2

Figure 7.7: School Environments' Conduciveness to Creative Thinking. (Data from *OECD PISA Report Volume III*, 2024.) Adapted from Table III.6.

Figure 7.8 exemplifies (*PISA Report*, 2024, 194–95) that, in activities for science, drama/theatre, debate and being involved in publications, Singaporean students' participation rate in school weekly is less than either Hong Kong (China) or Korea in general.

The *PISA Report* provides several explanations.

On average across OECD countries, students who report participation in many activities at school scored lower in creative thinking than do those who do not participate in many activities, and there is no strong association between participation in activities and creative thinking performance except for a few jurisdictions.[13] These findings imply that students from advantaged backgrounds, and/or those who are top performers in core subjects, participate less frequently in school-based activities, because they prefer to focus on their academic abilities.

Steadiness and balanced participation is suggested as the better way to success in creative thinking. Those who do so regularly outperform those who do not, and those who participate excessively – as in daily or close to daily non-stop participation – do not fare well. Less is more. PISA suggests that activities that involve daily learning within the curriculum which engage students in tasks that require creative thinking on a regular but considered basis may be the best way forward.

PISA might have pointed to a possible hidden curriculum and systemic issue in Hong Kong local schools.

Our experience has shown that many from privileged families have become in-school and after-school activities chasers. We know of those whose mothers are their 'social secretaries' who occupy all their children's post-school hours, some with as many as twelve extra-curricular activities per week. A quick glance at the websites of various schools will reveal the extensive range of activities offered to students.

For schools with economically disadvantaged students, activities are in abundance as well. In an era of low birth rates, non-stop provision of learning pursuits to advance a student's portfolio for next-step schooling is likewise popular. All this excludes tuition to bolster weak subjects or to further grades.

Exhausted students cannot be creative children.

Burnt-out teachers cannot accommodate creative thinking and learning in their classrooms during or after school.

In other words, this is likely to be a reason why Hong Kong has performed lower than its students' potential in PISA's creative thinking test. From our observations, activities in visual arts, music, theatre, creativity writing, and so on, concentrate on having participated much more than having understood, having related them to life, and building capacities in life for life. Many of the arts activities provided to students

---

13. Table III.B1.6.17 in *PISA Report*.

Legend:
- ☐ Less than 25%
- ☐ Between 25% and 50%
- ■ More than 50%

	Percentage of students who report that they participate in the following activities in their school at least once a week							
	Art classes/ activities (e.g. painting, drawing)	Music classes/ activities (e.g. choir, band)	Computer programming classes/ activities	Creative writing classes/ activities	Science club	Drama, theatre class/ activities	Debate club	Publications (e.g. newspaper, yearbooks, literary magazine)
	%	%	%	%	%	%	%	%
Korea	60	55	29	27	16	8	12	8
Hong Kong (China)*	29	33	16	16	9	12	8	9
Singapore	15	18	12	15	6	8	4	6

Figure 7.8: Students' Reported Participation in In-school Activities. (Data from *OECD PISA Report Volume III*, 2024.) Adapted from Table III.6.1.

are highly skill-based with thinking geared towards techniques for exams and other utilitarian purposes (see chapter 1, note 8).

Thinking out of the box carries far less weight. With a culture that supports the quantitative in the main, creative thinking can be crowded out. Academic excellence, PISA cautions us, is not a prerequisite for excellence in creative thinking. Nevertheless, students need a baseline level of skills in core subject areas to excel in creative thinking (*PISA Report*, 2024, 204–5).

Part VI

Learning from Strong Performers

From 2022 to 2024,[14] two international keynote speakers were annually invited to our year-end Knowledge Exchange forum for the *Creative Learning* project. Of the six keynote speakers, Professor Sunah Kim from Korea (2022), Clara Lim-Tan from Singapore, and Sharon Foster from Australia, are from nations that ranked second, first, and fourth respectively in the PISA 2022 creative thinking test. It seems apt then to conclude the chapter by exploring reasons for their achievements.

As evidenced in these top-performing jurisdictions, achieving creative mindsets are both plausible and attainable. In Singapore, it is clearly also possible to be at the pinnacle academically (top scorer in the three core subjects) as well as in creative thinking. Korea is second on the league table, higher ranked in science and reading than Hong Kong (China) is, and thirteen points ahead in mathematics.

The report indicates that Korea, Singapore, and Australia (like Canada and Denmark) have all integrated creative thinking as foundational to their educational reforms, articulating its importance. All include the provision of high-level strategic documents and practical resources for educators (*PISA Report*, 2024, 205).

These countries support educators in understanding the importance of creative thinking by developing targeted and relevant documents which include evaluation in the form of learning progressions or rubrics, thereby offering a roadmap to achieving outcomes across the curriculum.

Australia

Sharon Foster, the executive director of the government entity ACARA (Australian Curriculum, Assessment and Reporting Authority) based in Melbourne, was instrumental in developing a critical and creative thinking learning proficiency continuum for different levels of proficiency from primary to secondary school. In her keynote

---

14. For 2022, when Hong Kong was still in COVID lockdown, keynote speeches went online.

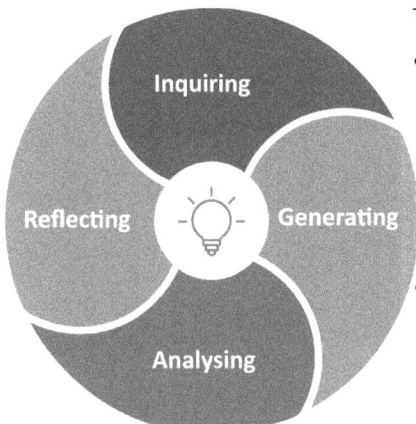

This Element is organised into 2 sub-elements:

- Develop questions - students narrow or expand the focus of their thinking and explore ideas and concepts critically and creatively. When they develop different kinds of questions, students can further their inquiry. they can find more information about a topic and form a better understanding of how something works or why something is the way it is.

- Identify, process and evaluate information - students seek information from a range of sources, make decisions about expert or personal opinion and understand which sources are trustworthy, relevant and useful.

Figure 7.9: Critical and Creative Thinking Learning Continuum. Courtesy of the Australian Curriculum, Assessment and Reporting Authority 2010 to present.

speech (Hong Kong, 2024), the continuum transformed the 2010 curriculum reform policy, which included critical and creative thinking, into actual practice.

Her address focused on the conceptualisation, formulation, and implementation of creative thinking in Australian schools.

Of the four capabilities in nurturing creative thinking,[15] figure 7.9 illustrates details to Inquiring, as in how to develop questions and the process in producing students' own opinions. In other words, the behaviours that form the thinking. AFTEC's creative learning system starts with the localised development of our seven tools and skills as a foundation, from which teachers and artists can launch into asking questions and sharing opinions guided by Lucas, Spencer, and Claxton's Inquisitive Habit of Mind.

One of the constant issues raised in creativity and creative thinking is assessment. Foster, in table 7.4, also shown during her keynote, extracted a section of the assessment progression rubric[16] from the Australian curriculum as an example for the audience to understand how the subset of Developing Questions and Identify,

---

15. 'Australian Curriculum: General capabilities – Critical and Creative Thinking Version 9.0 About the general capability', Australian Curriculum, Assessment and Reporting Authority, accessed 1 July 2024, https://v9.australiancurriculum.edu.au/content/dam/en/curriculum/ac-version-9/downloads/general-capabilities/general-capabilities-critical-and-creative-thinking-about-the-general-capability-v9.docx.
16. Curriculum, Assessment and Reporting Authority, accessed 1 July 2024, https://v9.australiancurriculum.edu.au/content/dam/en/curriculum/ac-version-9/downloads/general-capabilities/general-capabilities-critical-and-creative-thinking-about-the-general-capability-v9.docx.

Table 7.4: Critical and Creative Thinking Learning Continuum Version 9.0. Image courtesy of Australian Curriculum, Assessment and Reporting Authority, 2022.

Sub-element	Level 1 (Foundation)	Level 2 (Years 1–2)	Level 3 (Years 3–4)	Level 4 (Years 5–6)	Level 5 (Year 7–8)	Level 6 (Years 9–10)
			INQUIRING			
Develop questions	Develop questions to explore a familiar idea or topic.	Develop questions to explore a familiar idea or topic.	Develop questions to examine unfamiliar ideas and topics.	Develop questions to examine unfamiliar ideas and topics.	Develop quests to investigate complex issues and topics.	Develop questions to investigate complex issues and topics.
	Questions developed reflect their curiosity about the world.	Questions developed are fit for the purpose of the investigation.	Questions developed support the process of improving knowledge and understanding about a topic or investigation.	Questions developed focus on improving understanding about a topic and clarifying information about processes or procedures.	Questions developed assist in forming an understanding of why phenomena or issues arise.	Questions developed facilitate increasing understanding of abstract ideas and concepts.
Identify, process and evaluate information	Identify and explore relevant points in information provided on a topic.	Identify and explore relevant information from a range of sources, including visual information and digital sources.	Identify and examine relevant information and opinion from a range of sources, including visual information and digital sources.	Identify and examine relevant information and opinion from a range of sources, including visual information and digital sources.	Identify and clarify significant information and opinion from a range of sources, including visual information and digital sources.	Identify and clarify significant information and opinion from a range of sources, including visual information and digital sources.
	Prioritise the information that is most relevant to the topic of study.	Identify and explain similarities and differences in selected information.	Condense and combine selected information related to the topic of study.	Compare information and opinion that can be verified against claims based on personal preference.	Evaluate the accuracy, validity and relevance of the information and opinion to the topic of study.	Evaluate the information selected to determine bias and reliability.

Source: Australian Curriculum, Assessment and Reporting Authority 2010 to present.

Process and Evaluate Information are measured (2022, 3). Clearly, where there's a will, there is definitely a way.

This approach allows schools in Australia to create curriculum opportunities for students to engage in creative and/or interdisciplinary work. As with our work in Hong Kong, a major challenge is the pivoting of an ongoing and overcrowded curriculum (in which much is still based on prescriptive teaching) to a more progressive, creative learning convention.

Korea

In Korea, the determination of the government to implement its 2009 education reforms directed at nurturing creative citizens resulted in the crucial first step of reducing the compulsory curriculum portfolio to make room for creative experiential activities at primary and secondary levels. Although the initiative was not without its difficulties, by 2016, an exam-free semester was introduced across the country for junior secondary schools, to allow for further curriculum space for creative projects and to relieve exam pressure.

Sunah Kim is the Professor of Applied Art Education in Hanyang University. Her keynote in 2022 at the our Knowledge Exchange – *Cultural Arts Education as Transformative Pedagogy* – reflected on Korea's fundamental realisation of how twentieth-century-trained teachers were deploying nineteenth-century teaching pedagogies to educate twenty-first-century students and the resultant change in education policy in general as well as in the arts education curriculum.

In figure 7.10, Professor Kim reveals Korea's thinking in interrelating schools with intermediaries as bridges linking the former to cultural organisations and professionals across the country, consequently widening the learning network, promoting creative thinking, and developing a culture for creativity.

She cited and connected the vital role that intermediaries such as AFTEC play (top right-hand corner) in the pilot *Creative Learning Project*. The key matter, Professor Kim pointed out, is to move away from the traditional linear provision of artists and professionals by arts companies to symbiotic web-like synergies (my term). In this book, chapter 9 refers to this phenomenon as 'service provision' which is based on a restricted relationship that undermines the abilities of professionals to truly communicate and collaborate.

PISA spearheaded the creative thinking test by situating itself within the education continuum. Aside from Korea's leading role in arts education, its arts and cultural development merits an exploration at this juncture.

I believe that one of the reasons Korea is placed very high in creative thinking (with a score of 38) is the government's history of total commitment to arts

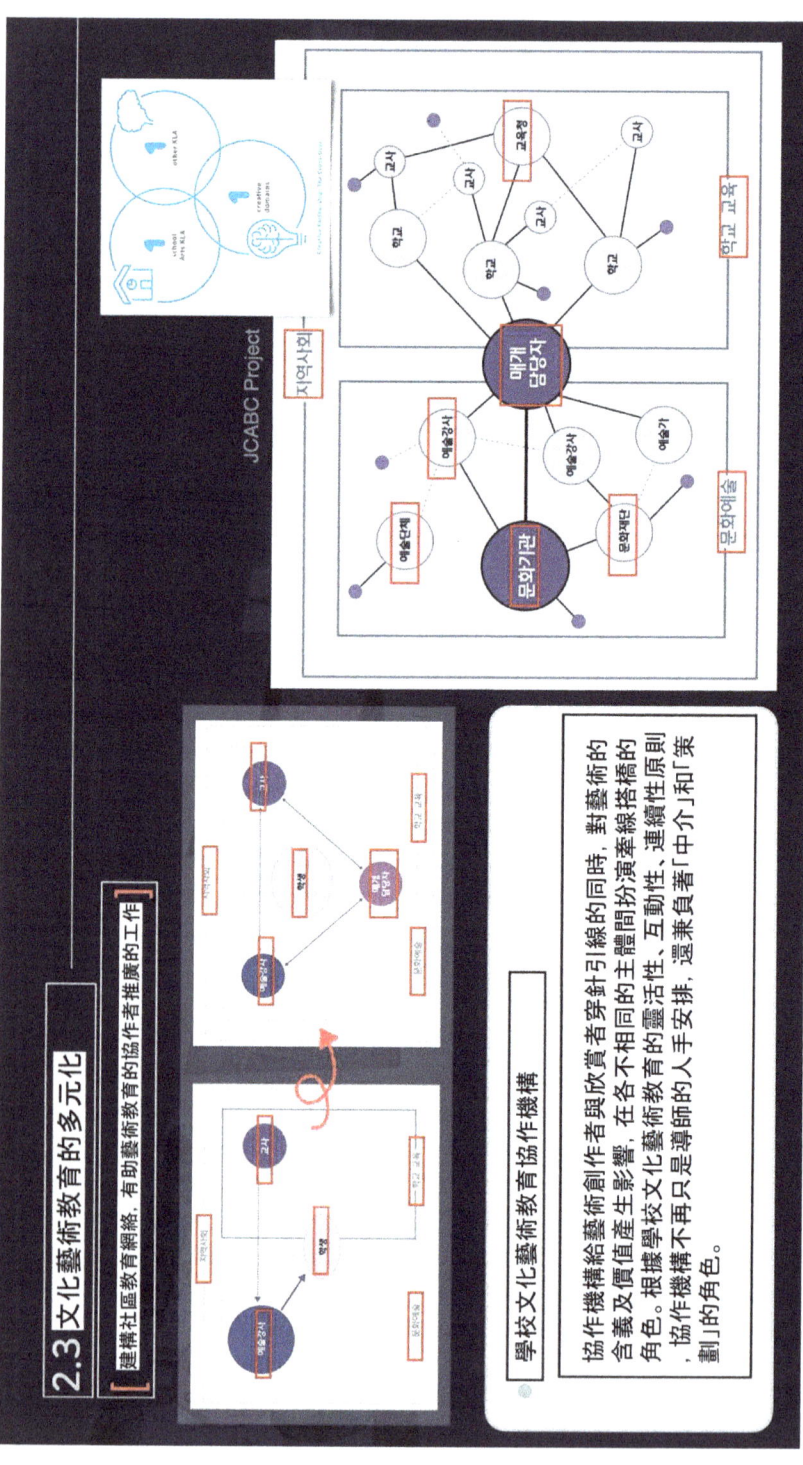

Figure 7.10: Cultural Arts Education from Schools to Arts Organisations. Image courtesy of Professor Sunah Kim, Hanyang University, 2022.

and cultural development as a matter of key policy. A few decades ago, there was no K-Pop and definitely no filmmaker who caught global attention.

Film director Bong Joon-ho's *Parasite* won the Palme d'Or at the Cannes Film Festival 2019 and went on to sweep numerous Oscars at the 92nd Academy Awards for Best Director, Best Original Screenplay, and Best International Feature Film. The years of funding the arts and cultural sector in Korea have evidently paid off handsomely. The country has sown an environment for the arts. How far has art education progressed?

In addition to being a part of Hanyang University, Professor Kim is a force at KACES, the Korea Arts & Culture Education Service, a government non-profit that was established in 2005 after the enactment of the Arts and Culture Education Act 'to revitalise arts and culture education, and to contribute to improving the quality of cultural life of the people and to strengthening the cultural capability of the State' providing equal opportunities for its people to 'systematically study and receive education on arts and culture throughout their lives according to their interest and aptitude regardless of age, gender, disability, social status, economic circumstances, place of residence, etc.'[17]

In the same year, KACES, with initial funding to the tune of HK$50m (US$6.3m), co-hosted the UNESCO Asia-Pacific Regional Conference in Preparation for the World Conference on Arts Education (Seoul, Korea) and launched national arts and cultural education policy projects in schools and welfare centres. From there, it has expanded arts education to the entire country in schools as well as in villages and even the military.

In 2011, the Seoul Agenda was adopted unanimously at UNESCO's 36th session of the General Conference in Paris and has since become the global beacon in arts education development. Today, KACES has a budget of HK$737 million or US$94 million and 5,000 teaching artists working nationally. Its Culture & Arts Education Instructor Certificate System has become a national qualification pathway cultivating arts and culture education experts with the necessary qualifications and expertise.

These endeavours all evidence the need for macro planning and solid implementation. The results speak for themselves. Korea ranked just after Singapore in the creative thinking test, and students in Korea were most successful in scientific problem-solving contexts and in tasks requiring students to evaluate and improve ideas. It also had a large share of top-performing students (45%), over 70% of students performing at or above Level 4.

---

17. 'President's Message', Korea Arts & Culture Education Service (KACES), accessed 11 July 2024, http://eng.arte.or.kr/about#presidents-message.

Singapore

Paired with the Australian keynote speaker was Singapore's Lim-Tan, the director of Arts Education from the Ministry of Education and a principal turned minister at the helm. Her address did not focus straightaway on arts education but took a panoramic perspective of the Singapore government's vision for education (figure 7.11).[18] We have to unlearn to relearn competencies for this century, says Lim-Tan.

'Adaptive and innovative thinking' are priorities. There is a clear throughline. But is policy implemented and practised on the ground? Wei Li Liew, director-general of Education at the Ministry of Education explained that, in 1999, 'Inventive Thinking' was incorporated into 'all subject curriculum, teaching and learning guides and even exam syllabuses where possible'.[19]

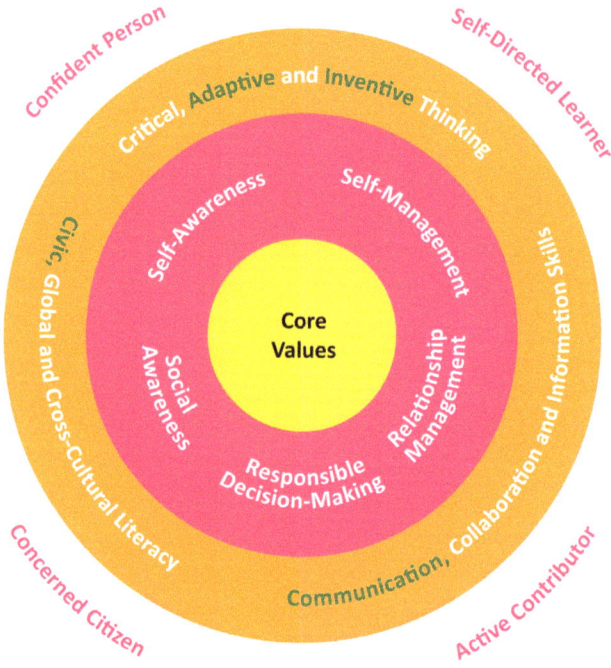

Figure 7.11: Singapore's Twenty-First Century Competencies. Image courtesy of the Singapore Ministry of Education, 2023.

---

18. '21st Century Competencies', Education in SG, Ministry of Education Singapore, accessed 30 June 2024, https://www.moe.gov.sg/education-in-sg/21st-century-competencies.
19. Wei Li Liew, 'Singapore's 15-year-old students score top marks in OECD's creative thinking test', LinkedIn, June 2024, https://www.linkedin.com/posts/wei-li-liew-98051044_singapores-15-year-old-students-score-top-activity-7209552308576141305h12-vI1c?utm_source=share&utm_medium=member_desktop.

From what can be understood in Lim-Tan's keynote, the ministry gave priority to professional development through STAR, or the Singapore Teachers' Academy for the aRts, in 2011.[20] STAR aims to build a community of arts teachers in music and visual arts by igniting passion and inspiring professional excellence in arts education. The academy offers year-round programmes to continuously generate interest and excitement in professional learning. Housed in a building, STAR provides specialised facilities including art and music studios, training rooms, and a recital room that support professional development activities.

By creating a local professional community network of arts educators, the academy also forges partnerships with other arts organisations locally and with overseas institutions. Inspire, connect, and build predicates arts education in an authentic environment. Schoolteachers and their professional practice are grounded in a support network, benefiting students in a continuous cycle of lifelong learning.

STAR's Professional Development Framework addresses the broadening teachers' perspectives, widening their repertoire of pedagogies, and developing their practice. Teachers develop an understanding of how their arts disciplines support holistic education, the 'strengthening of cultural appreciation and the Singapore national identity.'[21]

The Professional Development Programmes meet diverse needs, from in-service teachers with a specialism in visual arts and music to non-specialists who are aiming to cultivate themselves in the art forms. Teacher leadership training is available, as are programmes for teachers who wish to develop their future competencies. The latter concept is created under the *Skills Framework for Arts: Arts Education, a Guide to Occupation and Skills* developed jointly by the National Arts Council and SkillsFuture SG.[22]

It is through partnership engagement within the government and across *other* ministries that networks for building on strengths are formed and expertise is shared. SkillsFuture Singapore[23] drives and coordinates the implementation of the national SkillsFuture movement, promotes a culture and holistic system of lifelong learning through the pursuit of skills mastery, and strengthens the ecosystem of quality education and training in Singapore.

---

20. 'Home', Singapore Teachers' Academy for the aRts, accessed 12 July 2024, https://star.moe.edu.sg/.
21. 'STAR Professional Development Framework', Singapore Teachers' Academy for the aRts, accessed 21 August 2024, https://star.moe.edu.sg/programmes/star-professional-development-framework/.
22. 'Skills Framework for Arts (Arts Education)', National Arts Council Singapore and SkillsFuture Singapore, accessed 15 July 2024, https://www.nac.gov.sg/docs/default-source/skills-framework-documents/skills-framework-for-arts-(arts-education).pdf?sfvrsn=69556f56_4.
23. 'About SkillsFuture Singapore', SkillsFuture Singapore, accessed 21 August 2024, https://www.skillsfuture.gov.sg/aboutssg.

To ensure vibrancy and a constructive eco-system in arts education, professional development is not restricted to schoolteachers. Teaching artists are vital to the picture as well. In response to changing learning environments, the National Arts Council, in collaboration with the National Institute of Education, a leading Singaporean tertiary institution, offers *Essentials of Teaching and Learning*,[24] a platform designed for teaching artists working in schools.

Deploying both asynchronous and synchronous online teaching approaches, this programme equips teaching artists with the skills and knowledge to conduct arts programmes in schools covering five broad areas: the psychology of learning, curriculum planning, lesson planning and assessment, 'facili-acting' and e-pedagogy.

It is obvious by now that Singaporean success in PISA's creative thinking test points in the distinct direction of the existence and implementation of an overarching strategy that is continuously updated.

Lim-Tan and her team link and connect the arts education portfolio enabling different government ministries to move towards similar twenty-first century competencies for the nation as an integrated and comprehensive whole. Holistic development is not meant solely for students' growth. When public administration embraces it at the core, the positive effect becomes much more than the sum of all its parts.

Coordinated policies cascade across and down. In Singapore's planning between primary schooling and tertiary level, the training of secondary schoolers in the arts is as significant as academic prowess. The School of the Arts, or SOTA,[25] as it is often known, the national pre-tertiary specialised arts school, has a fierce overseas reputation of driving teenagers (13 to 18 years) very hard to aim high and achieve considerably.

SOTA, under the aegis of the Ministry of Culture, Community and Youth, provides a dedicated development path for those who have passion and show early talent in the arts, providing a learning environment where both the artistic and academic potential can flourish. With a vision to nurture creative citizens, the school identifies and nurtures artistic and creative learners who can 'positively impact Singapore and the world'.[26]

On top of academic studies that are premised on the International Baccalaureate, known for its impressive critical thinking curriculum, SOTA students focus on specialised art forms in dance, theatre, music, visual, and literary arts. This stream of

---

24. 'Arts Education – Essentials of Teaching and Learning', National Arts Council Singapore, accessed 15 July 2024, https://www.nac.gov.sg/support/capability-development/training-opportunities/arts-education-essentials-of-teaching-and-learning-module-(em).
25. 'About SOTA', School of the Arts Singapore, accessed 15 July 2024, https://www.sota.edu.sg/.
26. 'School of the Arts Singapore', Create For _____, accessed 15 July 2024, https://www.sota.edu.sg/wp-content/uploads/2024/08/a3fe529b-e333-48aa-9f4d-eeb18ce0e1a3.pdf.

young talents are in the making for the crucial six years, and by the time they are accepted into both arts-based universities and general universities, they are likely to be the cream of the crop.

In Hong Kong, this intermediate layer is partially taken over to a small extent by local arts companies but without the education aspect. As an institution, the Hong Kong Academy of Performing Arts would be a natural vehicle to network and coalesce independent companies as they plan to develop their second campus in the city's upcoming Northern Metropolis.

In the two decades and more of Hong Kong's participation in the PISA tests before 2022, it always scored high, in the top five consistently. Like a few other jurisdictions, including Czechia, Macao (China), and Chinese Taipei, Hong Kong (China) performed above the OECD average in mathematics, science, and reading although for creative thinking pioneered, it was below the OECD average.

As seen in this chapter, there needs to be a serious understanding of arts education and the arts-in-education, a commitment, a policy, and authentic inter-bureau collaboration. Equipping teachers for teaching creatively is now a growing global trend. Singapore and Korea's achievements have also shown the means by which academic learning and arts and culture can form strong alliances, paving the way for creative thinking across the city.

Some live for international league tables; others read them with a huge grain of salt. Whatever the preference, a widely referenced scale like PISA provides meaningful insights that should not be disregarded.

8
Museums and Performance Spaces
Sites of Creative Learning

Summary

This chapter investigates alternative and inspiring spaces for creative learning beyond traditional school perimeters and parameters.

　　Part I defines what a Site of Creative Learning is, its physical, mental, and emotional components and nature. Part II closes in on four globally renowned museums for their physical and cognitive visitor relationships. Part III assesses diverse theatre configurations in performance spaces. Part IV integrates museums and performing spaces as sites for affective learning. Part V explores schools as transition locales for teaching that could extend into museums and theatres as a unified system, citing one of AFTEC's recent signature projects as an example.

Part I

The Frame of Mind (figure 8.1) is a page from my thinking notes. The notes were sketched out in a comparatively short time, the thoughts having bubbled in the head for a relatively long while. The fascination at work has been with merging as opposed to bisecting, criss-crossing instead of maintaining a linear focus. Why is that?

　　Because the arts are, in and of themselves, fecund and all-encompassing; because life and learning are not about silos but about generating ideas from a range of catalysts and inspirations around us; because if we are looking to nurture a creative city, we need creative mindsets. These do not happen overnight. Imagine if a ten-year plan was created and implemented back in 2005. It could be that the understanding of creativity called for in 2015 would have been so much more impactful and, by 2025, we would see a bumper crop.

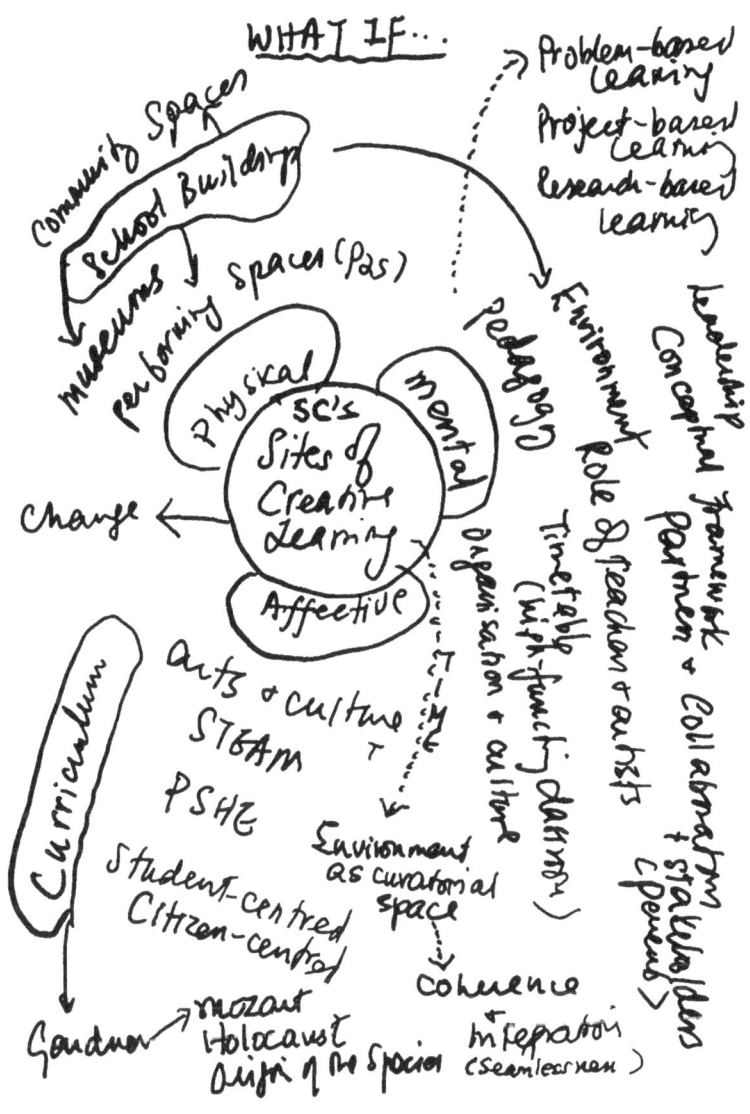

Figure 8.1: A Frame of Mind. Image by author, 2024.

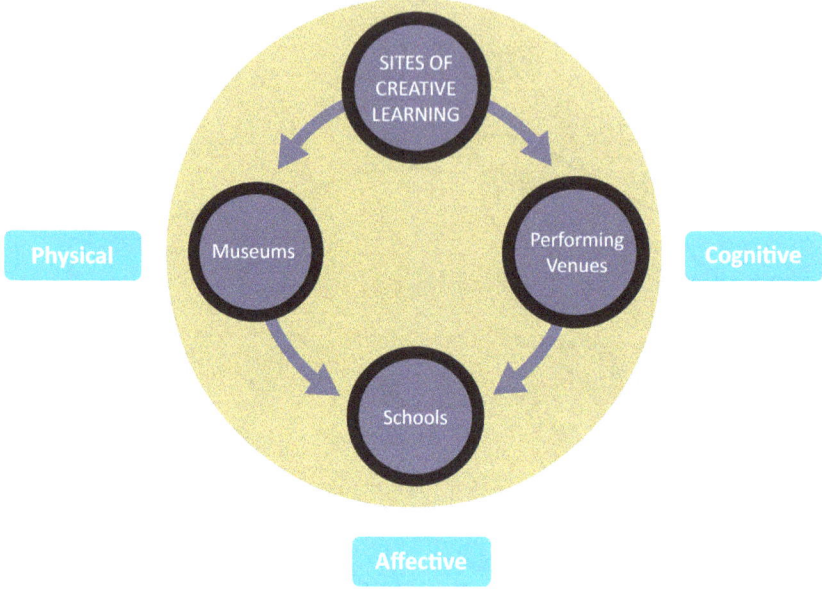

Figure 8.2: Interconnected and Permeable Sites of Creative Learning. Image from AFTEC, 2024.

To those who may not be familiar with Hong Kong, we are a bustling, crowded place. That is probably why most of us go about our daily lives at speed, getting out of each other's way mumbling 'No time, no space, done' as a mantra. This chapter will deal with space, time, and whether some things are ever done. It will address possibilities in the arts and creative learning, amalgamating two major sets of components found in various Sites of Creative Learning (figure 8.2).

Sites of Creative Learning is a term coined to represent places, conceptual and actual, where creative teaching and learning occur beyond obvious educational establishments, to augment schools' collaboration with arts companies and artists. In a world where competencies and capabilities are increasingly called for to maintain and enhance the competitive edge, the four walls of a classroom need to be extended to include the cultural community. Premised on the three spheres of learning, visual and performing arts locations are significant spaces whose potential should be fully maximised beyond transporting coaches of schoolchildren there.

There are three influences on an individual's growth: the physical environment in which we live, the mental or cognitive affordances given the individual, and finally, the affective or the inner emotional and external social lives that navigate a person in life. The darker shades list spaces that pertain to this book's coverage in the arts (visual and performing sites) interconnecting with teaching and learning (arts-in-education/creative learning).

This chapter first visits museums as a concept, their internal environment and the cognitive space imparted, before advancing to performing venues to examine the same concerns. Linking both types of arts establishments are considerations of the affective disposition or the place where feelings exude. Genuine sites of learning intersect and interact. That is why museum visits should be more than drop-ins, whirlwind tours, worksheet-filling, and mechanically fulfilling a task. That is also why performances are storytelling and more. These, I believe, can influence learning and the nature of our audience (see chapter 9).

What does it mean, though, to champion a Site of Creative Learning which encourages 5Cs of creativity, critical thinking, communication, collaboration, and contribution to social capital?

Part II

Museums as Sites of Creative Learning

Physical Space

Museums past and present

Museums have come a long way from the nineteenth-century idea of august buildings, where the space was considered sacred and the audience viewed as pilgrims, heads bowed before imposing artefacts, engaging in hushed conversations about great names and price tags. While old masters are still to be revered, the awe associated with them is broadened because of the comparatively easy access for most advanced nations to compare and contrast then and now, past and present.

The space in traditional museums generally only serves one purpose – how best to display the collection. I remember my younger self feeling and thinking that museums were churches; they were quiet, and masterpieces were simply there to be studied, preferably moving along chronologically. Then a plethora of extraordinary museums appeared.

The Guggenheim Museum Bilbao[1] (figure 8.3) in Spain opened just one month before the Miho Museum in Japan. The museum in Bilbao was choreographed, and made to dance, by Frank Gehry, unlike I. M. Pei's in Shiga prefecture, Japan. The Guggenheim's stunning design resembles a ship at the dock by the river, titanium

---

1. 'View at Dawn Across the Nervion River Towards the Guggenheim Museum. Iberdrola Tower in Background, Bilbao, Spain', *Alamy*, accessed 2 May 2024, https://www.alamy.com/view-at-dawn-across-the-nervion-river-towards-the-guggenheim-museum-iberdrola-tower-in-background-bilbao-spain-image332650486.html.miho.

Figure 8.3: Guggenheim Bilbao. Photo from *Alamy*, 2024.

skins shimmering like fish scales in the sunlight. Its cavernous atrium is flushed with glass and light. It clamours to be seen as a spectacle far before visitors take to its collection of contemporary art from the mid-twentieth century till the present.

The Miho[2] (figure 8.4), by contrast, reflects the source of the inspiration. When I last visited, the first visual indicator after alighting from public transport was the entrance to a tunnel that began the imagined trip of the famed fable by Chinese Poet Tao Yuanming (365–427 CE), *The Peach Blossom Spring*.

From there, one transferred to silent buggies and travelled through a long dark passage into the light and the entrance to an otherworldly, almost utopian site. The building itself is coddled and buried in the mountains. It calls for anonymity and quiet contemplation. The Miho Museum's thinking, initiated by its founder, Mihoko Koyama, was for beauty, peace, and joy through art. The architecture reflects this, as does the collection of ancient Japanese and Asian art of diverse materials.

Innovating the thinking

Traditional museums used to be top-down establishments when the buildings served as placeholders for the collection. Both the Guggenheim and the Miho, one calling out to be noticed and the other shy and reserved, offer the same concept of space – its exploratory nature. Taking the cue from the two museums and transferring this

---

2. 'Architecture of Miho Museum in Kyoto, Japan, Designed by Architect I. M. Pei', *Alamy*, accessed 2 May 2024, https://www.alamy.com/kyoto-japan-jul-16-2015-architecture-of-miho-museum-in-kyoto-japan-the-museum-designed-by-architect-i-m-pei-is-a-17400-m2-building-carved-image33-9593560.html.tate modern.

Figure 8.4: Miho Museum Tunnel Entrance. Photo from *Alamy*, 2024.

notion to teaching and learning, we can shift the conservative, prescriptive paradigm of education of the nineteenth to twentieth centuries.

This is moving from a linear to a curvilinear notion, from the instructive to the constructive, more personal and experiential. After all, when policy documents detail learning as being 'holistic', the engagement would need to be different, would it not?

Looking at the new thinking behind the two museums, suddenly one is made acutely aware of the play of the imagination being a central tenet. The architecture is now playing a different role, opening up the mind for discovery. Museums are oases of opportunities. The role of the visitor has changed. We are now asked to involve ourselves, to engage with the space and not just the objects.

Not all museums have to be newly minted to offer a journey for those who throng through. The Tate Modern's launch[3] in South Bank, London, in 2000[4] (figure 8.5) offers another level of excitement.

The Bankside Power Station constructed between the 1940s and 1960s became the Tate's gallery for international and contemporary art. Herzog and De Meuron, the architects, kept the old structure and its original character. In 2009, the Tate

---

3. 'View of Tate Modern Gallery and the New Len Blavatnik Building in Bankside, London, UK, *Alamy*, accessed 2 May 2024, https://www.alamy.com/london-uk-a-view-of-tate-modern-gallery-and-the-new-len-blavatnik-building-in-bankside-image557745851.html.
4. The concept was mooted in 1992.

Figure 8.5: Tate Modern. Photo from *Alamy*, 2024.

embarked on a major project to develop Tate Modern. Working again with the same architects, the Tate this time transformed the power station's spectacular redundant oil tanks to increase gallery space as well as improve visitor facilities.

What changed was the very idea of curating in museums. The radical thinking of distancing itself from chronological and movement-based layout for exhibitions to theme-based[5] across objects, materials, and historical periods was nothing short of heart-racing. Twentieth-century artworks were grouped around four main themes instead: *Still-Life/Matter/Environment*, *Still-Life/Object/Real Life*, *History/Memory/Society*, and *Nude/Action/Body*.

Looking back, my time at Tate Modern in 2010 may have marked the moment when a pathway beyond categorisation became apparent. This experience reinforced AFTEC's early vision of bridging divides, a principle we continue to pursue to this day.

Unlike the singular, convergent lines of thought typically found in traditional museums, Tate Modern allows visitors to explore exhibitions in a divergent manner, leading them to their own conclusions. This is not to say there is little complexity or choice in the traditional mode. Multi-layering is far more exciting to the imagination

---

5. The MOMA in New York, the Centre Pompidou in Paris, and Essl in Vienna were also planning and executing along the same lines as the Tate Modern.

when a host of thinking strategies can be used. This way lies creativity when one needs to work a multitude of apparently heterogeneous thoughts into a coherent whole or, purely, to end up asking a host of open-ended questions, one powerful approach to thinking critically and creatively.

As traditional synchronous hangings and placements go, there is a starting and an ending point. When artworks are thematically treated, the Tate's then-senior curator, Francis Morris, explains, they open up the conversations among the displays and not narrow and flatten them.[6]

Eccentricity personified

If one is looking for outlandish and mind-teasing museums in which the objects as well as the space are as compelling and they are 'confusing', where every attendee is in a way alone, or free, to work out the exhibitions, then the Museum of Old and New Art[7] (MONA, figure 8.6) in Hobart, Tasmania, is the spot.

Opened in 2011 as a private museum, MONA was founded by art collector David Walsh. It is best for MONA to describe him, to understand the tone of the museum. 'MONA is the playground and megaphone of David Walsh, who grew up in Tassie (just down the road from MONA), dropped out of uni, played cards, won, did some other stuff, and opened a small museum of antiquities to which no one came. He declared it a triumph and decided to expand. The result is MONA, a temple to secularism, rationalism, and talking crap about stuff you really don't know very much about. We won't tell anyone. Come and play.'[8]

It is truly laid-back Australian even in the writing along the hoardings and the website. The often tongue-in-cheek displays make an individual either love it or hate it. As one can surmise, the MONA space is nothing short of eclectic. It is underground, and gallery walls are the unadorned, natural bedrock. There is also no timeline to follow.

Objects seem to be intentionally placed as contrasting – an Egyptian mummy next to a twentieth-century artwork – that may or may not be thematically linked and which ask the visitor to decipher. It is great fun, as diverse interpretations can happen. Amongst a group of friends, many intriguing conversations can be struck.

Physical spaces in museums are very special not only because of their imposing buildings. In fact, size is relative. It is the placement of the artefacts in relation to the

---

6. Louisa Buck, 'Curator Interview: Tate Modern's Thematic Hang', *The Art Newspaper*, 1 May 2000, https://www.theartnewspaper.com/2000/05/01/curator-interview-tate-moderns-thematic-hang.
7. 'A Beautiful View over the Mona Art Museum, Hobart in Tasmania by Water', *Alamy*, accessed 3 May 2024, https://www.alamy.com/a-beautiful-view-over-the-mona-art-museum-hobart-in-tasmania-by-water-australia-image489258835.html.
8. 'About', Museum of Old and New Art, accessed 21 August 2024, https://mona.net.au/museum/about.

Figure 8.6: Museum of Old and New Art. Photo from *Alamy*, 2024.

galleries that is important or, to put it more succinctly, it is the actual space between the displays and the passage for visitors' traffic which is crucial to the experience. This 'third space' is where subtle exchanges can happen between visitor and artwork.

This is why emerging new museums play with different concepts of space. Opened in 2024 is the Goodman Gallery's fourth space within Cheetah Plains Lodge in South Africa. As tourists roam the lodge during their safari stay, they interact not only with their surroundings but also the lodge, conservation ideas, and sustainability issues. Any sales resulting from the gallery are a cause for good, as a percentage goes towards benefitting local communities to provide clean water.

The 'third space' is community and communal, increasingly a far cry from the nineteenth to twentieth-century concepts of what museums were.

Building relationships

Museums are by and large object-based, the majority of pieces from time past and increasingly numbers from time present. Discounting movable installations, artefacts/artworks are mainly static. As if time has captured and frozen them in a large volume of air molecules that hold and embrace all time enveloping intergenerational visitors, allowing objects and people to look, observe, stare, gape, and wonder at each other, interminably, until closing hours. The still nature of the artefacts commands the attention of object (artefact) and subject (visitor), building a relationship forward.

The four international museums referenced – Guggenheim Bilbao, Miho, Tate Modern, and MONA – are so empowering because they palpably break the usual conventions and thus mindsets for visitors. The body experiencing a different atmosphere stimulates the mind to reconfigure a different relationship. Museums are very much sites of creative learning.

We know that the four museums are in cities where there is available land and deep vision. Here in Hong Kong, there are museums with physical space which can equally captivate minds. The various public museums, including those in the West Kowloon Cultural District, spring immediately to mind.

Here locally, can we re-envision how existing space and/or buildings can be utilised? Can we enhance village revitalisation to include museum ideas? Can we change a disused space into a museum, like the Muzeum Susch in the Swiss Alps, which transformed a monastery into one showcasing modern art? Even better, can we take the profusion of empty schools built over decades (now defunct) and morph them imaginatively into museums?

Our museums may be comparatively smaller in physical size. Yet the tightness of space need not hamper the expanse of the mind. Their evolution as sites of creative learning has immense possibilities.

Cognitive Space

Object-based learning that encompasses an inquiry-based approach in museums is a useful entry point for cultivating creative mindsets. The approach to exhibitions is a crucial factor in nourishing and opening up thinking. The environment influences the space in which the curators plan and the objects displayed influence mindsets.

When art is hung chronologically, minds will follow in a linear fashion. Of course, if the learning team is curious and playful, then activities and clues can be across rooms and multipronged. The idea is to unfurl possibilities. I hear from many who work in museums that they have no time. True as it may be, it is half an illusion. Time is what we make of it. Changes will, at first, take time although once mindsets have adapted to shifting to an alternative mode of planning the learning, the time required will become increasingly reduced.

Tate learning

The physical space and exhibitions of the four museums stand out naturally. The Tate Modern's learning, however, is head and shoulders above everything else. Anna

Cutler, the director of learning and research in 2010, undertook a major review with her team to transform Tate Learning over a few years.

The core of the review focused on how learning could be better integrated into the organisation, and by implication to the work it does. To enable that, the team dived deeper into the concept of learning – what is it for them, what is learnt or not – in addition to questioning the assumptions and the values offered. And that was a journey not only for Tate Modern but across all the Tates, in St Ives, Cornwall, Liverpool, and Tate Britain in London. In short, an arts establishment turns to action research to gain ground within and outside the organisations.

In advancing the relationship between the museum's work and visitor learning, the Tate reflected on existing practices and developed a values-based evaluation framework. Often we forget that *evalua*tion means the values within the organisation or project. With the support of critical friends, Tate identified five values-based and process-based frameworks to drive learning forward.

- Identify core values and consider the necessary conditions for learning.
- Articulate in detail how values are to be manifested in practice.
- Identify processes and mechanisms to be put in place to understand what is happening and to account for participants' experiences.
- Draw together and analyse findings to develop broader understanding and to build theory.
- Ensure that findings are fed back into practice and disseminated.[9]

Its resultant publication, *Transforming Tate Learning* (2014) is still captivating ten years on because of the revelation of the very intricate and complex process of change. Cutler and her team turned the routine notions of what a museum should be on their head, re-examining the rationale, and validating the arts in a way that few had attempted to do then.

Tate's approach influenced AFTEC by emphasising the importance of process and the careful consideration of organisational objectives and learning, rather than treating learning as secondary to arts productions or merely an afterthought. Ever since 2010, after enlightening conversations with Emily Pringle, then head of learning practice and research, our pedagogy has evolved alongside the processes of creative teaching and learning. Very simply put, if we want participants to have the arts rooted in daily life as a matter of habit, then experiences that involve the minds and hearts are pivotal, making encounters with the arts deeper, longer lasting, and sustainable. This enables us not to have to reinvent the wheel at every juncture once a frame of mind founded on creative encounters is established.

---

9. Emily Pringle, ed., *Transforming Tate Learning* (Tate Learning 2014).

Tate influence

AFTEC continuously seeks to understand and investigate the meaning of process and values of creative learning year on year. In the last quarter of 2023, we explored the concept of family creative adventures at three local museums.[10]

There, we ran two-hour workshops based on prior registration and/or walk-in families. A total of sixty-three participants joined us, making up twenty-nine families, and a 48% response rate from the survey we sent out subsequently. Three families who responded to the survey attended workshops at two museums, and one family attended workshops at all three.

Based on what colours jumped out at us during early site visits to the museums (white, red, and green), we wanted to explore if creative teaching could be adopted in a public arena as in schools through a choice of artworks across diverse rooms in hands-on, interactive modes without being didactic, to kindle the innate curiosity and spontaneity in discovery.

Families engaged in a meet-and-greet warm-up activity before the activities started, in which fun and collaborative tasks were meted out before they roamed specific galleries or areas. They then regrouped for dialogues on their discoveries, leading to further conversations. Over the three workshops, the key tools and skills of observing, imagining, questioning, and dialoguing were fundamental, used by teaching artists to elicit discussions among the same family members in separate groups and then across families.

Results from the survey of this initial exploration in the three museums were encouraging, families showing continued desire to locate workshops that are distinctive (92%), enhance family bonding (77%), and allow experiencing creative learning (77%).

The process offered – observations, discussions, making, and asking – were found by a large majority to be helpful although according to questioning techniques, a small proportion thought otherwise. Along the same lines, in post-workshop surveys, many were able to transfer some skills, redeploy observation, and imagination, ideas followed by sharing feelings and asking questions. Again, a small number found expressing feelings challenging, which we actually anticipated, as this is a common area of challenge.

Many replied that they would like to return for similar creative workshops in the future. Overall views ranged from calling on the museums for further similar activities to being able to understand artworks from multiple perspectives, learning how to guide children at other exhibitions, and calling for smaller workshop size.

---

10. Hong Kong Heritage Museum, Hong Kong Museum of Art, Hong Kong Science Museum.

These fledgling workshops proved highly informative to us. In debriefings, we were able to analyse activity details, their success and need for adjustment, where mismatches occurred, and where the gaps surfaced, predominantly in the lesser abilities to describe and engage feelings and deal with open-ended questions.

Part III

Performing Venues as Sites of Learning

Physical Space

Performing venues are dynamic sites of learning if they are regarded as being at the other end of the 'mobility' spectrum. Unlike museums in general, which in the main deal with produced immobile objects that stem from humans, on the stage we see human beings as performers and characters that inhabit the performance area in real time, expressing themes that are ideas-based.

Consequently, performers on stage seldom stand still, and if so, not for very long. The exception is in music, when the playing of instruments requires more stationary postures although movement is still apparent in the playing by musicians and in the scores where 'movement' denotes a section of the composition. Artificial Intelligence is changing the human-bot relationship but this is topic for another time.

Performing venues are not better or worse spaces than are museums; they are simply spaces for different purposes. In the ensuing discussion, we will focus on theatre and dance. Space for orchestras and how they affect acoustics, for example, will take us into a very different realm of discussion, one in which I am not knowledgeable.

Performing spaces are varied. For theatre directors, there are many reasons for the choice of space depending on the play, the interpretation, the choice of intended impact, and here in Hong Kong, availability, given extreme booking limitations.

Many Hong Kong venues are proscenium arch theatres in which all members of the audience are seated on the same side, their gaze directed in the same forward direction to a box-like stage with one wall missing. This is known as the fourth wall, as it enables the audience to watch the action on stage as if through an invisible wall. Figure 8.7 illustrates this.

Separately, figures 8.8 to 8.11 show four more kinds of staging.

Very, very broadly speaking, the more an audience is fixed in one physical area (proscenium theatre), the less they are able to connect with the tangibility of the stage area. This is very general and is untrue when an excellent script is created. As the seating arrangement diversifies (traverse, thrust, arena), the more involved

Figure 8.7: Proscenium Theatre, Sai Wan Ho Civic Centre. Image from digiAFTEC's online *Young Person's Guide to the Theatre*, 2022.

Figure 8.8: Traverse Stage. Image from digiAFTEC's online *Young Person's Guide*, 2022.

Figure 8.9: Thrust Stage. Image from digiAFTEC's online *Young Person's Guide*, 2022.

Figure 8.10: Arena or In-the-round Stage. Image from digiAFTEC's online *Young Person's Guide*, 2022.

Figure 8.11: Jockey Club Creative Arts Centre Black Box. Photo from AFTEC, 2024.

they may be though in actually moving around. Perhaps black-box theatres top it all. Without fixed seating or none at all, the audience has physical freedom[11] around the actors.

Immersive spaces for theatre are at the opposite end to proscenium space, in which the audience changes from passively watching the show to becoming active bystanders and even participants. Punchdrunk, formed in the UK in 2000, and a leading immersive company, takes over entire buildings, changing every single space and room into a set, decorating it to a specific era and theme. The audience are free to explore as they roam, touching, sensing, playing with their imagination.

The distance of the moving objects – be they actors or dancers and furniture and props – and their interaction all mean something, except, unlike museum artefacts, these are multiple happenings. In performance spaces, movements are converging or diverging, constituting ongoing and changing relationships. Their proximity (thrust or arena stages) or distance (proscenium arch) to the audience matters. The closer the more intimate as a rule of thumb. Diverse space means distinct possibilities.

---

11. See Passoverdance segment.

The imagination is where the magic begins. It is here, in this ephemeral space that the performance meets the audience. Because of the fleeting nature of moving pictures on stage, an audience absorbs the surface impact immediately and is likely to remain at the narrative level throughout if they do not care to look closer or are not given the appropriate tools to explore further.

Where a performer is placed, when and how that actor or dancer changes position can speak volumes about the director's and the choreographer's intentions. The performing arts can be very appealing, as the mind is kept constantly busy. This is also one reason that diving in at depth to understand the work is not always easy. This is the mental space for creative learning and teaching to work.

Physical to Cognitive Space

As a result, at entry point, it is probably better to start with museums before moving to the performing arts. Like museums, theatre and dance reflect life. Dissimilar to museums, the variables are in constant flux, making understanding theatre and dance more complex. This is the exuberance of the performing arts. The nature of learning here is layered though grasping it ultimately comes down to experience and practice.

AFTEC resides in the Sai Wan Ho Civic Centre for theatre productions and workshops. We set out over a decade ago to explore the theatre as a learning space. Things happen in a performing space as a result of intent as much as the realisation of the imagination, a value that could merit much more recognition in Hong Kong.

After all, how does one explain this string of development using AFTEC's 2024 stage production? From changing a bare stage at the Yuen Long proscenium arch theatre (figure 8.12),[12]

---

12. Major renovation at the Sai Wan Ho Civic Centre from 2021 to mid-2025 meant AFTEC became itinerant and produced its events in other venues, including the Yuen Long Theatre. Technical drawing from the theatre.

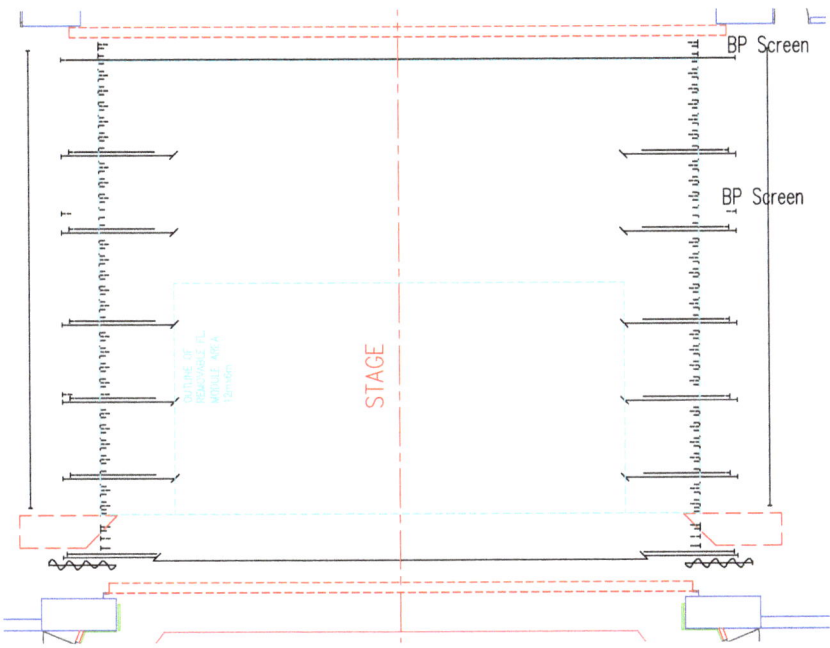

Figure 8.12: Yuen Long Theatre Stage Technical Drawing. Image courtesy of the Leisure and Cultural Services Department, 2024.

to a design as in figure 8.13,

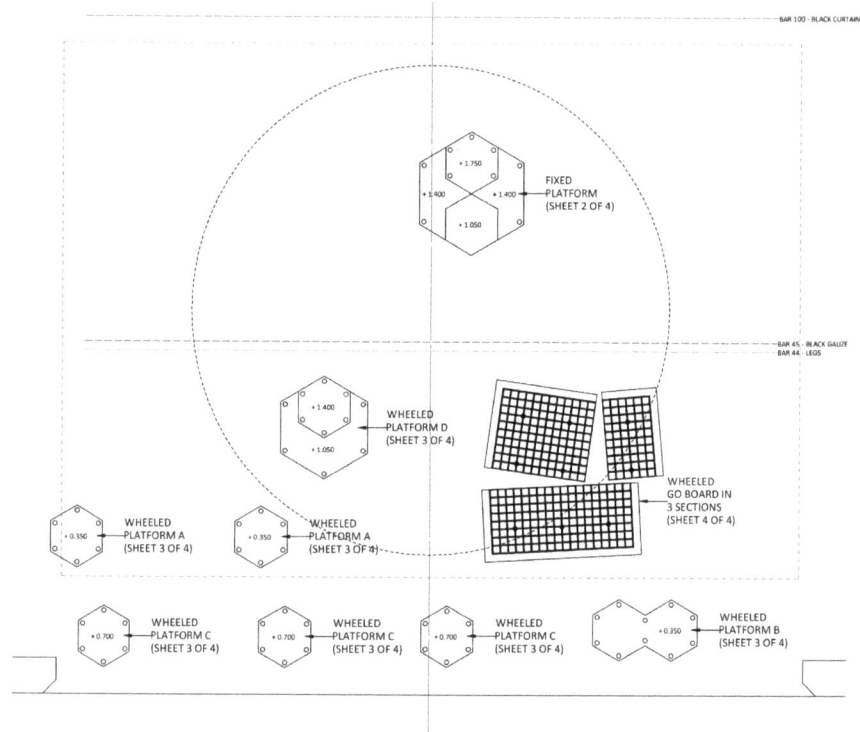

STRATEGY
The Absolutely Fabulous Theatre Connection Ltd
Yuen Long Theatre, 26 February to 17 March 2024
SHEET 1 OF 4 - STAGE/KEY PLAN - 10 November 2023

Figure 8.13: Set Designer's Initial Drawings. Image by Andrew Ritchie for AFTEC, 2024.

to 3D rendering (figure 8.14),

Figure 8.14: Set Designer's Model Blocks and Broken Go Board. Image by Andrew Ritchie for AFTEC 2024.

to the final set actualised on stage as in figure 8.15.

Figure 8.15: Final Set on Stage. Photo by Liu Ka Lam for AFTEC, 2024.

The set design photos from the technical drawing of the stage to the 2D plan then 3D model before the built set encompass the visual symbols of *Strategy*,[13] were from the re-imagination of the key strategic scenes in the Chinese classic *Romance of the Three Kingdoms*, in the battle of wits between real-life Chinese strategist Zhuge Liang and his arch enemy, Zhou Yu.

The large physical space (stage) actualised the interpretation of the script using a 3D Go board, the two protagonists playing out their battle moves and testing each other along the way.

Thanks to innumerable scenes across mountains (hexagonal granite-looking blocks), indoors (table and chair), on ramparts (highest blocks), land (stage floor), and floating on the water (soldiers rowing with oars on a block), the mind followed these signs in the production as different portable parts (the blocks, banners, flags, and furniture) were moved around the stage with, and sometimes without, the help of hydraulics such as a revolving stage.

Added to that set were colour-coded costumes and stage props denoting the three factions at war (red flags and military gear in red for the kingdom of Wei, pink for the kingdom of Wu, and blue for the kingdom of Shu). Huge physical confrontations were played out on a limited stage space as a result, covering what would have been vast terrains and contrasting topography. The actors in the production, the lighting, and the single Chinese opera musician's percussive instruments all forcefully brought the entire play to life that first took shape as one integrated concept in the mind of the director, Vicki Ooi.

Strategy is the sixteenth season's production under the *From Page to Stage* banner, a theatre-in-education programme that has seen over 250,000 students and teachers come through our doors firstly in pre-show learning in school, then watching as the audience, then progressing on to the stage as participants for activities, and finally returning to the school for post-show discussions. The underlying idea, though, is more than that from page (the Chinese classic) to stage (in a theatre). From reading and research, to concept, scripting over many drafts, design (set, lighting, sound, costume, make-up), auditions to rehearsals, script adjustment, and finally, to the stage.

The stage is the learning space that is an extension of and interconnected to the usual school learning environment. Imagine the abundance of content and activities that can evolve from a single production. The standard education pack for *Strategy* at two levels includes factual historical knowledge, themes, plot introduction, characterisation, in-class and post-show activities, a glossary, etc.

The theatre in its entirety is a site for learning. We use front- and backstage for creative learning, from the floor to the ceiling and the wings and other rooms in

---

13. *From Page to Stage* production, March 2024, Yuen Long Theatre.

the building. It is, in effect, a 'school without walls'. The learning in the theatre and other spaces is framed by the school curriculum, specifically here in English language teaching. With a production like *Strategy*, we look to reposition the audience's perception, from focusing on the plot, costumes, and naturalistic sets[14] delving into themes, characterisation, plot development, the correlation between visual symbols and dialogues among characters, to issues of historical, geographical, psychological, and emotional interests such as loyalty, friendship, betrayal, and commitment.

Another interpretation of the theatre space as a school without walls is the original, eponymous programme created by The Egg, a children's theatre[15] at the Theatre Royal Bath in the UK. When we met in 2010, Kate Cross, the director, had just initiated this format with the group $5 \times 5 \times 5$ = creativity and St Andrew's Church School.

Instead of routine schooling, St Andrew's took the whole of Year 4 (eight-year-olds) for six weeks to The Egg, learning core curricular topics, from new and different creative perspectives. After two years, the success of inquiry-based learning expanded to the whole school. Subsequently, the children lived the same concept at the Holburne Museum, Central Library, St Swithin's church, the Bath Spa University College of Art and Design, and the Museum of East Asian Art.

The immersive learning experience offered by Punchdrunk Enrichment is likely to be the most luxurious form of schools without walls. Like the original Punchdrunk, their charity arm invites schools, families, and communities into immersive learning spaces on site in schools where experiences are provided and are teacher-led.

Part IV

Museums and Performing Spaces for Affective Learning

As both museums and performing spaces are arts-based, they are strongly anchored to and situated in human objects and situations. Schools are human-centred or have student-centred learning as a core focus. The obvious common denominator between arts-based establishments and educational ones is human beings. In schools here though, one facet is infrequently dealt with daily, that of emotional expressions as socio-emotional development.

This limitation can be redressed and balanced through forming a relationship with museums and arts companies, in which readily available subjects are within

---

14. A naturalistic set shows realistic places and objects (a bedroom with a closet and bed), which is different from a non-naturalistic one, which is symbolically abundant. *Strategy* is one such example.
15. The Egg's facilities are all child size (seating) and child friendly (washrooms, tables, chairs) with quiet rooms available as the need arises.

sight and reach. The key question is how these sites of creative learning can become appropriate, illuminative, and mutually beneficial to all stakeholders.

Tate

Tate Learning, having had a head start of almost twenty years under Anna Cutler, seems to have travelled much farther along this road. At AFTEC, we have, for example, values that have sprung from programming practice over the years that are articulated. We have moved very much into 'process for learning' as opposed to 'product for learning'. But we have yet to document in writing the stages and the correlation between values and process. How far has Tate progressed by 2023 with its learning culture?

One of their core values is 'inclusivity', which is not a surprise given that this is a term often seen across the arts in ever expanding frequencies, in London, Hong Kong, and elsewhere. Nevertheless, Tate Learning seriously took up being inclusive from an incident at Tate Britain in 2013 through to developing an ongoing partnership for ten years between the Southwark Inclusive Learning Service and the museum's Schools and Teachers team.

The principal, Yomi Adewoye, explained that the Learning Service is a small alternative provision school for many students who are excluded from mainstream schools for complicated reasons. The Southwark borough in London, where the service is located, is an area where socially deprived families live. At the service, however, being underprivileged does not equate with underachievement. Inclusivity is a strong value there, and equal access to opportunities is offered to reduce the gap in education, thereby empowering the students to achieve success.

In 2013, at an artist-led workshop in Tate Britain with support from the museum's Schools and Teachers team member, a group of students encountered negative feedback from a visitor at the museum who regarded their freeze-frame drama activities[16] in front of artworks as behaviourally disruptive. A complaint to an attending security officer led to an attempt to terminate the activity. The security officer apparently labelled the group's activities as 'wrong'. Post-incident, the students were not astonished that they were not welcomed there.

After a Tate apology to the school, the Learning Service was offered another opportunity to work with the museum. From contacting the visual arts teacher initially, a relationship began to develop based on the premise of mutual learning to foster a more welcoming ambiance for all. The shared value of collaboration has since evolved into more regular interactions in the museum and the school.

---

16. Also known as tableau, this is a drama game in which participants use their bodies to create still images to illustrate an artwork or a scene.

A breakthrough emerged as Tate and the Learning Service teachers in a professional development workshop shared their views on a photograph, not from a curriculum but personal viewpoint. This object-based exercise brought about discussions, connections, and relationships in a new way, the teachers realising that the creativity behind doing so was being able to support better conversations with their young people.

The resultant outcome was to engage with each other for more days at the museum, everyone learning in the same physical and cognitive space, thereby elevating both sets of practices to another level. Over time, Tate invited a researcher to capture the process and support reflection along the journey.

The main *IDENTITY* project cemented relationships among the staff at the Tate and the school, reducing the space between the two institutions, the professionals, and the students. One of Tate Learning's values is not for one-way prescriptive factual knowledge dissemination but to engage participants in continuous, upcycle, correlative learning in which the process for museum and school is as vital as understanding the artwork. In other words, the movement is two-way and the learning is reciprocated.

The original visit by the Learning Service saw less than desirable emotions from different sides in a public space and yet, because Tate staff stepped up to become a catalyst for redressing and improving matters for less-privileged people via creative learning, the emotional disruption grew into a positive association. This is a case in point for affective learning in a museum with inclusivity at its heart.

Passoverdance

In the performing arts sector, like theatre, dance is an excellent vehicle for emotions. Contrary to popular belief, contemporary dance is not impossible to comprehend. It is, however, challenging if the audience only expects a storyline, a linear one that describes the beginning, middle, and end without the need to relate to what is happening on stage.

In other words, if an audience anticipates a straight narrative (as in many classical ballets) to be discerned immediately, then contemporary dance will be perplexing. By developing the imagination and working with visual symbols instead, non-narrative-based dance can be grasped.

A maze, as we all know, can be a physical entity or a mental state. The former is a space in which different paths and barriers create twists and turns for participants to find an exit after going past the entrance. The latter, the mental 'feeling like being in a maze', denotes a state of confusion and bewilderment.

What if a choreographer explores both aspects? What if dancers interact with walls in motion on stage? What emotions will emanate? The feelings of pressure, of being overwhelmed, of dealing with life's barriers, not being able to find immediate solutions can be experienced.

Pewan Chow, the artistic director and choreographer of Passoverdance in Hong Kong, has been working on the *Maze* concept for over eight years. With a deep interest in the idea of space, physical, mental, and emotional, she delved into limitations in life and in relationships. Through playing with the space in a black-box theatre, Chow wanted to invite the audience to share those boundaries, solid and otherwise.

As the dancers worked with moving white walls, changing the space from tight (three walls closing up, forming an oppressive triangular space) to broad with infinite variations, the audience watching were also caught up as they walked around the space with the dancers (figure 8.16). The internal feelings of the dancers coupled with those of the audience and the external observation of each other made for opening up, reducing, and occasionally stifling moments alternated with those of release.[17]

Taking the audience to the learning realm, connecting them to personal development, the curriculum becomes possible when we can conceive and envision the abstract as part of our human feelings. Movement allows us to be introspective and to connect with our inner emotions to understand them and articulate them in order to relate to the outside world.

Figure 8.16: Reproduced by permission from Passoverdance. *Maze: Pushing Boundaries*, 2018.

---

17. 'Maze: Pushing Boundaries', Passoverdance, June 2018, https://www.passoverdance.org/maze-2.

Part V

The space in museums serves more than just exhibitions and displays. Immovable objects offer head room for thinking, feeling, and learning. They build relationships with visitors through internal dialogues. For those who become participants, relational conversations happen between two or more people, thereby amplifying the idea of a community.

Performing venues and their spaces are at once very palpable and filled with creative thinking possibilities. The shows that are produced in varying spaces are ideas-based, constituting constant changes on stage which dazzle the audience as they can also bewilder. Long after the show is over, a bit of confusion can be meaningful, as the mind can return to recapture moments and rethink instances. This is part of an ongoing process to accept ambiguity, try and puzzle it, and continuously learn. This is part of what creativity is, sorting out and iterating ideas. Ambiguity is part of life.

Creativity and learning go hand in hand. Museums and performing venues are two evident spaces to be considered. This is not asking curators and artistic directors to forego exhibitions and productions. On the contrary, adopting a learning lens in museums and arts companies in addition as a matter of policy with regular reviews foregrounds serious intentions for audience development, quantitatively and qualitatively. Ultimately, we all want a larger audience, one that enters the space with the prospect of minds, hearts, and spirits being augmented to engage the artworks in front of them.

In the short term, high attendance figures and significant box-office earnings are impressive and should be maintained through various strategies. In the long term, fostering creative minds may help reduce audience attrition. Voting with one's feet is detrimental and fast; voting with one's mind is beneficial though it takes longer. With creative learning constantly and continuously at the core of cultural institutions' intent, a more solid foundation may be built to sustain the existing and groom a new audience.

Museums embrace static displays that are object-based, while performing venues harbour ideas-based dynamic offerings. Schools traditionally are didactic, where knowledge is inculcated as part of subject-based teaching. What if teaching and learning morphed to become more organic, adapting, adopting, and reflecting the myriad of objects and ideas available in museums and performing venues as resources for the development of creative mindsets?

In actuality, schools are the 'transition sites' for those within them to traverse formal, non-formal, and informal learning via the arts. Schools are fertile grounds for cultivating creative mindsets. The pilot *Creative Learning* project (2021–2024), as an example, emphasised training the trainers (schoolteachers and artists) for collaboratively engaging and encouraging students in creativity. Final evaluation results from the project's impact study illustrate its continuing possibilities.[18] Table 8.1 is an overview of data from teachers and creative practitioners, whereas table 8.2 gives the students' perspectives.

This project blends the kind of learning that AFTEC has been investigating for some time. Among the creative habits of mind foundational to the project is being imaginative, an adjective that is sprinkled throughout this book. This and other aspects of cultivating creative habits of mind require writing about separately and at length. From the preliminary results, the possibility is definitely there.

In the end, the call is not for local cultural establishments to helicopter in and copy overseas examples directly for the sake of efficiency and instant results but rather to contemplate the learning perspective that is specific to their establishments, to their learning and participation intentions, and create a bespoke approach. By doing so, museums and performing venues can elevate their purpose beyond great entertainment and scintillating sensations, embracing a greater social role for the advancement of creative capital.

---

18. The pilot project has now been extended by four years and renamed *AFTEC Jockey Club Creative Futures Project*.

Table 8.1: Pilot *Creative Learning Project* Impact Study Final Results: Teachers and Creative Practitioners. Image from AFTEC, 2024.

Pilot Project Final Evaluations — Teachers and Creative Practitioners		2021 – 2022	2023 – 2024
Teaching Methods	Encourage thinking	74.2%	90.4%
	Encourage students to ask questions and make suggestions	90.3%	96.2%
Designing & Implementing Creative Education Plan	More confident in their abilities	80.6%	96.2%
	Improvement in team collaboration	90.3%	98.1%
Cross-curriculum Creative Education	Had the connections and resources needed	74.2%	92.3%
	Able to apply learning to the teaching of the school curriculum	83.9%	92.3%

Table 8.2: Pilot *Creative Learning Project* Impact Study Final Results: Students. Image from AFTEC, 2024.

	Students' Views
Above 90%	**Empathy, respect & care for others**
80 – 89%	**Widen horizons** Enjoy creative learning through the arts. Raise learning motivation in the arts & cross-curriculum. Try to use the knowledge acquired to serve the community. **Application of creative strategies in other subjects** Understanding 5Cs is a creative learning style. **Enjoy *JCABC* class** Have more confidence in expressing oneself. **Express one's feelings in different ways**

9
Contextualising Human Resource Planning
A Triumvirate Concept

Summary

Chapter 9 explores the qualitative relationships among three parties – the audience, schools, and creative practitioners (CPs). It analyses supply and demand, then presents possible ways forward in the light of Hong Kong being given the mission to become an East–West Centre for International Cultural Exchange (the Centre) in arts and culture.

Part I gives the context to the writing of the chapter as well as sets out a vision for the triumvirate concept. Part II looks at the development of audienceship, offering five segments for consideration. Part III moves into schools, their arts provision, and a five-level progression chart for advancement. Part IV completes the tripartite idea with a perspective on current practitioner development in the arts. Part V draws together the chapter through the supply-and-demand imbalance in the arts and presents a phased-in CPs' human resource development approach to rectify the situation through bridge organisations. Part VI concludes the chapter, reiterating the crucial need to increase and cultivate CPs enhancing the overall quality of the arts all round.

Part I

Context

In 2023, the Labour and Welfare Bureau commissioned PricewaterhouseCoopers and the consulting firm InnoFoco to undertake a study in human resources projection for Hong Kong looking into the personnel needs of Hong Kong to develop as the Centre under China's 14th Five-Year Plan. We joined the session for the

Performing Arts Sector, and that session became the impetus for this chapter. The result is a concept for developing human resources in the arts sector pivoting on educational practices in schools, planning for advancing audience maturity, and training teaching artists.

Since 2014, in order to positively make a difference, we have seen that a train-the-trainers pathway will have to happen. Our efforts in nurturing creative thinkers on our own to directly affect more young people, though ardent and laser-focused, are limited, given that we are an organisation with limited resources. However, the choice was never not to start because it was challenging. We believed we should embark on the journey anyway to scout the landscape, to understand it, and make inroads where viable.

In 2017, we did just that, collaborating with individuals and arts organisations as a catalytic base. At that time, we did not think too deeply about the need for research data on the existing numbers of arts educators. We simply launched a three-year project targeting youth centres, working with social workers, and drawing together artists from diverse backgrounds, developing the training curriculum, and adjusting as the months passed and experience grew.

By 2020, as we were planning for the *Jockey Club Arts-Based Cross Curriculum Creative Learning Project* (the *Creative Learning Project*) in schools, mining data became a regular affair. Without such knowledge, planning was insufficiently solid.

This project formally dovetailed our years of experience into a creative learning model based on overseas research and then localised. Final data from the impact study, released in November 2024, clearly demonstrated to us that some extraordinary and wonderful work was indeed occurring as teachers and CPs collaborated, shared and merged ideas, and, along the way, changed children's level of motivation and interest, growing progressively as imaginative learners. Two insights emerged.

Insights

First, in spite of having read about what the teacher–artist relationships in theory and practice achieved abroad over time, we now embody the significance, potential possibility, and momentousness of cross-sector partnership in full. That was a lived experience, now branded into the company's DNA.

In preparation for the second Knowledge Exchange forum in 2023 for the *Creative Learning Project*, where all stakeholders spent two days discussing their achievements, concerns, and challenges together, colleagues in the company conducted an internal survey to prove what we had held to be true but lacked evidence for.

Then, a long-buried second realisation surfaced. Arts education, the arts-in-education, creative learning continue to be a realm that is peripheral even in the sector. There are many 'It's' out there. *It* is outreach in companies. *It* is in the Education Bureau's Key Learning Area guide, and *it* is one of the Hong Kong Arts Development Council's art form committees.

Thanks to the various project and matching grants schemes provided by the government, arts education[1] is a listed category to which applications can be made. Steadily, as the Culture, Sports and Tourism Bureau's bimonthly email updates attest, more is being done in arts education by grantees though the nature and extent cannot be diagnosed from the brief descriptions.

But what links it all together? Is it a connected, concerted, comprehensive, integral whole, or disbursements of concepts and grants for each to dispense of under its own radar, enabling a multitude of happenings? How can we capitalise and maximise this to advocate, advance, and adjust the status of arts education to benefit the city? What needs to be done?

This chapter proposes an investigation of an interconnected triumvirate: part I, the nature of the audience, part II, educational arts practices in schools, and part III, the categories of CPs. They form a tripartite alliance, as the interlinking relationship is interlocking and one affects the other. The thesis put forward in relations to human resources planning is that, when we have mapped out existing and probable scenarios in the three areas and a vision is set for a future in the next five to ten years, then human resources planning for the arts and cultural sector can be contextualised and a solid foundation can be built. The horse before the cart is the logic, and figures will only make sense if we commit to common goals.

It would be wise for me to say at this early juncture that I do not know of any research or sectorial discussions in Hong Kong covering the subject at hand and, for this reason, the concepts proposed are borne out of AFTEC's experiences and observations. This chapter consequently hopes to lay the groundwork for the field.

A Vision

The comparatively newly established Cultural Commission, promulgated by the chief executive in his 2022 Policy Address, was given the mandate to develop a blueprint for the arts. This encompasses the growth of culture and creative industries, as well as the improvement of the ecosystem. This will be accomplished by developing facilities, content, platforms, and a diverse talent pool, serving as both the software and hardware for Hong Kong's emergence as an East-West Centre. This particular focus will be explored in greater detail later in the chapter.

As part of the East–West policy, the Hong Kong Academy of Performing Arts is tasked with creating internships alongside the growth of other artistic and technical

---

1. Arts-in-education is not differentiated or mentioned.

talent. The Leisure and Cultural Services Department working alongside the West Kowloon Cultural District will groom more professionals to develop Hong Kong into a regional centre for arts conservation and restoration.

As a city, we are very experienced in constructing cultural buildings for performances and exhibitions, as they are countable. Probably less so is our ability to work with qualitative concepts that define the quality of who we are and the standard of how we are faring.

This is why I would like to delve into the hypotheses of 'quality audienceship' and creative thinkers as two principles to be planted into the Cultural Commission's equation. The first concept is across the board by training teaching artists as a focused, respected, and recognised professional subsector. To a very large extent, arts educators are currently a by-product of artists waiting in the wings for work they are trained for. As to arts educators' numbers, there seems to be no data as yet.

No one will dispute quality, but why audienceship? What do they have to do with the blueprint?

Part 2

Triumvirate Part 1: The Audience

I regard audienceship as the concept of a collective audience and its inherent nature. The audience and its attributes form the calibre of that group of people whether at performances or exhibitions. Figure 9.1 is an example. It has been created from observations and experiences of the local audience over the years and serves as a foundation for discussion.

The progression can be read from left to right and viewed from two angles. As a start, in a linear fashion, someone who starts as a Snapper (1) due to nil or low interest in the arts can advance to becoming a Follower (2) or a Taster (3) one day. Additionally, a multi-perspective lens on this diagram is possible.

At any one point, a member of the audience at different arts events will demonstrate varying stages of understanding and engagement. For example, I am an avid theatre-goer and am currently an Explorer (4) because I am ready to go further. In a textiles exhibition, however, I am at entry point, so I am only a Follower (2) of Reiko Sudo's highly imaginative creations, for example.

The key is whether there is any scaffolding to support qualitative audience development. At this point, probably not. Audienceship is thus crucial in that an ever-discriminating audience will become well-informed catalysts, who will in turn make demands on companies and festivals to spur them on their qualitative journeys. With ever-higher-quality events, the audience is taken to another level, and so

Audienceship & Its Characteristics

 Social media upload & ticking the box; one-off

 Social media, star power & company attraction; one-off

 Sometimes at docent-led tours & performances focusing on the surface level in general, asking for factual descriptions at post-show discussions/at exhibitions

 Curious, starting to engage creatively & reflectively; regularly at events; want more than descriptive facts; offering views, having a discussion; interested in being involved

 Knowledge savvy; habitual reflective thinkers; multi-artform frequenters; self-directed; in discussion with professionals

Figure 9.1: Observed and Projected Audience Attributes. Image from AFTEC, 2024.

the virtuous cycle repeats itself, driving the arts in Hong Kong upwards towards the standards that the city requires to mature into the eventual East–West Centre.

At the opposite end of the spectrum, if we continuously remain at Snapper level and not facilitate the audience's intellectual mobility – mainly stating that there is little interest, or that the audience is not ready – then the audience will make low to stagnant demands on artists. Worse still, even when top international and local happenings are available, the audience will not be as engaged as their untapped potential allows them to be.

Arts Appreciation

At this point, I would like to turn to the term 'arts appreciation', which is liberally sprinkled in our arts education and cultural programmes. This term does not appear anywhere in figure 9.1. This is intentional because 'appreciation' is, again, based on our local experiences, prescriptive, or at a distance.

Prescriptive learning can be regarded as convergent thinking in which the instructor provides very clear, black-and-white tasks to complete, with limited possible responses. It is definitely one kind of learning. This is, for example, a docent-led tour in a museum, in which hard cultural and historical facts are provided along the way, which hopes to contextualise the artwork and its understanding.

In schools, this transforms to the teacher being at the front of the class teaching from a textbook with minimal interaction and very seldom seeking responses from the students for their understanding. This is passive reception. Along the audience continuum, a person on a docent tour would be a Taster at best.

Nearer the other end of the spectrum, appreciation occurs when someone is equipped with a reflective ability and habit to gauge and thus understand the artwork. As an Explorer, the person prefers to move away from the prescriptive and use facts at a docent-led tour to jump further intellectually. Aficionados rely mostly on themselves to experience and engage with artworks and performances, with or without docent tours. Consider how AI learns, by amalgamating and learning from the data, and this is how Aficionados do it.

Arts appreciation is more than a tour. It involves developing the skills and knowledge to:

- understand the formal elements, techniques, and historical context of different art forms;
- recognise and interpret the meanings, themes, and emotional expression conveyed through artworks;
- critically analyse and evaluate the artistic merits and significance of works of art; and
- appreciate the cultural, social, and personal values that the arts can provide.

At Aficionado level, appreciation is highly interactive, from one's own thoughts to interacting with others, on stage and off. Borrowing from the formidable educator and writer, the late Elliott Eisner's writing on the arts and education, his equivalent of aficionado involves

> the ability to see, not merely to look. To do this we have to develop the ability to name and appreciate the different dimensions of situations and experiences, and the way they relate one to another. We have to be able to draw upon, and make use of, a wide array of information. We also have to be able to place our experiences and understandings in a wider context, and connect them with our values and commitments. Connoisseurship is something that needs to be worked at – but it is not a technical exercise. The bringing together of the different elements into a whole involves artistry.[2]

---

2. Elliot Wayne Eisner, *The Enlightened Eye: Qualitative Inquiry and the Enhancement of Educational Practice* (Merrill, 1998).

In short, 'appreciation' is a complex term that needs careful negotiation. This is where the need for creative thinkers as self-starters emerges. The Eisner definition offers a good glimpse of the qualities of a creative thinker. Ideas that are important and applied in AFTEC's work have been rendered bold:

- To **see**, not merely to look
- To **name different** dimensions of situation and experiences
- To see the way they **relate** to one another
- To **draw upon** and **make use of** a wide array of information
- To place our experiences and understandings in a **wider context**
- To **connect** them with our values and commitments.

This is the convergent/divergent thinking approach. where factual knowledge may be a prerequisite and catalyst from which a person is able to communicate with the artwork directly without an intermediary.

From a schooling perspective, this is self-directed learning, and if a teacher is present, the teacher is the facilitator much more than being the harbinger and vessel of knowledge.

Why are these qualities cardinal? When a young person, an adult member of the audience, practises these skills, creative thinking sets in, and this elevates the person to a stage in which there is rapport and intimacy with the arts, irrespective of whether the work in front is liked or not. When there is a critical mass of creative thinkers in the population, this is the level at which quality audienceship occurs.

Creative Thinking Skills

Critical thinking is essential. Giving evidence can happen within oneself (introspection) and with others. Post-show conversations can be swiftly directed from the factual (What was that?) to an exchange of ideas and opinions (If that could change, then . . .). At conferences, speakers can resist from only dealing with the descriptive (Our company's programmes are . . .) to authentically engaging with other panellists (Perhaps our common aspirations could . . .). Then arts organisations and producers will understand the audience. Their work will be different as a result, because mutual inspiration is a cornerstone of ascending quality.

Contrary to some views, creativity and critical thinking – collectively termed 'creative thinking' – are not only for artists and arts frequenters. Everyone needs creative thinking. The world view is forcefully inclining in the direction of creative thinking for education, future employment, and thus the fabric of societies to come (see chapter 7). The arts are the natural and optimal vehicles for achieving this.

The World Economic Forum *Future of Jobs Insight Report*[3] published in May 2023 provides data from organisations globally. Figure 9.2 indicates the share of skills deemed to be increasing or decreasing.[4] Almost three-quarters (73.2%) of organisations have allocated creative thinking to be the fastest-growing skill required in their workforce. Analytical thinking, curiosity, flexibility, motivation, and self-awareness are in the top eight. These nine together are part and parcel of the Eisner formula though the words used are dissimilar.

Also on the increase at 26.4% are reading, writing, and mathematics. However, they are ranked twenty-third out of twenty-six. Compared with creative thinking and the other leading constructs, this unequivocally spells out where the priority is. The indicated competencies required for future jobs should be cultivated in teaching and learning, incorporated into the curriculum, not simply as part of arts subjects but part of curriculum pedagogy. Creative thinking is generic and not subject specific.

The arts are natural bedfellows as evidenced in PISA's June 2023 report, *How Are Education Systems Integrating Creative Systems in Schools*,[5] whereby a large majority (over 88%) of jurisdictions surveyed from primary to secondary schools listed the visual and performing arts as domains in which creative thinking occurs (see chapter 7).

It is, therefore, unsurprising that PISA added creative thinking to its test in 2022 in addition to the age-old reading, sciences, and mathematics. Hong Kong has been a long-time participant and one of the top scorers in the core subjects. As we have witnessed in chapter 7, the city has much room for improvement in creative thinking.

In the 2023 PISA report, which relied on self-reported data from each jurisdiction, the city stands out as one of many where creative thinking is included in the curricula or learning standards for primary and secondary schools in more than 75% of subjects.

In figure 9.3 Cignetti and Rabella provide the overview for developing and assessing students' creativity at primary and secondary school levels. In a whole-system creativity approach, PISA examined progress as demonstrated by the existence of system-level teacher qualifications and training requirements related to creativity.

Two segments are extracted for presentation here: one giving Hong Kong's replies and the other Singapore's.

In the area of system-level formal guidelines or requirements related to the contents of initial teacher training, the authority in Hong Kong (presumably the

---

3. *Future of Jobs Report 2023*, World Economic Forum, May 2023, https://www3.weforum.org/docs/WEF_Future_of_Jobs_2023.pdf.
4. *Future of Jobs Report 2023*, figure 4.3, p. 39.
5. Marta Cignetti and Marc Fuster Rabella, 'How Are Education Systems Integrating Creative Thinking in Schools?', *PISA in Focus* (2023), https://doi.org/10.1787/22260919.

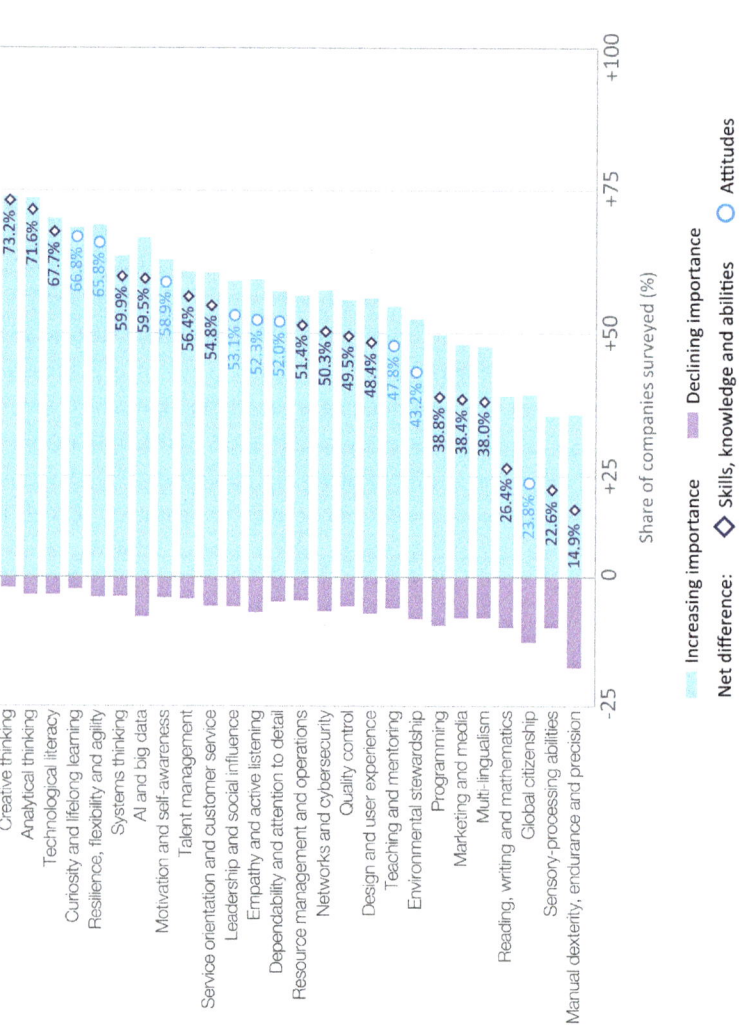

Figure 9.2: *World Economic Forum Report*. Image courtesy of the World Economic Forum, 2023.

Taking a whole-of-system approach: A snapshot of jurisdictional progress [1/3]

Existence of system-level teacher qualifications and training requirements referring to creativity, by level of education, and of system-level guidelines (e.g., learning progressions, rubrics) or evaluations of creativity, 2022

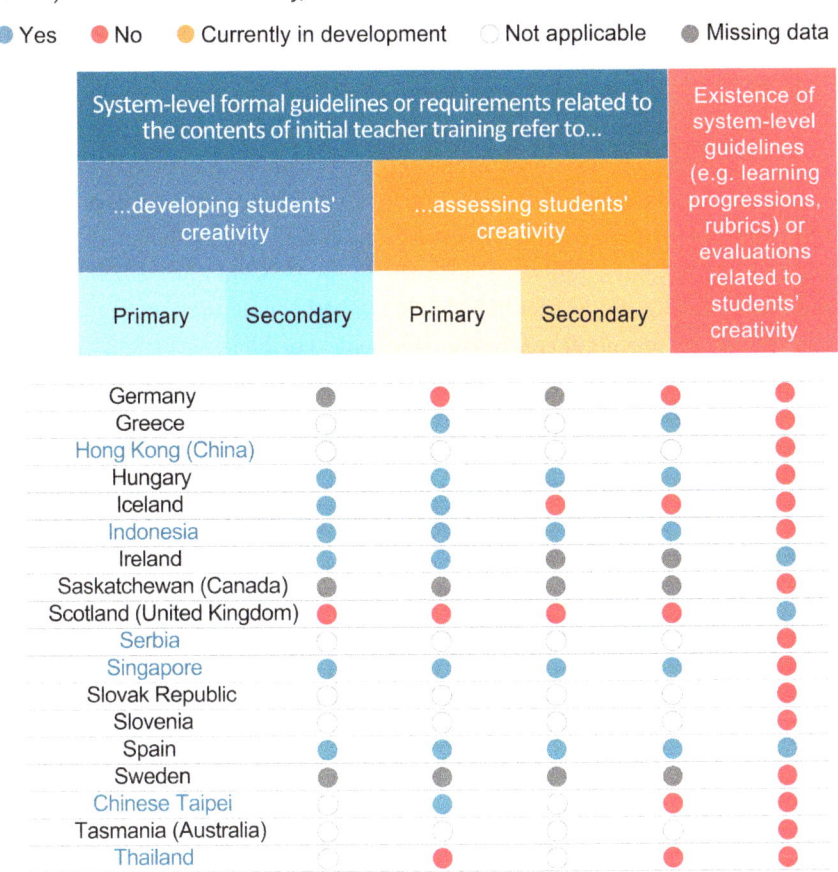

Figure 9.3: Taking a Whole-of-System Approach: A Snapshot of Jurisdictional Progress. (Data from *PISA in Focus*, No. 122, OECD Publishing, Paris, 2023.) Adapted from 2023: 5–7.

Education Bureau) reported 'Not applicable' for developing students' creativity at primary and secondary levels and assessing students' creativity at both levels, whereas Singapore indicated 'Yes' for all.

The reasons for both cities' answers were not explained in the report. If Hong Kong ticked 'No', then it would indicate that no such guidelines existed. Why did the city choose 'Not applicable'? Does this mean that another approach is being applied in Hong Kong? Or that guidelines are informal? Or that we are not intending to integrate creativity into our education system? But we have been informed that teachers' in-service training by the bureau includes creativity handled via PowerPoint.

In the availability of system-level guidelines or evaluations (learning progressions, rubrics), related to students' creativity, the answer from both Hong Kong and Singapore is 'No'. For clarification, an email[6] to the OECD in July 2023 drew this response: 'what the report tries to highlight is whether education systems offer the opportunity for students to be creative in the context of different curricular domains or subjects. In this sense, the analysis subject by subject reveals that overall, there is still [some] way to go to integrate creative thinking across all or most curricular subjects.'

System-level protocol across many jurisdictions is very much a work-in-progress because it is no mean feat to develop one. Australia's Australian Curriculum, Assessment and Reporting Authority, however, has done just that (see chapter 7). In Hong Kong, creativity as a word appears in numerous documents both in arts-education-related and in other domains. It is undeniably present. The hope is that the education and other bureaux will see the importance of formally and actively nurturing this competency system-wide. All things considered, compared with two countries that gave the same responses across the board as did Hong Kong – Serbia and Slovenia – we are the affluent city by far, based on international standards and GDP per capita.

Part III

Triumvirate Part 2: The Schools

In May 2023, a two-day Knowledge Exchange forum produced at the award-winning heritage site Tai Kwun in Central district brought together educators and CPs who collaborated with the primary schools in the *Creative Learning Project*. This annual event celebrating the close of another academic year also saw a host of invited guests from both the arts and education sectors unconnected to the project but who were invited to kick-start a panel on cross-sector collaboration.

---

6. Email to OECD by author, 2 July 2023.

The forum discussed matters of common concern for different stakeholders. Two interrelated themes came into play in Panel Three on cross-sector collaboration premised on the nature of the current relationship between the arts and education in local schools and the kind of training afforded to university students in the arts and arts education.

As a result of there being no existing data in the public or private realms known to us being readily available, we undertook simple research to understand the current arts and education interconnection.

To contextualise, Panel Three, comprising school principals and invited guests from both spheres, dialogued on the theme of *Talent Development: Cultivating Cross-Sector Collaboration*. Its remit was to review general and current practices between schools and artists, and then to discuss resource needs of the two sectors and whether/how there might be further room for building existing relationships.

In the survey, the AFTEC team randomly selected forty arts organisations according to available website information and pooled knowledge of institutions that have education or learning in their remit. Both the performing and visual arts companies were chosen though many more of the former had ready-made information.

The research investigated the purpose and provision of arts learning in schools outside of the regular curriculum in music and visual arts lessons. We looked at schools' interaction with arts organisations and the degree to which learning manifested in itself. In other words, what kind of relationship is presently predominant?

Arts-Sector and School Relationships

Figure 9.4 reveals that over ten companies do not interact with schools at all, while the majority of the others offer after-school activities which show rich offerings. Compared with the UK and the US where their large populations are spread across a wide terrain, in Hong Kong (China) extra-curricular offerings are numerous, with many schools boasting extraordinary quantity.

Data also show that all activities are knowledge- and skills-based, making specific art form learning generally the single focus. Students learn to play instruments, act, practise Chinese calligraphy, and dance.

These are also time-limited activities. In addition, intentionally or not, few relate to the core curriculum although some pertain to schools' arts subjects. In Hong Kong, the greatest proportion is visual arts and music, as these are official learning areas. Learning materials and kits for subsequent learning in the curriculum also appear rare. It seems clear that extra-curricular programmes are specifically designed

In-school Programmes

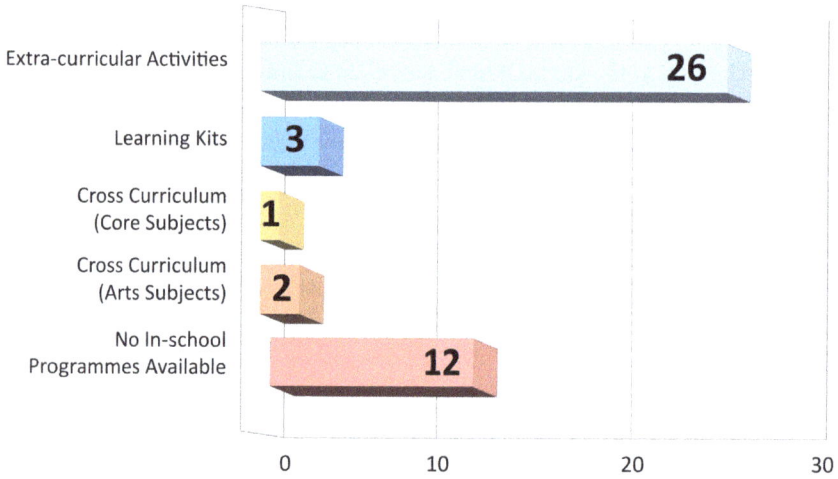

Figure 9.4: Overview of Arts Organisations' Activity Provision in Schools in 2023. Image from AFTEC, 2024.

to be one-offs for students to be exposed to the Chinese aesthetics philosophy[7] as part of the whole-person development policy.

Wherever possible and when circumstances permit, a large number of schools arrange tenders for and/or commission arts groups to train students and produce school year-end showcases, preferably in a public venue although school halls are often the contingency plan. And more often than not, these productions are musicals in which an inordinate number of students can be involved.

Separately, inter-school and other public competitions also require artists to be the trainers for music and drama, in which trophies are awarded. The focus is for the experience and, if possible, on winning the prize.

Reviewing the general view of how schools have been working with artists, it seems evident that little has changed in decades. Arts organisation professionals are service providers. The school 'buys' service and the artists cater. There is nothing intrinsically at stake here except for two concerns. This pattern has dominated the school–arts relationship for decades. Aside from the knowledge and skills acquired, how much understanding is there? For musicals and competitions, the product is the sole goal. The question to ask is whether this is sufficient in the twenty-first century.

---

7. The five Chinese domains are: ethics, intellect, physique, social skills, and aesthetics (德智體群美 in Chinese).

The more worrying fact is that demand for arts education is, in the main, largely about showcases and competitions. In this equation between schools and arts companies, supply and demand is restricted on this single level.

It is understandable that, because teachers here in local schools are seldom given the opportunities to go beyond such routines, and artists are able to create only as much as the schools' imaginative parameters allow, the former has low comprehension of the arts, and the latter, of teaching and learning.

This is a pure relationship of 'co-operation', defined here as situation in which teachers are present as administrators and to make payment while artists fulfil their end of the transaction by training students to perform. Co-operation is more mechanistic aiming for working together to fulfil one's own individual goals, each doing what is asked of them. A second more pertinent point is whether 'collaboration' – shared ownership to build a relationship for common outcomes – is another way forward.

Data from figure 9.5 are also derived from the AFTEC team's quick survey. It illustrates the degree of teacher training given by arts companies in schools. Given the rudimentary demands made by schools, 44% of arts companies polled do not offer any training to schools at all.

The second largest slice (35%) includes talks and workshops as training. They are art form-based, the acquisition of knowledge and skills as the goal. Teaching guides, when produced, apply to the work at hand. These occasional forays mean sustained learning is not the objective, and any legacy that could have been developed is not.

Teachers do not seem to be sufficiently well informed or experienced to be discriminating in the selection of artists and arts companies on programmes that are beyond skill-based. Many choose on the basis of logistical convenience and

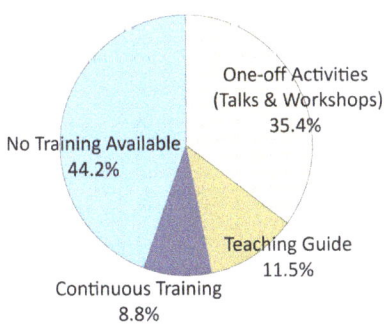

Type of Train the Trainers	Number of Groups
One-off Activities (Talks & Workshops)	16
Teaching Guide	5
Continuous Training	4
No Training Available	20

Figure 9.5: Arts Organisations' Training Provision in Schools 2023. Image from AFTEC, 2023.

affordability, which are important, but which in no way equate with demands made of the arts sector to flourish and schools to understand a different perspective of the arts.

In actuality, the *PISA Report* (figure 9.3) queries our readiness as a city and as an education system to adopt creativity and learning along that line, given that arts education and arts-in-education are basically at 'service provision' level.

Clearly, there is no clear-cut generalisation here. However, we can advance by creating a 'progression table' for the kinds of arts practices seen in local schools currently. Perhaps from there, an answer can be teased out as to why 'Not Applicable' was Hong Kong's response to PISA.

Arts Readiness in School

To the best of our knowledge, there is no available data on the macro levels of arts practices offered in local primary and secondary schools here.[8] In the UK, there have been a few recent studies on 'arts-rich' schools. However, in 2017,[9] the Royal Shakespeare Company saw an information need. Their joint research with the University of Nottingham on arts-rich schools,[10] and the subsequent report, encouraged others to follow suit in examining the context of such schools at both primary and secondary levels.

As part of a nationwide study[11] by the Royal Society for the Encouragement of Arts, Manufactures and Commerce, the definition of an 'arts-rich' school provides a good reference to those of us interested in exploring the subject.

> All students, whatever their heritage, status or family income, have access to and participate in arts and cultural education. The school sees arts subjects and cultural education as vital to the compulsory school curriculum. It therefore ensures that:
>
> A range of arts subjects is offered at all Key Stages.
>
> The school timetable makes it possible for students to choose arts options.
>
> - Students are actively encouraged to take arts subjects.

---

8. AFTEC launched its own survey in 2024 to ascertain arts provision in primary and secondary schools.
9. 'There is also no nationally recognised set of recommendations about what good arts learning provision in schools looks like. It's a significant gap', Jacqui O'Hanlon, 'Evidence Informed Decision Making About the Importance of Arts Rich Schools', Royal Shakespeare Company, accessed 16 November 2023, https://www.rsc.org.uk/learn/research/research-blog/evidence-informed-decision-making-about-the-importance-of-arts-rich-schools.
10. 'Tracking Arts Learning and Engagement', *TALE Project*, accessed 16 November 2023, https://researchtale.net/.
11. Sam Cairns, Fran Landreth Strong, Elinor Lobley, Claudia Devlin, and Laura Partridge, *Arts-Rich Schools* (Royal Society for the Encouragement of Arts, Manufactures and Commerce, 2020), 5.

- Specialist teachers are employed to teach arts subjects.
- Arts facilities are well maintained and equipped.
- Budget allocations recognise the actual costs involved in arts and cultural education.
- Careers advice incorporates careers in the arts and cultural sectors.
- Teachers participate in professional development opportunities provided by local and national arts and cultural organisations.

Students are supported to participate in cultural activities and arts learning through:

- Partnerships with local and national arts and cultural organisations
- Subsidised excursions, visits and performances in school
- A range of cultural activities through clubs, lunchtime and after school activities, in addition to timetabled lessons.

In addition, deploying our own experience, our longstanding relationships with local schools,[12] and from years of observation, we show in table 9.1 arts practice readiness in local schools. This overview proposes five levels of arts education practices (reading from left to right), denoting applicability, level definition, and suggested adjectives that describe that specific status. 'Untrue' denotes no correlation, 'True' as correlated, 'Some' meaning from time to time, and 'Not yet' suggests that that level of arts engagement is not occurring at the point of writing.

This table aims to scope from our understanding where local schools are in 2023, possible future attainments given the injection and development of appropriate resources, including training for human resources. Because there are notable differences in culture, set-up, and levels between Hong Kong and the UK, table 9.1 is localised for Hong Kong and only took reference from the Royal Shakespeare Company/Nottingham and Royal Society.

The UK is a nation, and Hong Kong is a city in China. We are at different stages of understanding the values of the arts and hence, aspiration, policy, and implementation. The UK started over four decades ago[13] in arts education and arts-in-education. While we are abundant in offerings, we seem to be without a clear plan for quality enhancement. It would thus be inequitable to apply the UK's definition to Hong Kong's situation though referencing Western development is a good springboard. The various stages of arts education and arts-in-education development have now been reconceptualised in table 9.1 to fit our local culture and characteristics.

---

12. Local schools in Hong Kong include government public schools, those with government subsidies, and under the fee-paying Direct Subsidy Schemes. They exclude international schools and those from the English Schools Foundations that operate with curricula from diverse countries.
13. Ken Robinson, *The Arts in Schools: Principles, Practice and Provision* (Calouste Gulbenkian Foundation, 1982).

Table 9.1: Arts Practice Readiness in Local Schools. Image from AFTEC, 2024.

Hong Kong Local Schools are...	Status	Description	Adjectives
Arts Poor	Untrue	Arts unavailable in schools	Non-existent, unaware
Arts Provisioned	True	Arts in local school curriculum. Schools instruct on needs with artists & companies as service providers (year-end showcases, competitions). In the community, shows & activities that are art-form based generally	Linear, top-down, singular, uni-directional, exams-based, functional
Arts Connected	Some	Building relationships with artists/companies moving beyond the Arts Provisioned stage to deeper understanding and learning to explore the diverse properties of the arts through creative thinking	Multi-perspective, exploratory, diverse
Arts Rich	Not yet	Starting to consolidate solid relationships with artists/companies on a regular basis. Teachers' professional development as regular communication and training	Strong communication, give and take, mutually inspiring, working on concepts and principles
Arts Empowered	Not yet	Schools taking on the active role of commissioning arts in education & creative learning. Internships opportunities available in the arts sector	Multi-layered, encompassing, collaborative, synergistic, proactive

The five descriptors have an inherent progressive nature created from our present comprehension of local schools and from some international approaches in personal and first-hand experiences, in addition to publications, reports, and literature.

The left-most column indicates the level which schools are at, while the column next to it under Status is an opinion on whether, and to what extent, the level applies. The Description column gives a brief overview of the level. The right-hand column includes adjectives that illustrate arts practice readiness.

Hong Kong is definitely not Arts Poor and has not been since the 1950s, when music and visual arts were taught in schools, irrespective of quality or quantity. In this city, it is a blessing that this level of arts education is possible. In the UK, although they are very much ahead of us in arts and cultural learning depth, they still struggle with basic accessibility to the arts for students in some regions. It is well-known that the further away from London, the more challenges there are, especially where there are high cases of free school meals[14] for students.

In this respect, Hong Kong is doing very well because we are a compact place, all schools being reachable by an efficient public transport system that is relatively affordable compared with systems in larger jurisdictions.

As at 2023, we surmise that local schools are mainly at the Arts Provisioned status, the assumption being that the education reforms in 2000 gave credence to the arts as part of holistic education and whole-person development. AFTEC's experience also supports the view that arts activities are abundant. From an arts practitioner's viewpoint, the nature of arts education locally is confined to two layers.

The first layer calls on the *intrinsic* properties of the arts, that is to say, arts for arts' sake. Here, they are art form and skill-based, heavily inclined towards examinations. The practicality of this form of learning is efficient and gives rise to the second layer, whereby artists involved in schools are 'service providers' commissioned by most schools to coach students and schools for exams, shows, festivals, and competitions.

Arts Provisioned schools offer a clear, linear top-down direction in arts learning. Income-bearing for companies but, in the long run, remaining as service providers is a disservice to arts organisations, given that the powers of the arts are far more than what they are perceived to be by schools (see introduction).

Future Indicators

Three more levels are mapped out in table 9.1 enabling the arts and education sectors to jointly reflect on the quality of arts offered in schools presently and the goals they may like to achieve.

These layers draw out the *extrinsic* nature of the arts where, for example, the arts' characteristics are deployed for education (in the arts and in subjects), well-being, employment, etc. We understand that, in addition to AFTEC, there are a handful of arts companies working within the Arts Connected layer.

Through practices in this third phase, a singular perspective is replaced by multiple possibilities. Students begin to take on the role of explorers in the classroom, and learning becomes more diverse as individuals emanate expressively as they engage with the arts.

The crucial question for this discussion is why more schools are not working with artists, arts educators, and companies along these lines.

One possibility is that schools are satisfied with their current offerings from the arts sector. Another reason might be that they are unaware of the additional benefits

---

14. The equivalent of economically underprivileged students in Hong Kong.

of the arts and thus unable to explore further opportunities. A third explanation could be that teachers are aware but are at a loss to pursue actions beyond the existing arts provision. Additionally, some teachers may struggle to integrate the arts into their teaching because their professional development during university did not include arts education. Lastly, there is the expectations gap between teachers and teaching artists, as discussed in chapter 1.

From a larger perspective, there may also have been little knowledge, direction, and incentive for schools to progress further than their Arts Provisioned status. At the time of writing, there has been only one known update to the Key Learning Area Curriculum Guide in 2017, formalising the tone and content of the original document. Despite the fact that global changes have been huge and international documents have called for much more from the arts, employment, and education, they do not seem to have been encompassed or actively pursued.

In an email discussion with an education official in July 2022, on the existence of an arts education policy prior to 2000, the response was that there are other approaches. 'I would rather not say "there is no overall arts education policy" since there were actually different pathways to promote arts to school (speech, dance, etc.), not limited to subjects nor lesson time.'[15]

Conceivably, this is a reason why schools have still maintained their Arts Provisioned status quo by and large. Is this also the rationale for a 'Not applicable' reply in the self-reported PISA survey in 2022?

Compared with the UK definition of arts-rich schools, in Hong Kong, schools that desire to become arts-rich will need to rise above the ideas of arts companies and teaching artists as mere providers of service to one which is more dynamic and mutually beneficial. This would entail schools understanding the innate characteristics of the arts more and arts practitioners further encouraging this layer of involvement.

The relationship required will be more than ad hoc, more regularised, with each potential long-term partner sitting down to discuss a broader perspective of how the arts can play a stronger and larger teaching role in the school. From piecemeal encounters in a pocket of school life, the arts and learning can grow to become embedded in the school culture.

In time, these schools will become Arts Empowered, whose body of professionals from the principal and top management to the teachers and the CPs will see the value of the arts and creative learning through them. As I write in the summer of 2024, two Lead Creative Schools have emerged from the pilot *Creative Learning Project* (Arts Rich schools). Both are located in the New Territories and cater to children from low socio-economic status. From August 2024, professionals will be

---

15. Email by author, 13 July 2022.

offered online and face-to-face professional development locally, before a study trip to London that includes principals, vice heads, and curriculum heads, on top of the core teachers and artists.

Conversations will be ones in which the schools will begin to explore planned personal and whole-school creative learning development. One day, they may even be able to commission projects with arts organisations, integrating creative learning into the curriculum.

Vitally, the arts will become the centre of school life. In primary schools, this may involve the arts deployed as a means to teach curriculum subjects. In secondary schools, the arts will be connected to possible internships and career pathways linking students with cultural institutions and building their portfolios from there on.

If Hong Kong is to strengthen its competitiveness, then we need to heed global developments.

Particularly post-pandemic, arts and culture in other jurisdictions are shifting into far more than performances and exhibitions, into the community, into education, into well-being and social mobility through the arts. By repositioning themselves as Arts Empowered, schools will deeply engage everyone and offer alternative paths to creative learning. They will likewise play a part in grooming quality audienceship along the way.

Triumvirate 3: The Practitioners

To build a deeper relationship between the arts and education sectors, what would training for artists resemble then? To begin looking at this, we need to understand the present-day infrastructure for cultivating teaching artists.

To decipher this, we need to review macro-picture training offerings in tertiary education in Hong Kong for arts education and arts-in-education and, via that avenue, creative teaching through the arts. How, we can ask, can teaching artists support a more fecund environment for the widening and deepening of sectorial collaboration?

Exploratory Research

As part of the research also for the Knowledge Exchange 2023 for the *Creative Learning Project*, colleagues reviewed the official websites of core universities in Hong Kong. This was a complex segment to the research, as there were many variables that could not be teased out clearly, and information available was not always sufficiently clear for us to analyse similar values. Nevertheless, figure 9.6 gives us a bird's-eye view of the current status.

Tertiary Education

Of 11 local universities, 6 offer BA degrees in arts subjects and BEd degrees & above

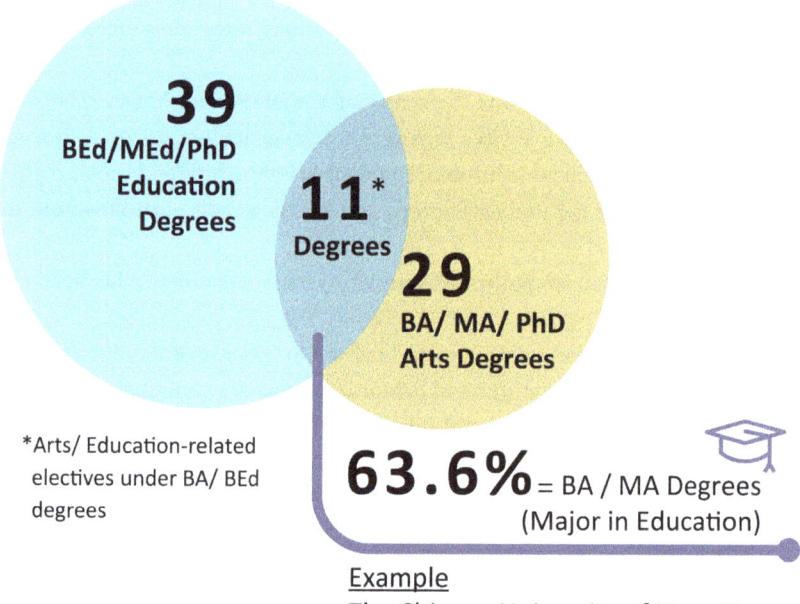

Figure 9.6: Tertiary Sector Degrees in Arts and Education. Image from AFTEC, 2023.

We came to the following conclusion with the data mined:

- Six out of eleven institutions provide undergraduate and higher degrees in arts- and education-related disciplines with some encompassing pedagogy.
- Arts or education-related electives are available under BA and BEd degrees.
- The exception is the Hong Kong Academy for Performing Arts, in which all degrees are art-form-based or technical arts-based.
- The Education University, at present, seems to be the only institution offering taught arts subjects in teaching for schools, bachelor's and higher degrees in Creative Arts and Culture, and a PhD in Creative Arts Education that resembles basic research in the area for a doctoral candidate. There is also a Creativity Module at the Department of Curriculum and Instruction, Faculty of Education and Human Development.

After the forum, we were able to garner further data from the Faculty of Education at the University of Hong Kong. Under the Centre for Advancement in Inclusive and Special Education is the Laboratory and Program for Creativity and Talent Development. Within the centre are professors who teach MEd modules that pertain to *Nurturing Creativity: Theories and Practices* as an elective in 2023–2024.

In mid-2024, we connected with a lecturer at the Hang Seng University who recently started a module in creative thinking.

One of the obvious routes is to build a stronger and more meaningful relationship between schools, arts companies, and teaching artists. The third diagram to complete the triumvirate of audienceship and educational practices is a rough overview of the kinds of arts practitioners we now have, their nature, and the road ahead.

Figure 9.7 consists of five segments derived from experience and then further developed. It illustrates a spectrum of practitioners, ranging from those who may still be students to those pursuing trophies and awards, whether as amateurs or professionals. It also includes job holders at various arts organisations, along with two additional tiers that resemble those in the audience diagram presented in figure 9.1.

Kinds of Practitioners & Characteristics

Under & over 18, in school or at work, they have little interest in the arts and learn them because they are instructed to. Almost never at artistic events

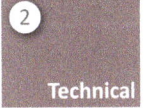
In school or not, they are skills-, exam- and competition-focused for the next accreditation & trophy. Sometimes at artistic events

Professional artists whose job is to perform and create. They may be passionate about their artform

Passionate about their practice, involved in mind, body & spirit, constantly renewing their craft

Passionate, dedicated, with deep knowledge & astounding abilities, always pursuing perfection

Figure 9.7: Observed and Projected Practitioners Attributes. Image from AFTEC, 2024.

The schematic is self-explanatory. In our experience, many emerging practitioners here in Hong Kong (from left to right) are at Rote (1) and Technical (2) status due to parental and/or institutional demand. This may be for the purpose of ensuring that knowledge and skills acquisition are the sole foci. It may also be for the sake of sharpening their drive by enlarging an ever-growing portfolio of achievements.

In one university where I was a guest lecturer, at pre-career levels, final-year undergraduates in music were hard pressed to go beyond rehearsing their own young students for exams and competitions or to explain why music is so meaningful. Instrumentalism was the driver behind their taking on pupils. Even as upcoming Career (3) professionals, passion for the art form was not always a given though many undoubtedly do enjoy what they do.

As with figure 9.1, I have intentionally replicated the Explorers (4) and Aficionados (5) classification titles though adjusting for attributes. Like the most ardent audience member, a Segment 4 and 5 practitioner's mindset is one which is curious, if not inquisitive, imaginative, and always pursuing goals they or their artistic directors have set. These practitioners are self-motivated, constantly absorbing and learning to perfect their artistry, their teaching, and always taking inspiration from others, even other art forms.

If we compare the traits of practitioners and the audience (figure 9.1), a few questions arise:

- Where are we currently in the quality of both audience and practitioners?
- Why are we there?
- What can be done if we want to engage more of the public in the arts as an audience?
- What is the city's vision in 2035, for example, and the prerequisites should we want to travel from Segment 1 towards 4 or even 5?
- How will this vision be coordinated across the board (as far as possible), from training institutions to the terms and conditions that arts organisations are funded, to the way the arts in schools are run, understood, and valued?

Part IV

Supply and Demand in the Arts

The visualisation of the triumvirate discussed thus far presents a fundamental spectrum that ranges from basic practicality to increasing interest and ultimately to strong, sustained enthusiasm. Our capacity to qualitatively nurture and develop schools, audiences, and practitioners along this classification ladder aims to create a better balance between supply and demand in the arts.

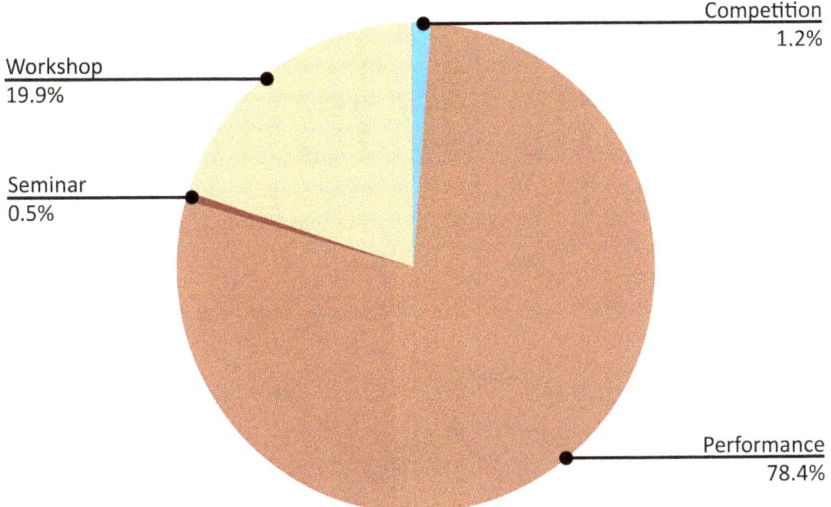

Figure 9.8: October–December 2023, Supply- and Demand-Side Events. Image from AFTEC, 2023.

Currently, the arts in Hong Kong are supply-strong and demand-weak. Physical events such as supply-side programming are much easier seen and quantified than are fundamentals such as arts-in-education, arts research, and arts criticism (demand side). A random survey (figure 9.8) that we conducted on programming and events in both the performing arts and exhibitions in the city from October to December 2023 supports this viewpoint.

A total of 475 arts programmes/events (supply) were produced in the last quarter of 2023, of which 88% were in government venues, 86% were in the performing arts, while 14% were exhibitions. In the former category, 78% were performance-based across diverse art forms (figure 9.9); regular classes and one-off workshops made up 20%, and the balance consisted of seminars and competitions.

Research on 407 performing arts programmes revealed that only ten (2.5%) had extended activities – none for exhibitions – fifteen activities between them (assume demand side). There were eight workshops, five seminars, and two guided tours. All but one were presented by the government's Leisure and Cultural Services Department as part of its *New Vision Festival*.

From a citywide perspective, the Hong Kong Arts Development Council's Annual Arts Survey[16] data present straightforward and illuminating information

---

16. 'Annual Arts Survey Result Dashboard, Performing Arts', *Hong Kong Arts Development Council* (2024), https://www.hkadc.org.hk/en/research.

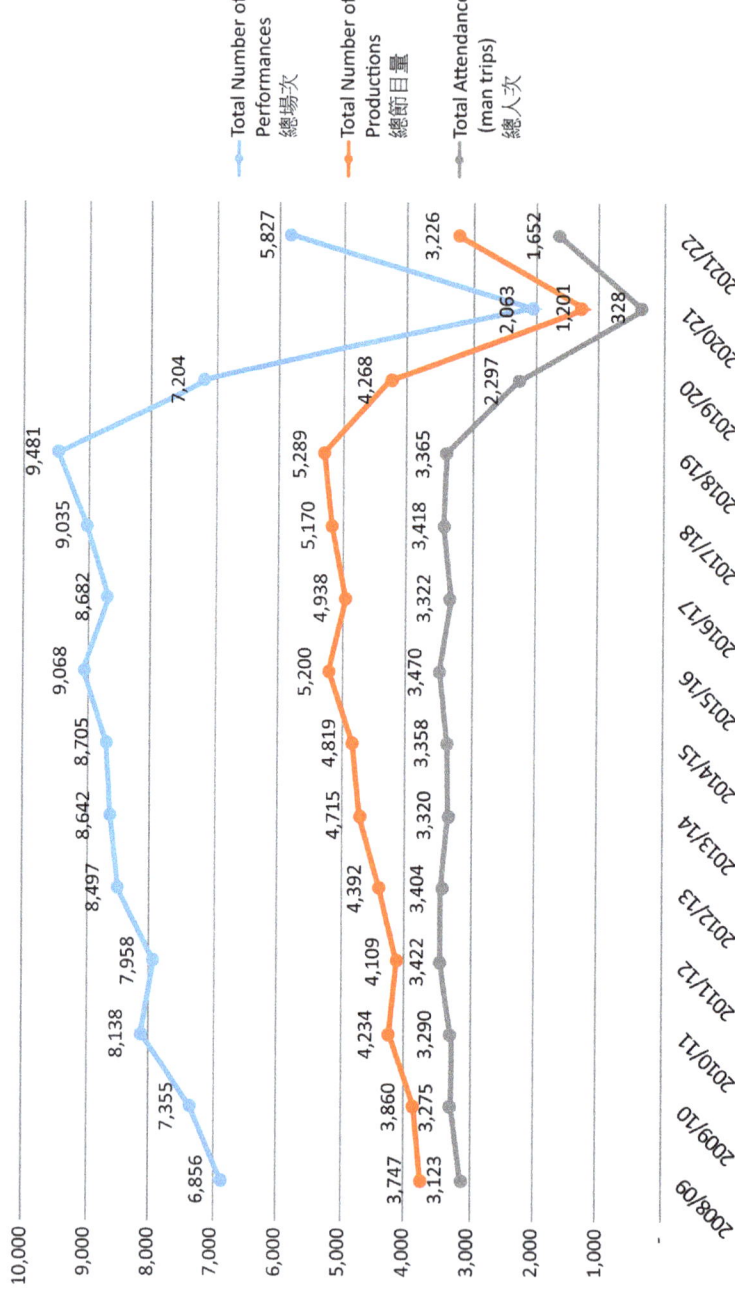

Figure 9.9: Annual Arts Survey Performing Arts 2008–2021. Image courtesy of the Hong Kong Arts Development Council, 2024.

as well. A consolidated overview[17] of performing arts productions, performances, and audience attendance from 2008 to 2022 in figure 9.10 attests to the supply-and-demand situation. As far as we can ascertain, there is no arts education data in Hong Kong that reveal supply and demand. As such, while the data is not the exact information we seek, it is nevertheless helpful to understand the broader view.

The graph sets out the number of productions, the equivalent number of performances or shows per production and audience attendance by person trips, not unique individuals. The Arts Council's year on year data begin in 2008–2009 and take into account the next thirteen years to 2021–2022 (figure 9.9).

On the whole, performances[18] were on the rise almost year on year until they peaked in 2018–2019[19] with 9,481 performances (5,289 productions) and a total of 3.365m person trips. Understandably, the COVID years saw a drastic fall in numbers although pick-up began from 2021 to 2022, which, when compared with the crest in productions in 2018–2019, fell 38.5% (productions), 39% (shows), and 51% (attendees).

Discounting huge COVID losses, growth in audience numbers have lagged behind increase in productions and performances. Supply has outstripped demand. From the random micro survey that we carried out to the official picture, it is evident that demand-side activities were paltry in comparison with the enormous supply of performances.

Perhaps we are on par with some major cities in this respect. However, it does not mean we should remain indifferent and complacent. How we as a city get ahead is to avoid being complacent even if other jurisdictions have similar issues. In fact, it is precisely in redressing this imbalance that we can stand up, stand out, and stand taller.

Creating a healthy and higher-quality demand from our audience, our schools and practitioners, funders, and individuals who are well informed and conversant is a uniqueness that the vision of the East–West Centre can aspire to. Our people, as a whole, should be regarded to be as valuable as our programming.

---

17. Number of programmes in 2021–2022 are based on those held in twenty-nine arts and cultural facilities during the financial year from 1 April 2021 to 31 March 2022. The Hong Kong Coliseum, Queen Elizabeth Stadium, Hong Kong Convention and Exhibition Centre, AsiaWorld-Expo, Kowloon Bay International Trade and Exhibition Centre, etc. are excluded.
18. Shows include those by subvented companies largely funded by the government plus those subsidised at a lower level of funding.
19. Performing arts include dance, music, theatre, *xiqu* (Chinese opera), variety and pop shows, multi-art forms, and competitions.

Basics to Cultivating Demand

As early as 2008, the US-based RAND Corporation[20] produced an all-too-important report under the RAND Research in the Arts banner on *Cultivating Demand for the Arts – Arts Learning, Arts Engagement, and State Arts Policy*. While the US then was very unlike Hong Kong, there are still principal ideas that merit our scrutiny today. Figure 9.10 lays out a template for a strong and buoyant arts sector in supply, access, and demand.

For RAND, the aesthetic experience plays a central role in the equation. On the supply side is a host of actors that create the works for public consumption. These we are familiar with in Hong Kong as well. On the demand side are those who, as individuals and institutions, engage people with the arts and give them the skills and strategies in their encounter with artworks. Both arts and educational institutions play a large role here. They are present in the city although arts critics and arts researchers are few and far between.

It is noteworthy that RAND makes an important distinction here which Hong Kong needs to seriously consider: that cultivating demand is *not* 'primarily about marketing campaigns and public outreach; it is about giving people the skills and

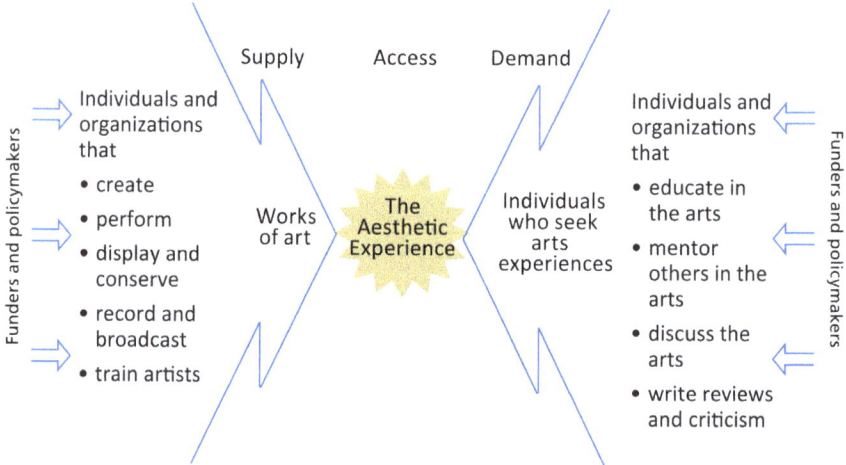

Figure 9.10: Reproduced by permission from RAND Research. *Concept of Supply, Access and Demand in the Arts.* 2008.

---

20. RAND is a non-profit, non-partisan research organisation that develops solutions to public policy challenges and is committed to the public interest. Laura Zakaras and Julia F. Lowell, 'Cultivating Demand for the Arts – Arts Learning, Arts Engagement, and State Arts Policy', *RAND Research* (2008), https://www.rand.org/pubs/monographs/MG640.html.

knowledge they need to have encounters with works of art that are *rich enough to keep them coming back for more*.'[21]

This is where the sector is sometimes confused and believes erroneously that arts education and marketing are one and the same (see chapter 10). The operative phrase is deliberately italicised. Are our productions fecund enough? Do our schools have rich enough arts practices? What are our audience/schools coming back for? Are they demanding more quality? If yes, what is the nature of that request? These are crucial questions we need to reflect on now as part of the East–West Exchange planning and for the Cultural Commission to consider.

Cultural well-being, coined by RAND, has a three-prong objective:

- Expand supply by increasing the production of high-quality works of art.
- Expand access by creating more opportunities for people to encounter such works.
- Expand demand by cultivating the capacity of individuals to have aesthetic experiences with works of arts.

I have less concern about production increase, as the government is injecting a substantial amount of new funding into cross-border and international exchange projects, including HK$24 million into the 2024 Performing Arts Market and a recent announcement of $70 million[22] for further programming supply. Access can always be expanded though it is not necessarily a given that with supply there will be the audience. For example, how often do arts teachers and their students frequent events and for what purpose?

The apprehension is in capacity cultivation because even with the best productions in the world, they can be lost in translation if the audience are only there as Snappers and Followers (figure 9.1), or for schools, if they are continuously at the Arts Provisioned levels (table 9.1).

Perhaps we can substitute the central feature of RAND's *Aesthetic Experience* in figure 9.11 with the East–West Centre idea and reinterpret the diagram, bearing in mind four arts learning areas listed by RAND which apply equally to us:

Area 1: the capacity for aesthetic perception, or the ability to see, hear, and feel what works of art have to offer

Area 2: the ability to create artistically in an art form

---

21. *RAND Research*, xv.
22. 'The Chief Executive's 2023 Policy Address', The Hong Kong Special Administrative Region of the People's Republic of China, 25 October 2023, https://www.policyaddress.gov.hk/2023/public/pdf/policy/policy-full_en.pdf.

Area 3: historical and cultural knowledge that enriches the understanding of works of art

Area 4: the ability to interpret works of art, discern what is valuable in them, and draw meaning from them through reflection and discussion with others.

In our city, Area 3 learning is prevalent in museums and performing arts events. Area 2 occurs frequently in formal, informal, and non-formal settings. Area 1 is the Explorers and Aficionados classification, the characteristics of which were quoted earlier from Eisner and in much of relevant literature. Area 4 describes the intent to dive beyond surface understanding of a story or immediate perception to connect value in relationships between the individual and the artworks.

Moving beyond skills-based teaching towards creative thinking by re-skilling, up-skilling, and increasing the existing pool of professionals is one route to develop the aesthetic experience. Yet that will be insufficient for us as an East–West Centre. We have to reach outwards from the present to connect with other creative industries and even non-arts and culture sectors. In other words, to add an approach aiming to redress the supply-demand imbalance somewhat.

Part V

East Meets West Centre for International Cultural Exchange

In the National 14th Plenary Session Five-Year Plan, Hong Kong was tasked with elevating itself to an East–West Exchange, an ambitious and yet not impossible notion.

The city is strategically positioned along the coast of Eastern China and is well versed in Western customs and cultures, having played a historical role in trade and finance. Geography alone does not define us as a hub for cultural exchange. Our performances, exhibitions and cultural heritage reflect our cultural wealth. As a result of international visitors – both cultural and otherwise – the dialogue extends far outside the confines of concert halls and exhibition spaces.

The conversations on, about, and through arts and culture can be more pervasive and be heard everywhere, in the community, on the streets, in schools, in homes. In other words, the very nature of the city needs to breathe arts and culture. This calls for events definitely, but above and beyond that, how each individual, how our people relate to and embody the arts as lived experiences.

Quantitatively, rapidly injecting enormous funding caches to create tangible products is the easier highway. The less-travelled road, however, may not always be immediately discernible for the uninitiated. This is the journey towards a legacy that ensures the return on investment is meaningful.

Human resources planning, properly thought out and integrated into the cultural policy, is indispensable. Quantity may be good as long as funding lasts; quality delivers higher sustainability through investing in current and future generations. Needless to say, money and human resources wisely spent is the ideal.

Hong Kong is renowned for its efficiency. A fast pace of life has been how we have kept up and charged ahead. Pragmatics and practicalities served us well in the past when working hard meant achieving much. The world has changed, however, especially after COVID, and ever evolving geopolitical tensions. We can no longer rely on the same formulas indefinitely. It is time to prioritise working smARTer.

From a fixer mentality and a service provider, we need to cultivate mindsets that connect seemingly disparate sectors for creative integration. These minds are synergistic and collaborative, having reciprocity and mutuality as the main tenets. These creative thinking mindsets benefit the arts intrinsically and sectors where new thinking and solutions can serve Hong Kong. They will be instrumental in buoying demand-side expectations and provision.

Capturing the Creative Flow

Figure 9.11 offers one view of the developmental flow linking the city and its culture to creativity, its people for exchanges through tangible arts-producing offers and towards dialogic communications.

To incorporate and personify the East–West Centre principle, arts educators will be pivotal and more than just skills-based. At the very core, they must be

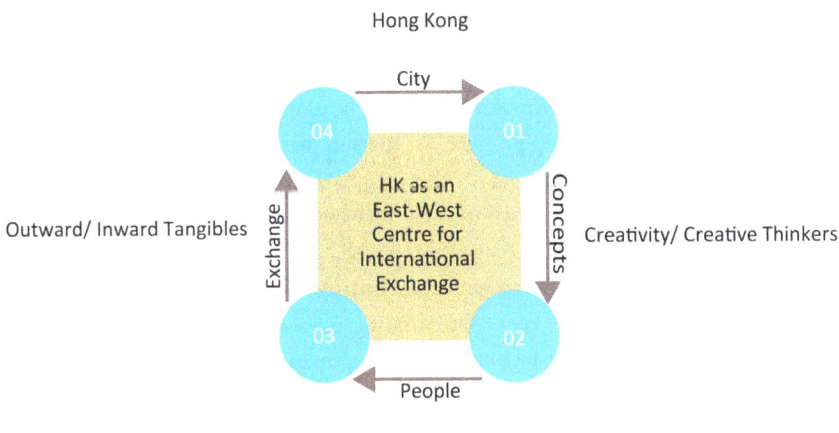

Figure 9.11: Four-Pronged East–West Cultural Development. Image from AFTEC, 2024.

creative change agents. For this reason, 'creative practitioners' is the preferred term, as it is much more expansive and all-encompassing. CPs as the alternative takes in non-artists who are flexible minded, imaginative, and ingenious (see introduction).

The chief executive promulgated the East–West Centre concept in 2022. Citywide consultations took off in 2023, the aim for a blueprint from the Cultural Commission in 2024. In the space of five years from 2024 to 2030, for Hong Kong to be on the road to become such a centre, a short-term plan necessitates initial development that paves the way for mid- to long-term development of CPs and creative community consolidation. Figure 9.13 represents a possible development of a web of practitioners within and outside the arts sector at varying levels, allowing permeation of creativity and creative thinking to enhance the current levels of:

- general audienceship growing from Tasters to Explorers,
- schools' arts education and arts-in-education practices from current Arts Provisioned level to Arts Connect and on to Arts Empowered for teachers,
- arts practitioners from Career to Explorers, enabling them to facilitate and develop creative thinking and learning in schools and elsewhere, and
- the nurturing and development of CPs across the board to enrich beneficiaries in other fields.

Cross-Sector Creative Practitioners' Development Web

The Web (figure 9.12) puts forward a concept of developing and networking CPs across the city. The goal is to build a broad-based creative thinking platform for collaboration not restricted to the arts sector. The participatory nodes in this web share diverse strengths and expertise which, collectively, can ignite creative learning.

The largest circles illustrate the two core sectors in which CPs as a group of professionals lay the groundwork for potentially large employment prospects. These sectors are hence accorded top priority due to their immediacy and from which arts and education expertise arises.

Phase 2 accommodates a total of three phases spread over ten years, including those in youth development and community NGOs. Once phase 1 is set up and piloted in the arts and education, time, space and, resources can flow towards others.

Phase 3 sees the health care system being embraced, as are diverse creative industries. While the initial impression of health care may raise eyebrows, the arts in health for well-being has been a long-term practice in, for example, Arts on Prescription in the UK (see chapter 6) and the Center for Arts in Medicine, University of Florida, USA.

The creative industries seem to be given a lower priority for no other reason than the buy-in. That is to say, the understanding that CPs beyond the arts are

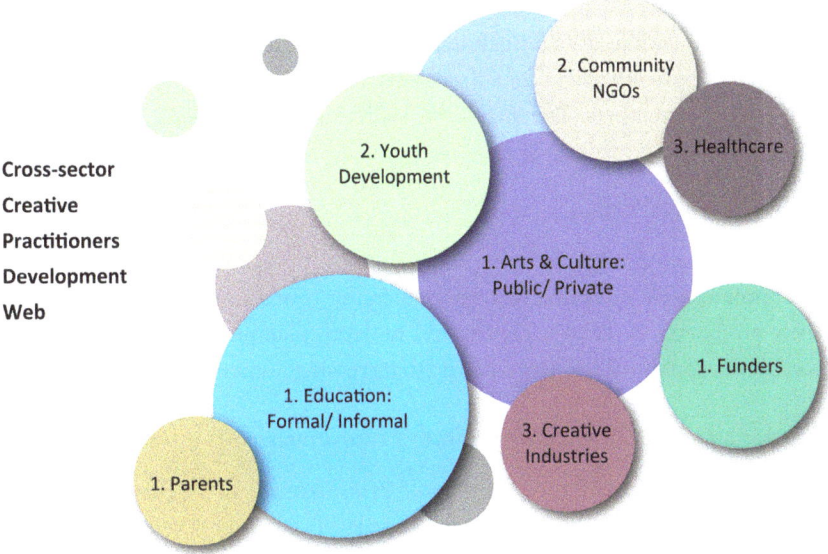

Figure 9.12: Ten-Year Phased-in Approach for Hong Kong as a Creative Community. Image from AFTEC, 2024.

important to the industries' development. Advocacy to these industries will need to be done in phases 1 and 2 before implementation in the final phase. This Web is therefore a cross-government bureau and community initiative.

Education involves those in formal, non-formal and informal learning. Parents are a group fundamental to this, as they need to understand the importance of the arts in learning in order to support their children and their schools.

Quantitatively, it is tempting to inflate numbers to create the noise. In reality, it is best to begin the first year with a core group that will be solidly grounded in the work to come before implementation. It is envisaged that core members will be drawn from the performing/visual arts and education fields with a track record in arts-in-education and a keen interest in collaborative planning, design, and enactment.

Whenever this begins, it will be a ten-year journey in qualitative nurturing and quantitative growth. Challenges will abound, ranging from the understanding of the rationale to quality audienceship and CPs and thinkers; the willingness of companies and institutions to think beyond a set routine to breakthrough teaching; and above all, the patience to see a new adventure take shape. Contrary to naysayers, it is an entirely possible proposition if there are sufficient resources for this expedition.

Although teachers abound in the city, mindset shifts from the traditional to incorporate creative thinking will demand time. However, it is also evident that CPs may not be well versed in articulating creative thinking either. However, on balance, as they reside within arts and culture, the driving force should be located there. While organic growth allows for adjustments in number, human resources planning needs concrete numbers. This final section will explore some ideas.

Phased-in Approach

Tables 9.2, 9.3, and 9.4 encapsulate the phased-in approach to growing CPs across the community at varying levels from emerging (undergrads) to early and mid-career professionals. With sufficient and in-depth planning, the pace of growing these professionals will pick up and lead to increasing numbers.

Phase 1: 2026–2027 – Arts and culture + education sectors + funders

The number of current arts educators and CPs is unknown, to the best of our knowledge. The city is very likely to start at the basic level as a result. The year 2026–2027 will be for planning and design (table 9.2), in which the framework for cultivating CPs, including advocacy and training, will be mapped out for roll-out from 2027 to 2030.

Bridge organisations – borrowing a UK term – are those with current creative thinking expertise and those with the propensity and ability for immediate pick-up and take-up to train associates, teachers, and CPs. They will lead across art forms and cross-sectorial thinking, and they are strong and flexible in co-planning and co-designing the framework within a year.

Table 9.2: Phase 1 Planning and Design. Image from AFTEC, 2024.

Arts and Culture + Education Sectors + Funders	
Planning, Design and Pilot Framework for Creative Practitioner Development	**Components**
Arts & Culture	• Bridge organisations • Associate organisations • International & local trainers
Education	• Tertiary institutions • Lead Creative Schools Cultural Leadership Champions (top management) • Schools (teachers & parents)
Funders	• Public & private policymakers • Advocacy (workshops)

Associate organisations are those with potential to become Bridge organisations in a few years to train existing creative agents and become lead CPs. Those keen will move from only skill-based to incorporate creative thinking in their portfolios and support training the trainers.

In addition to trainers, the views from beneficiaries like schools should be part of the planning and decision-making. As such, the suggestion is for representation of Lead Creative Schools, which will upgrade to being Arts Connected and Arts Empowered to be in this opening phase. Representatives will be able to speak to other schools of their experience and needs. Their input will be needed for the master plan.

While funders are not CPs per se, they too need creative mindsets. They play a crucial role in the advocacy and understanding of the rationale and importance of CPs.

Phase 2: 2027–2030 – Extending to community NGOs and youth development sectors

CPs need training in creative thinking so they can reflect, articulate their artistic thinking, organise, and extract relevant ideas for their specific art form to be incorporated in school and community settings. It is not enough now to simply 'do and make'; they need to make sense of their practice and communicate this, so that the audience/participants progress along the audienceship continuum.

In this next phase, exploring and expanding into the non-profit and youth sectors means we can introduce the concept of 'para' Creative Practitioners (para CPs) – inspired by paramedics – in phase 2 to indicate additional human resources that are not at a fully professional level and/or full-time (table 9.3). These will be professionals not specifically in the arts or education fields but who have the interest to facilitate in community contexts, youth centres, corporates, etc. Training could occur from 2027 to 2030.

Museums are the optimal spaces to grow Learning and Participation teams whose single portfolio is in learning and not diluted by other administrative duties as many seem to be presently.

Arts organisations should consider creating Learning and Participation teams in earnest. There is no optimum number because it is dependent on the extent to which companies want to seriously adopt creative thinking as opposed to solely undertaking outreach. The government as a funder should take the lead in launching this concept. Its threshold for support should be significantly higher, given their resources and ability to connect with a large segment of the audience, including schools. It should act as a catalyst and establish Bridge organisations.

Table 9.3: Phase 2 Early Training. Image from AFTEC, 2024.

Extending to Community NGOs & Youth Development Sectors	
Planning, Design & Pilot Framework for Creative Practitioner Development	**Components**
Community NGOs (Para-CPs)	• Social Welfare sector NGOs • District organisations • LCSD/WKCDA/Tai Kwun docents
Youth Development (Para-CPs)	• HK Arts Development Council Arts Ambassadors (Secondary students) • Tertiary Institution Common Core/General Education

Phase 3: 2030–2035 – Extending to health care and the creative industries

It may seem odd that the creative industries are placed in phase 3 (table 9.4). In Hong Kong, however, these are sectors which are generally commercial and, as such, it will take time for them to absorb and understand the necessity for across-the-board cultivation of creative practitioners and para-CPs. As case studies from phases one and two show, their on-boarding may become more accessible.

While the health care field does not seem immediately relevant, in the UK, for example, arts and medicine have had a constructive relationship of over forty years. Social prescription through the arts is popular in London as preventative health care, and Clod Ensemble, for example, is an award-winning company that is heavily influential in training health care professionals.

Table 9.4: Phase 3 Further Training. Image from AFTEC, 2024.

Extending to Healthcare + Creative Industries	
Planning, Design & Pilot Framework for Creative Practitioner Development	**Components**
Healthcare	• Hospital Authority • University of Hong Kong & Chinese University of Hong Kong Faculties of Medicine
Other Creative Industries	• Combination of CPs and Para-CPs

Part VI

The chief executive's 2022 and 2023 policy addresses pivot on hardware development in arts and culture to a huge extent. In software, talent development, the aim is to cultivate artists, playwrights, and administrators. Aside from such specific roles, to facilitate these aspirations, a balanced and sustainable ecosystem is required. Figure 9.13 explains this visually.

CPs are the vital link needed to connect the arts and education sectors. This role is not merely a short-term or fallback option; it involves dedicated professionals whose expertise, skills, and commitment are both acknowledged and valued. They will serve as catalysts for citywide transformation.

In schools, CPs will inspire, engage, and guide creative learning by utilising the arts as driving forces for innovative thinking. By establishing a strong foundation for demand-side development and fostering inward enculturation – immersing oneself in the language of the arts – we can continuously cultivate creative thinkers of all ages. As we consistently build an audience of higher quality, the resulting outward expressions (in the standard, nature, and value of events) will enhance the city's sophistication and elevate its international reputation.

Over decades, so much investment has been poured into arts and culture annually. Let us refrain from simply duplicating existing roles without carefully considering new ideas and novel approaches. Careful consideration has to be given to the fast-changing circumstances that envelop us daily. In arts learning, to be an East–West Centre, creative thinking is one golden key to unlock innate talent. Set the vision and accompanying parameters first, and then quantitative human resources planning will fall into place.

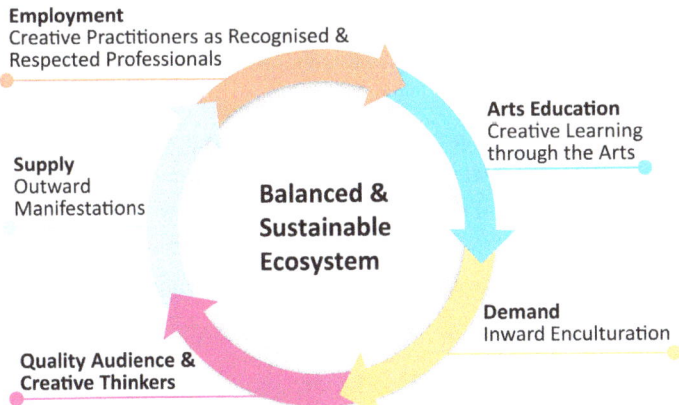

Figure 9.13: Cultivating Supply and Demand in the Cultural Ecosystem. Image from AFTEC, 2024.

10
Myths and Misunderstandings
Musings and Replies

Summary

This final chapter shares firsthand and overheard moments over the years in arts and cultural spaces, revealing a basket of misconceptions about the arts. They are categorised under three headings: Learning, Arts Sector, and General.

Context

With the passage of time, there have been many opportunities to engage with volunteers, beneficiaries, their friends, and the wider public. I regularly visit schools in our programmes as an eyewitness and as a member of the audience in public events also as an 'ear witness'. There, the chances of overhearing remarks and having conversations as one is seated before the curtains rise on performances, and when strolling through exhibitions, also afforded an understanding of what others believe in and what they think about the arts.

I eavesdrop humbly, often with gratitude for being given very different perspectives of what I take for granted, said feelingly with such honesty that I am often filled with the burning desire to, if not counter-argue, then at least to offer a practitioner's perspective.

This final chapter seems an opportune time to redress, if not dispel, some miscomprehensions and apprehensions about the arts, arts education, and creative learning from a library of long-embedded sound bites.

This (inexhaustible) list may tickle your fancy or annoy, but hopefully give food for thought. These are just my chance encounters, not representative of anyone else's. They are written for the record, for edification, and to acknowledge how much more still needs to be done in audience building, arts advocacy, arts engagement, and arts learning. That is, if we want current and future generations to be truly motivated to *know* the arts personally rather than to simply *view* performances and artworks at a distance – physically, mentally, emotionally – when a ticket is purchased or at a mandated school outing.

At each heading is a short comment and, where appropriate and able, a recommendation or two.

Learning

Myth 1: The Arts Should Stay Peripheral in Schools

Although music and visual arts have been firmly planted in the local school system since the 1950s, the unofficial understanding is that they can be sacrificed when needed, in place of core subjects and preparation for exams. This, I am told, happens regularly today. This very act sends an erroneous signal to stakeholders that the arts are dispensable when, in actuality, the properties of the arts go far beyond show time. They can become the very essence of learning. The arts can be the foundation to creative learning in school across the curriculum.

Change initially requires time. However, a key step to adapt our mindset and achieve meaningful, sustainable benefits is to promote creative teaching through the arts across various subjects, ideally at the whole-school level. By motivating learning, we empower students to take charge of their own education. This can be achieved by offering more authentic in-service training for teachers, enabling them to transition from and move between the traditional and creative classroom environments.

Another added and misguided related notion is that, because there is insufficient expertise overall, creative thinking, learning, and teaching is impossible. Other jurisdictions have disproved that. We can at least make an attempt. AFTEC's programming over the years is able to provide some proof of concept.

Myth 2: Creating Worksheets for Factual Recall Is Learning

One conventional approach is to start with the seemingly efficient and proverbial worksheet enamoured by many teachers. These factual quizzes are most convenient during school outings. Through them, teachers are able to verify whether key factual points have been captured. Their work seems to be done. Yet, would it not be more exciting and valuable to see how students think? I know some teachers and many artists do ask open-ended questions, and these are progressive educators. They wish to know the 'how' to the 'what' and the 'why' to the answers, enabling them to assess the individual and follow up in areas that are unclear. Illumination and fun can be powerful tools.

Myth 3: It Is Best If All Students Get the Same Materials Pack

The price one sometimes pays for efficiency can also be demonstrated in the common packs of materials provided to students. Homogeneity can dull the senses, leading to a habit of mind that can easily replicate a neighbour's work because thinking out of the box can be very hard when provisions are exactly the same. Creative classrooms cultivate creative thinking and promote diversity.

Giving the same pack of materials is administratively handy though the results are often less attractive because minds are less engaged. Of course, in the capable and creative hands of good creative practitioners, the same materials can do magic. In general, the easier way is to provide choice.

Seeing eyes light up when there is choice must be one of the most pleasurable sights in a creative classroom. It is to us. We have groups that literally plunge into materials of assorted textures, colours, and size to design and make costumes, for example. The inherent inclination to ask questions, take risks, and engage in deeper thinking arises from having guided choices. Choice elicits conversations. As many individuals as there are in class, there will be a host of unexpected artworks waiting for you *when* there are options.

Of course, at the end of the day, facilitation through the learning process is the core to teaching creatively. Is facilitation currently a training module for pre-service teachers and artists? Do in-service teachers and teaching artists obtain regular updates and refresher courses in their careers? These are questions that demand serious consideration.

Myth 4: The Arts Are Only Good for Certificates, Competitions, and Showcases

One outcome of only serving a large dose of constant prescriptive instruction is in how adult values affect children.

A friend's son smashed his violin as a 'celebration' after passing the Associated Board of the Royal Schools of Music Grade 8 violin exams in school. That is sad. While that was clearly a singular incident, it goes to show the intensity of negativity that can be caused. More acutely, the perception of the arts as being solely instrumental (no pun intended) to upward mobility in school and performance as achievement is misleading because it does not mean that, once certified, we have arts lovers who will engage continuously and beyond exams.

This kind of thinking only touches the very surface of what the arts are when, in truth, they are meaningful, valuable, and life-sustaining. By all means, enter the arts world via examinations and exhibitions, but product-oriented objectives can be tempered with the joy of exploratory processes. At the same time, it will be good to instil a sense of wonder through experiences that have lingering recall, not merely for fun but to teach for understanding. Good parental intentions in giving resources, time, and effort will see better return on investment.

Myth 5: Cultivate the Arts and Creativity Only in Schools

Schools are not meant to be the only arena to cultivate the arts and instil creativity in students. A home is an equally suitable space for arts and creative activities. Nothing very special is needed. A mark of being creative is to use available resources.

For example, pots and pans, forks and spoons are very percussive. Odd pieces of paper or cloth can become a texture garden. Mops and broomsticks are the very stuff of drama and in addition to clothing in the wardrobe, an evening in the home theatre is possible. Perhaps the crucial factor is how parents and guardians can be part of their children's lives in the evening or at weekends. The arts and creativity are everywhere. It only depends on whether there is an open mindset to rediscover and reignite them.

Arts Sector

Myth 1: Arts Organisations Size Matches the Venue

This conversation occurred at a concert when I had the privilege of being seated next to a member of the performing company's board. 'So you run a small organisation. That is why you are resident in a small venue.' The undertone and subtext, though genuinely pleasant, pointed at ability. 'Actually, not necessarily', I replied. The larger the company does not mean it is more successful and thus is able to perform in bigger spaces. Size does not matter; artistic 'fit for purpose' does.

AFTEC is a small medium company, and we chose the Sai Wan Ho Civic Centre because of the flexibility of the space and the area's demographics. A larger company, for example, the Hong Kong Sinfonietta's *Tiny Galaxy Concerts (@ Wontonmeen* concerts were staged in a very small space, in a hostel, in the heart of Sham Shui Po, a district in Kowloon. To free the imagination, we need to review our idea about size.

Myth 2: Running Fun Arts Activities Is Everything

Perhaps we tend to reign in our collective imagination because current formulas work. AFTEC had to think beyond running fun arts activities being sufficient. Making the audience happy is a major endeavour so that they will return. It is thus logical to make activities fun, and the more this idea works, the more we rely on the vicious cycle.

This is not to say that the arts should not be joyous; they *are* fun. At AFTEC, we often ask ourselves, 'So what happens after that? What are the takeaways that will help to build, over time, an understanding of the arts and their connection to life?' Sheer fun is energy, yet can we do more for the arts? Do participants learn something? What does that constitute? What, in fact, are we trying to achieve? What does Fun+ look like? Arts companies can regularly review their offers, and stakeholders can ask what else companies can do with their fun activities. When the audience practises Fun+ as a matter of routine, they will keep those of us in the sector on our toes.

Myth 3: Arts Promotion Is the Same as Arts Education

Fun+ can be supported by arts education to a large extent and arts promotion to some degrees. Regrettably, the two are often confused.

As an example, a food *promotional* event means there is information, tasting, and merchandise. Any cooking may only be demonstrations using the ingredients and the recipes. A culinary *course*, by contrast, is learning through a structured framework, not necessarily to sell but definitely to educate. Similarly, while there is an overlap between arts promotion and arts education because of the similar intention to cultivate further knowledge in the arts and enlarge the audience base, the two are quite distinct.

The focus is different, the planning is dissimilar; the former is broader, the latter needs more depth; the former creates awareness, the latter develops understanding. Arts promotions aim to get the customer through the door; arts education is teaching and learning for life to keep the customer returning because they are energised, given meaning to view the world differently, and thus want more.

Myth 4: Grant-Giving Is the Only Responsibility of Funders

Sponsors and funders will do well to bear this distinction in mind, especially post-COVID when economies lack buoyancy and dollars are from hard-earned taxpayers and shareholders' hard-earned effort.

Contrary to general belief, grant-giving is not the single responsibility of funders in an 'apply, assess, accept' refrain. Far from it, grant-giving is the cumulative action taken by a funder to reflect its own organisational policies and values. Casting the widest possible net is one approach; specialising is another.

Research offers the rationale. This is fundamentally lacking in the arts and arts education here. With data, we will be so much clearer on why we fund and who we fund. Research can be on the ground, such as action research and practice as research.

For the latter, it is crucial that findings are disseminated externally in written form or otherwise and not merely performed. Research is networking, capacity development, communications, and impact development. Higher education academics and the arts sector can gravitate to become solid partners, to cultivate a common language of enrichment.

Myth 5: Attrition Is Unacceptable

Grants granted do not mean plain sailing from there for arts entities. No one wants to misstep, but life happens. In the arts, there is no single or constant solution. It's the variables that make the arts fascinating; hence, there is no blueprint for avoiding attrition.

For our long-term projects, we have seen that, consistently for varying programme scales, there has been roughly a 20% dropout rate. Well-meaning funders normally focus on the reasons, and this is fair. Wise funders look at the 80% who are still committed and persevering, to gauge how resources can be concentrated to bolster their learning further and what quality of candidates complete the journey. This is learning for facilitating top-class participants who deserve higher plus deeper cultivation.

Myth 6: Quantity Tops Quality

Accountability to boards, shareholders, and stakeholders is uppermost in the minds of funders. This is understandable. Numbers are also much less laborious and are immediately obvious 'success' factors. Quantity is success is predictably unquestioned.

The issue with this thinking is that we only ever work on one level: mass and basic. While at entry point, this is reasonable, it does beg the question of what quality audience and practitioners and performers we desire to cultivate for the future. Over time, if this policy is adopted, then it can affect the city. This is not a zero-sum game, but it needs to be a *gradated* one, in two senses of the word.

Firstly, developing a more sophisticated audience leads to a progressively higher return on investment; they are drawn not only by the story or the costumes. Secondly, quality graduates come from demands made on them. Otherwise, we keep playing to one set of needs. As with sports, so in the arts, we can begin with huge numbers for awareness and buy-in, but there has to be sequential, upward-building quality. Do not blame the arts for not having Olympic-level performers if quantity is all we want to cultivate most of the time. The need for an integrated ground-up policy cannot be further emphasised.

General

Myth 1: The Arts Are Not for Me

'The arts have nothing to do with me' is a perception that many have. One reason is that very possibly their lives have not been touched by the magic of the arts. They have not been exposed at all or, more so, the engagement was factual and instructional, lacking in hands-on exploration, immediacy, and relevance. The arts have everything to do with everyone if only we manage to open up, through creative learning, to create curiosity and subsequent inquisitiveness. In our homes, we want aesthetically pleasing decorations and furnishing, no matter the size of the space. That is already a small foray into the arts.

Myth 2: I Don't Understand the Arts; Therefore They Are Boring

Coming a close second is this idea.

David Perkins of Project Zero, Harvard University's Graduate School of Education, succinctly captures the four routines[1] that should not be applied to looking at the visual arts and by extension, to any art form.

In day-to-day routines, he says, our thinking is too hasty, often narrow, sprawling, and sometimes too fuzzy. We do not understand the arts immediately because of this habitual mindset. We like obvious answers, fast conclusions, we like to be right immediately. I refer to this as the 'instant noodling' culture to satisfy present bias. This will not do for the arts. What is needed is reflective thinking, more of a 'steam, double boil, and stew', to borrow a Chinese cuisine phrase.

Myth 3: The Arts Are Abstract and Cannot Be Understood

Very often, the issue is that many members of the public believe the arts are inaccessible. Actually, the arts are very tangible most of the time, notwithstanding the perceived enigmas. But why should you bother? Answering this question leads to another question: why must everything be immediately understood?

If understanding needs to be instantaneous, then notices and instructions would suffice. If the arts are to be grasped straightaway, then the viewer must be at an aficionado level. Most of us are not. We should bother because it is fun, stimulating, inspiring, and invigorating to see ideas from unusual angles. Discovery through the

---

1. David Perkins, *The Intelligent Eye: Learning to Think by Looking at Art* (Getty Publications, 1994).

arts makes for the little bright lights in life. Learning the strategies to be inquisitive and imaginative is always a start.

Myth 4: You Need Training to Understand the Arts

Is training the only way into the arts then? That is to say, unless one is trained (preferably with a certificate to show for), you cannot partake in the arts. That is a great misunderstanding.

If one wants to turn professional, then the answer is 'yes'; otherwise, approach the arts with a sense of curiosity and receptivity, attend arts events, partake in them, and volunteer. It is about imagining, interpreting, and exploring possibilities and perspectives.

What is on offer much of the time to the widest public and easily accessible is often taken to be the only approach. Delving into more than one type of performance, one type of theatre, for example, is the equivalent of opening doors for oneself.

Myth 5: Theatre Equals Musicals

One regular comment I have heard frequently over the years is that theatre means only musicals. Many adults think this, and consequently their children believe this. In Hong Kong, musicals abound because they are in demand and bring in revenue for companies.

An honest sponsor once commented that the way spoken lines are delivered by actors in serious theatre are over the top and exaggerated, with a lilt that is not normal speech. Musicals are much more palatable and appealing to her because of their innate components of catchy tunes, snappy dance numbers, and realistic acting.

There are two issues worthy of deeper thought here: the degree of knowledge in those who hold the purse strings, and how the many other types of theatre productions can be brought to the forefront in addition to musicals. The misconception that 'theatre is musicals' is very much like the hidden curriculum in schools – unwritten, unofficial, and very often unintended lessons, values, and perspectives. It is the culture of the offer that matters.

Myth 6: Beautiful Costumes Are All that Matter

The following is likewise a misunderstanding along the same vein that we need to dispel: 'Beautiful costumes are all that matter on stage'. One day, a member of the audience suggested that we did not have a sufficient change of costumes in the play for the main characters. Another day, a volunteer confessed that she had no idea what ballet was nor did she understand what she was watching, so the costumes are the sole focus. 'They are so beautiful', she exclaimed.

We go to great lengths to plan, fundraise, and produce. Are those comments enough for our efforts? Costumes are outward visual signifiers of characters, of their inner mindscapes, their relations to each other, the period in which the play is set, and the overall aesthetic effect. Watching a production is to understand the whole in relation to the parts before the entire picture can be captured.

Myth 7: Only Artists Are Creative

Ultimately, many believe that creativity is only for artists. Giants like Bach, Picasso, and Wu Guanzhong are creatives with a 'Big C'. Big C people are also outside the arts, like Steve Jobs and Pony Ma. On a daily basis, we are all creative in that we solve problems by thinking of alternatives, the 'little c'.

Artists are in the zone for creative work as part of their professional lives. Creativity for artists is a mindset that supports new thinking, new connections, and innovations. Yet, does the business sector not need creativity? What about health care? Why not create a Creative Thinking City Day to drive the message home and share the creativity? Or even a Bachelor of Creative Teaching and Learning in tertiary institutions?

Myth 8: Making a Living in the Arts Is Impossible

Compared with traditional professions like accounting, law, and medicine, 'making a living in the arts is impossible' is the constant cry. This is far from true. The world is now so complex that those with flexibility of thought, adaptability of mind, and ability to think on their feet will find jobs more likely to come by.

Employers now desire creativity, creative thinking, emotional intelligence, and ability to handle large amounts of data which are ideas, concepts, and abstractions. Creativity and critical thinking, communication, and collaboration are key. Data from Frey and Osborne's *The Future of Employment* (chapter 1) and the World Economic Forum (chapters 1 and 9) speak on this.

Values and messages emanating from the arts sector affect schools and the future of our audience. What and how we produce for our audience affects their understanding, acceptance, and support of arts and culture. We are unable to guide everyone all of the time through detailed docent tours or incessant information leaflets. The second and better option is to truly empower schools and the public. There are so many wonderful, powerful, and meaningful experiences in the arts that rationalising otherwise is akin to a poor excuse.

Epilogue
First-Class Humans

Andreas Schleicher, the director of the OECD Directorate for Education and Skills, posed a question that we should seriously ponder. 'How can we ensure our young people become first-class humans and not second-class robots?'[1] He was not being facetious.

In a bustling city like Hong Kong, where space is a scarce resource, the focus on nurturing first-class individuals transcends physical boundaries, uncovering a realm devoted to cognitive, mental, and emotional growth.

This realm is where the imagination can be put to good use since globally, the call and practice from education reforms has been for creativity and creative thinking in many jurisdictions. This zone is neither fluffy nor fanciful but one which offers essential tools that craft and generate a future that harbours immense possibilities.

We have been inspired by voids or less obvious spaces for programming that has supported the evolution of creative mindsets. Young people, schooling, and creative learning have been at the centre of the company's desire to manifest and showcase the powers of the arts for teaching and learning. It is in the exploration of inquiry-based learning via the arts that capacity-building viabilities have opened up in local classrooms that we serve.

Introspection and reflection are essential for realising and motivating qualitative improvements, which can then provide crucial context complementary to quantitative metrics. Ironically, the pandemic, though devastating, gave time and scope to AFTEC for deep review and contemplation, bringing out the camaraderie that normal routines may have buried. The growing emphasis on well-being has

---

1. Andreas Schleicher, 'First-Class Humans, Not Second-Class Robots – Andreas Schleicher on Learning and the Future of Work', hosted by Kate Lancaster, OECD Podcasts, OECD iLibrary, 23 June 2019, 14 min, 59 sec., https://doi.org/10.1787/87958706-en.

prominently manifested across all realms of work, the arts increasingly serving as vessels of hope.

Creative thinking has never been more urgent or practical, as shown in the 2022 pioneering PISA test. In space-constrained Hong Kong, physical limitations can inspire the growth of mental capacity when we nurture creative thinking and artistic expression. When a city's population embraces creative thinking, the entire urban landscape becomes an infinite canvas for innovative expression by first-class humans.

Questions to Ask

How does one differentiate a second-class robotic young person to the first-class counterpart? Is it a matter of academic performance? Or to show a long list of after school achievements made or overseas graded examination results to denote whole-person development?

What role does divergent thinking have in classrooms when high-stakes testing is still the main criterion for success, where textbook learning is single-subject-based in local schools, students' mindsets converging into giving the single, correct answers? Is linear teaching an adequate approach even in arts subjects such as music and the visual arts in local schools?

If being robotic can be summarised as routine, repetitive, replicative responses from young people physically present and less so cognitively, mentally, and emotionally, then what society are we looking forward to?

Along this vein, what can training the trainers in different sectors resemble? If there are good degrees in the core subjects — languages and mathematics — does it not also make sense at the present time to explore the prospect of a degree in creative teaching and learning?

If there are well-established undergraduate degree programmes in traditional performing arts disciplines like theatre, music, and dance, is it not plausible to have similarly robust, fully fledged degree programmes in arts education and arts-in-education that are not merely add-ons or minors, but stand-alone, respected areas of study?

Can there be investigations into transdisciplinarity in which the arts-in-education can seed and grow dedicated teachers and artists for education and cross-sectorial development and learning?

To what extent does technology serve the arts? Will the current Arts x Tech incentives suffice because of the sheer availability of technology for the arts sector in productions and performances? How can we further develop and expand the expertise and imaginative capacities of artists in order to empower humans to create *with* technology rather than be driven solely by its availability?

While STEM education is a forceful intent in local schools, can it be more than coding and the step-by-step manual approach to build a car that moves, a robot that picks up objects? How can creativity be infused into linear logistics nurturing first-class young people? Can STEM really see the significance of STEAM at work?

Can tertiary institutions step back from their current focus to step forward expanding to collaborate with arts and cultural institutions for academic and cultural exchanges, conferences and networking, knowledge exchange for public engagement, and broader connections between research and challenges, thereby eliciting groundbreaking developments?

The common gaps from research data in chapter 3 collectively present a stark reality irrespective of which sector we belong to. Change can no longer be on the surface; differences need to be set aside and overcome. The lack of attention to the deeper fortes of the arts, arts education, arts-in-education, and creative leaning need to be re-addressed expeditiously. There is much to consider with systemic shortcomings accumulated over decades. The creativity code can be and needs to be cracked.

Placing Creative Learning at the Heart

What might we need to put in place to boost all-round creativity in Hong Kong? At the outset there must be a strong recognition that creative learning via the arts has to become part of the city's fabric. Public–private partnership needs to be well planned and implemented authentically, continuously, and with commitment.

Formal education would be the natural choice as the principal nurturing ground for upcoming generations. The following recommendations are based on AFTEC's experience, particularly from 2017 onwards, when training the trainers matured in complexity and depth. These do not constitute a blueprint but rather ongoing inquiries and reflective explorations into developing creative habits of mind.

1. **Creative learning should be at the centre of the curriculum as a generic approach** and not only in arts subjects. Systemising a creative teaching pedagogy is crucial as it is fundamental. This will support cross-curriculum learning and if done well, will in time reduce teaching load as opposed to increasing it, as students will have agency and be more able to engage in self-directed learning.
2. A **conceptual framework** needs to be worked out with teachers and artists together to find common ground. Teachers and artists are the main protagonists collaborating closely in the creation of lesson plans and regular follow-up discussions. This will include common learning objectives and outcomes in teaching and to follow on, assessment rubrics that are agreed upon.

3. **Schools as a sector need to be given space and time to explore creativity** that is beyond the familiar coaching for standard exams locally and abroad and beyond skills-based learning. Critical thinking, communications, and collaboration can be embedded into projects that have creativity as a central prerogative and not taken for granted that they will happen anyway.
4. To achieve this, **collaborative partnerships on a longer term** between schools and arts organisations are required to organically create the desired creative learning environments in a school over time on exploratory journeys. One-off collaborative projects could provide an opportunity to explore mutual expectations, leading to the development of comprehensive, multi-year programmes to trial an initially agreed conceptual framework. This programme could be appropriately moderated by organisations and/or individuals deeply rooted in the arts and education. If there is institution-wide take-up and osmosis, the learning will cascade from a single project to the entire school or school-sponsoring bodies, thereby shifting the culture to one of creativity.
5. One goal that creative learning can work towards is **to focus on the processes of creating** leading up to the product and to avoid just working towards the product at speed. If school audits and sponsors adopt a creative learning concept and move beyond rote learning, then evaluation will adapt to avoid single correct answers.
6. **Training the trainers beyond skill-based teaching and techniques** is required. Pre-service training would do well to include sufficient time to embed creativity into the curriculum. This will include creative thinking models and strategies not as an elective but as a core module at vocational training level, for bachelor's and master's degrees. When there is a critical mass of graduates nurtured in this, practicum projects can be dispersed as they now are for subject-based pre-service teachers and in arts organisations that focus on the arts-in-education.
7. **Organisational leadership in arts companies and schools** would do well to take on broad creative teaching and learning intentions. Principalship studies could offer a course on creative teaching and learning, as top management's comprehension and buy-in will greatly increase the success of fostering school-wide creative culture not only restricted to arts subjects. Parents can benefit in regular year-round creativity introduction workshops, enabling them to see beyond academic results.
8. In **informal settings**, it would be advantageous as a step towards building a citywide creative fabric of quality if non-arts-trained professions and even volunteers could be provided with an understanding of creativity, the part it plays in their lives, training, guidelines, and recurrent updates. This large

group could include those working as administrators, programmers, marketing teams for arts-based organisations and institutions, relevant government bureaux and departments, galleries, and cultural establishments.
9. **Across other sectors**, social welfare, health care, and even businesses where employers call for more creative employees in the workforce, an inauguration into the arts for creativity and workshops for creative thinking can effect mindset change if a solid programme is in place.
10. **Shared applications**, in particular in good practices, could be centralised in a non-profit organisation. In formal education, a thoroughly mapped-out award for schools with a creative culture or those that formally embed creative teaching into their curriculum will give recognition and encouragement. The awards should not be competitive but criteria-based and sequential.
11. If there is any will to genuinely ensure that the **nurturing of creative habits** is the developmental core, then year-round and continuous advocacy is crucial to highlight and substantiate the powers of the arts, arts education, and creative learning.
12. Above all, **ensure synergies** across government bureaux and discard siloes that are too often seen in policymaking (figure 11.1). Enhancing the quality of audienceship does not fall on the shoulders of any one ministry.

It is pivotal to encapsulate creative learning as an essential building block to twenty-first-century Hong Kong. For first-class humans in a first-class city in a first-class country, a thoughtfully cultivated creative network across the arts is essential — one that enriches public and private realms, engaging young and old, as well as cross-sector professionals.

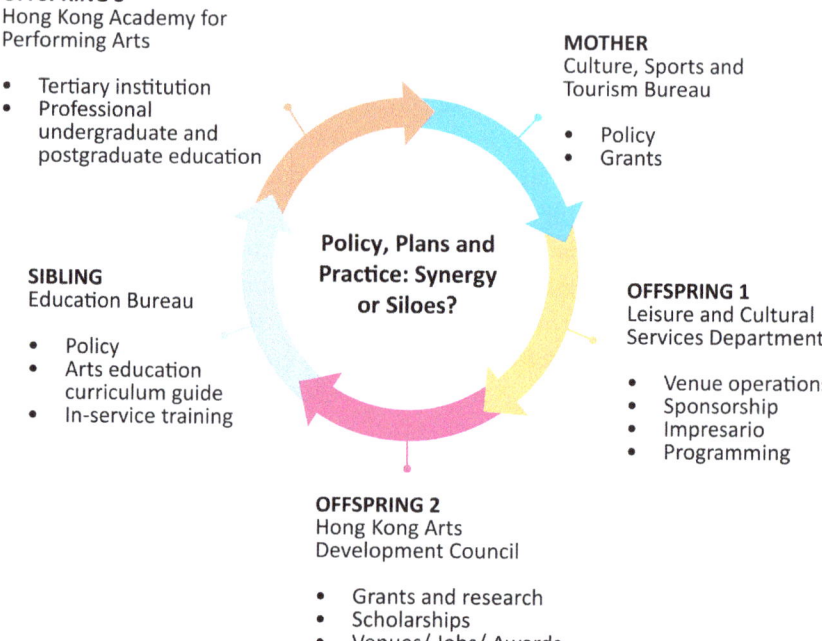

Figure 11.1: Policy, Plans and Practice – Synergy or Siloes? Image from AFTEC, 2024.

Appendix

The appendix lists projects in chronological order as they are implemented. Only projects that are discussed in this publication have been included here. Other projects can be viewed at www.aftec.hk.

1. Title: *From Page to Stage*
   Year: 2009–ongoing
   Target Group: Secondary students and teachers (main) + general public
   Overview:
   From Page to Stage Programme is a comprehensive Learning & Participation theatre education platform in English. Presented since 2009, this is probably the longest-running theatre-in-education production in the city that has reached to nearly 120,000 audience members. Six productions were produced under The Jockey Club from Page to Stage® Programme from 2012 to 2018. It was also one of the English Alliance programmes under the Standing Committee on Language Education and Research (SCOLAR) from 2018 to 2021. Tailor-made for local secondary school students, the programme is a fresh and unique educational adventure. Through high-quality drama performances and in-school pre- and post-performance workshops, we aim to nurture students' interest in literary classics and appreciation of the arts.
   Links:
   https://www.aftec.hk/zh/from-page-to-stage-zh/ (Chinese)
   https://www.aftec.hk/from-page-to-stage/ (English)

2. Title: *Sm-ART Youth*

   Year: 2012–2020

   Target Group: Primary 4–6 (9–11-year-olds)

   Overview:

   Beginning in 2012, *Sm-ART Youth* is designed to nurture creative learning for underprivileged primary students and aims to demonstrate arts for transformative educational change. Programmes include constant year-round exposure to diverse arts disciplines in and outside of the classroom, such as Cultural Days. The project is based on intergenerational teaching and learning. Participants of different age groups benefit from volunteer training and cultural outing participation. Practical opportunities were offered for interns from the University of Hong Kong's MA in Expressive Arts Therapy in the middle years.

   The 2018–2020 cohort marked the end of the project. *Sm-ART Youth* has enabled in total 155 underprivileged primary students to nurture a questioning habit of mind, to understand the self and beyond, and to locate meaning in their young lives.

   Links:

   https://www.aftec.hk/zh/sm-art-youth-zh/ (Chinese)
   https://www.aftec.hk/sm-art-youth/ (English)
   https://www.aftec.hk/smart/index.html (Main site)
   https://www.youtube.com/playlist?list=PLkEm7rC-5Jv6A5o7bWs3qLRiggtq0jpRl

3. Title: *Medical Humanities (Performance Arts Module)*

   Year: 2012–ongoing

   Target Group: Medical undergraduates Years 1 and 2

   Overview:

   AFTEC is a community partner in The University of Hong Kong Li Ka Shing Faculty of Medicine Medical Humanities Programme, which is a credit-bearing part of the medical curriculum. Through an imaginative encounter with the arts, medical students can explore the human aspect of medical science through engaging in drama and music in the early years and then movement and drama in recent years.

   Links:

   https://15.aftec.hk/zh/exhibition-vista-2b-zh/ (Chinese)
   https://15.aftec.hk/exhibition-vista-2b/ (English)

4. Title: *Bravo! Hong Kong Youth Theatre Awards*

   Year: 2013–2020

   Target Group: 13–19-year-olds

   Overview:
   Conceptualised in late 2011 for a 2013 launch, *Bravo!* is a bilingual acting and life-skills programme for full-time Hong Kong students aged 13 to 19 who are passionate about theatre. The project is eighteen months long with a *Bravo! Hong Kong* segment that includes workshops, theatre productions, and community services. A final selection is made after one year for further and higher-level training with AFTEC Learning Partners, the Cloud Gate Dance School in Taipei, and The London Academy of Music & Dramatic Art (LAMDA) in London as the *Bravo! Asia* and *Bravo! International* legs respectively. This project gives priority to underprivileged youth.

   Links:
   https://www.aftec.hk/zh/bravo-zh/ (Chinese)
   https://www.aftec.hk/bravo/ (English)
   https://www.youtube.com/playlist?list=PLkEm7rC-5Jv44L1Oirz9egnZJPJd-B6FS7
   https://www.aftec.hk/beyond-bravo/

5. Title: *Classics for Juniors*

   Year: 2014–2021

   Target Group: Primary school students and teachers (main) + general public

   Overview:
   Classics for Juniors is a tailor-made theatre and language learning programme for primary and junior secondary school students since 2014. This comprehensive educational programme comprises pre-show workshops, education materials, an interactive English theatre performance with a professional cast, and drama classes called the Creative Box. All the components create effective and meaningful learning experiences in a professional theatre setting for children. Public performances are also held for the public and families to be part of the experience.

   Under the same banner, AFTEC brings the very special Relaxed Theatre. Through this groundbreaking programme, AFTEC hopes to explore theatre and its potential to support individuals with Autism Spectrum Disorders and learning difficulties and raise awareness of their needs.

   Links:
   https://www.aftec.hk/zh/classics-for-juniors-zh/ (Chinese)
   https://www.aftec.hk/classics-for-juniors/ (English)

6. Title: *Plays for Young People*

   Year: 2016, 2018, 2021

   Target Group: International playwrights; emerging translators

   Overview:
   Plays for Young People is a project very close to AFTEC's heart. As a bilingual Learning Theatre for young people, AFTEC believes in widening the vision of young people to perceive other cultures.

   Since 2016, aiming at nurturing local talent creating quality translated or original plays for young people, AFTEC has organised numerous symposiums and workshops to connect emerging translators with overseas playwrights and dramaturges, veteran translators, and local directors.

   Through the *Young Theatre Makers* and other programmes, AFTEC hopes these outstanding plays from Europe and Asia, in original or translated versions, will be offered to schools, youth centres, and tertiary institutions for staging and meaningful discussions.

   Links:
   https://www.aftec.hk/zh/plays-for-the-young-people-zh/ (Chinese)
   https://www.aftec.hk/plays-for-the-young-people/ (English)
   https://www.youtube.com/playlist?list=PLkEm7rC-5Jv5330DmWmbFrWH7TbB12aEE

7. Title: *Young Theatre Makers*

   Year: 2016–ongoing

   Target Group: Secondary students and youth colleges

   Overview:
   Young Theatre Makers is a bilingual drama training programme that focuses primarily on analysing and understanding a play. Intended for secondary school students, the cross-curriculum scheme uses play scripts as a framework for discussion to develop students' critical thinking.

   Schools can choose from fifteen original plays by playwrights from around the world. The plays deal with coming-of-age themes that resonate with young participants, and aim to stimulate interesting debate and dialogue. By combining showcase and discussion, the programme uncovers just how much the arts can help us understand life.

   Links:
   https://www.aftec.hk/zh/school-young-theatre-makers-zh/ (Chinese)
   https://www.aftec.hk/school-young-theatre-makers/ (English)

Appendix 273

8. Title: *Jockey Club Arts for Change Project*

   Years: 2017–2021

   Target Group: Children and youth; professional social and outreach workers; artists

   Overview:
   This project has the ultimate goal of empowering social workers, young people, and youth organisations to become effective change-makers through the power of the arts. Led by AFTEC, a diverse range of local professional artists co-designed and co-created with social workers and young people from three NGOs. This three-year pilot programme focused on creating nine meaningful and effective community projects. This project came to an end with the showcases on 13 and 14 March 2021.

   Links:
   https://www.aftec.hk/zh/jcac-zh/ (Chinese)
   https://www.aftec.hk/jcac/ (English)

9. Title: *Jockey Club Arts & Action Project*

   Years: 2019–2022

   Target Group: Primary and secondary students and teachers

   Overview:
   This is a forty-four-month project focusing on developing an arts-based curriculum in conversation with teachers, social workers, and students from schools for Social Development from 2019 to 2022. As part of the Special Education Needs system, AFTEC created a diverse educational space for teachers, social workers, and students at two schools, Tung Wan Mok Law Shui Wah School and Caritas Mother Teresa School, as well as to assist the former in developing the Jockey Club Black Box Theatre.

   This project broadens the artistic horizon for teachers and students through Cultural Days, Continuing Professional Development workshops for teachers, and AFTEC Lab. The arts for change concept was adopted as an alternative approach, to facilitate students' self-understanding and the development of their individual potential through applying the power of the arts to foster layered and nuanced emotional connections.

   The final showcase depicted a three-year journey of arts exploration by students from these two schools. Every project has an end, but in life, every ending is just a new beginning.

Links:

https://www.aftec.hk/zh/arts-for-empowerment-zh/ (Chinese)
https://www.aftec.hk/arts-for-empowerment/ (English)
https://www.youtube.com/watch?v=pb9_Cr3mmbo (Highlights)

10. Title: *Jockey Club Arts-Based Cross Curriculum Creative Learning Project*

    Years: 2021–2024

    Target Group: Primary 4–6 students (9–11-year-olds); teachers; creative practitioners

    Overview:

    Funded by The Hong Kong Jockey Club Charities Trust, the project is a three-year-long endeavour designed to complement the Hong Kong school curriculum to foster whole person development and life-wide learning in students from Key Stage 2 (Primary 4–6).

    The project focuses on a thematic, cross-curriculum project learning approach to nurture self-directed learning capabilities in students through the integration of

    - fundamental subject knowledge based on Key Learning Areas;
    - generic skills such as basic skills, thinking skills, and personal and social skills; and
    - underpinned by a strong foundation of positive values and attitudes.

    This student-centred creative partnership project aims to prepare young people for the challenges of the twenty-first century by developing their creativity, critical thinking, communication, collaboration skills for contribution to social capital ('5Cs'), bringing about an increase in creative practices in schools through the training of teachers in collaboration with Creative Practitioners (CPs).

    Links:

    https://www.aftec.hk/zh/arts-based-cross-curriculum-creative-learning-project-zh/ (Chinese)

    https://www.aftec.hk/arts-based-cross-curriculum-creative-learning-project/ (English)

11. Title: *AFTEC Jockey Club Creative Futures Project*

    Years: 2024–2028

    Target Group: Mainly primary 3–5 students (8–11-year-olds); teachers; creative practitioners

    Overview:

    An expansion to the *Jockey Club Arts-Based Cross Curriculum Creative Learning Project*, this project extends creative teaching and learning to a multi-layer four-year-long extension that includes a higher level with tertiary institutions as Partners or Collaborators. Here postgraduates and undergraduates are offered workshops of different durations. On the other side of the spectrum, at entry point level, are the Associate Creative Schools in which continuous professional development sessions are provided to teachers from primary to junior secondary schools annually.

    The original creative learning schools who wish to advance are able to continue and 12 new creative schools will be recruited.

    Links:
    https://creativefutures.aftec.hk/home-zh/ (Chinese)
    https://creativefutures.aftec.hk/home-en/ (English)

References

Alamy. 2024a. 'A Beautiful View over the Mona Art Museum, Hobart in Tasmania by Water'. *Alamy.* https://www.alamy.com/a-beautiful-view-over-the-mona-art-museum-hobart-in-tasmania-by-water-australia-image489258835.html.

Alamy. 2024b. 'Architecture of Miho Museum in Kyoto, Japan. Designed by Architect I. M. Pei'. *Alamy.* https://www.alamy.com/kyoto-japan-jul-16-2015-architecture-of-miho-museum-in-kyoto-japan-the-museum-designed-by-architect-i-m-pei-is-a-17400-m2-building-carved-image339593560.html.

Alamy. 2024c. 'View at Dawn Across the Nervion River Towards the Guggenheim Museum. Iberdrola Tower in Background, Bilbao, Spain'. *Alamy.* https://www.alamy.com/view-at-dawn-across-the-nervion-river-towards-the-guggenheim-museum-iberdrola-tower-in-background-bilbao-spain-image332650486.html.

Alamy. 2024d. 'View of Tate Modern Gallery and the New Len Blavatnik Building in Bankside, London, UK'. *Alamy.* https://www.alamy.com/london-uk-a-view-of-tate-modern-gallery-and-the-new-len-blavatnik-building-in-bankside-image557745851.html.

All-Party Parliamentary Group on Arts, Health and Wellbeing Inquiry Report. 2017. *Creative Health: The Arts for Health and Wellbeing.* All-Party Parliamentary Group on Arts, Health and Wellbeing. https://www.culturehealthandwellbeing.org.uk/appg-inquiry/Publications/Creative_Health_Inquiry_Report_2017_-_Second_Edition.pdf.

Arts Council of Wales. 2017. *Lead Creative Schools Prospectus for Creative Agents.* https://creativelearning.arts.wales/sites/default/files/2022-07/Prospectus-for-Creative-Agents.pdf.

Australian Curriculum, Assessment and Reporting Authority. 2022. *Australian Curriculum: General Capabilities – Critical and Creative Thinking Version 9.0 About the General Capability.* Australian Curriculum, Assessment and Reporting Authority. https://v9.australiancurriculum.edu.au/content/dam/en/curriculum/ac-version-9/downloads/general-capabilities/general-capabilities-critical-and-creative-thinking-about-the-general-capability-v9.docx.

Bamford, A., Rachel Y. J. Chan, and Samuel Leong. 2011. *Quality People Quality Life: Developing Hong Kong into a Creative Metropolis through Arts Education*. Home Affairs Bureau, The Hong Kong Special Administrative Region of the People's Republic of China.

Buck, Louisa. 2000. 'Curator Interview: Tate Modern's Thematic Hang'. *The Art Newspaper*. https://www.theartnewspaper.com/2000/05/01/curator-interview-tate-moderns-thematic-hang.

Cairns, Sam, Fran Landreth Strong, Elinor Lobley, Claudia Devlin, and Laura Partridge. 2020. *Arts-Rich Schools*. Royal Society for the Encouragement of Arts, Manufactures and Commerce. https://www.thersa.org/globalassets/pdfs/reports/rsa-arts-rich-schools.pdf.

Campos, Luisa, Pedro Dias, Ana Duarte, Elisa Veiga, Claudia C. Dias, and Filipa Palha. 2018. 'Is it Possible to "Find Space for Mental Health" in Young People? Effectiveness of a School-Based Mental Health Literacy Promotion Program'. *International Journal of Environmental Research and Public Health* 15 (7): 1–12. https://doi.org/10.3390/ijerph15071426.

Census and Statistics Department. 2024. *The Cultural and Creative Industries in Hong Kong*. The Government of the Hong Kong Special Administrative Region. https://www.censtatd.gov.hk/en/data/stat_report/product/FA100120/att/B72406FA2024XXXXB0100.pdf.

Centre for the Humanities and Medicine. 'Centre for the Humanities and Medicine'. The University of Hong Kong. https://chm.hku.hk/medicalhum.html.

Cheung Yung, Jane Y. W. 'Integrated Arts Education in Hong Kong'. Paper presented at the Asia-Pacific Education Research Association (Hong Kong), 28–30 November 2006. https://citeseerx.ist.psu.edu/document?repid=rep1&type=pdf&doi=0f02cc11eaddc39517307036cf4cc1934aa949cb.

Cignetti, Marta, and Marc Fuster Rabella. 2023. 'How Are Education Systems Integrating Creative Thinking in Schools?' PISA in Focus. OECD PISA. https://doi.org/10.1787/22260919.

COVID-19 Thematic Website, The Government of the Hong Kong Special Administrative Region. 2020. 'Anti-epidemic Fund'. Coronavirus.gov.hk. https://www.coronavirus.gov.hk/eng/anti-epidemic-fund.html#:~:text=The%20%24120%20billion%20relief%20package,Council%20on%2018%20April%202020.

Curriculum Development Council. 2001. *Learning to Learn – Life-Long Learning and Whole-Person Development*. The Hong Kong Special Administrative Region of the People's Republic of China. https://www.edb.gov.hk/attachment/en/curriculum-development/cs-curriculum-doc-report/wf-in-cur/CDC_LtL_Report_2001(web)_e.pdf.

Durham Commission on Creativity and Education. 2019. *Durham Commission on Creativity and Education*. Arts Council England, https://www.artscouncil.org.uk/sites/default/files/download-file/Durham_Commission_on_Creativity_04112019_0.pdf.

Education Commission. 2000. *Learning for Life, Learning through Life: Reform Proposals for the Education System in Hong Kong*. The Hong Kong Special Administrative Region of the

People's Republic of China. https://www.e-c.edu.hk/wp-content/uploads/2000/09/Proposal_Edu_Reform_2000.pdf.

Einstein, Albert. 1940. *Einstein on Cosmic Religion and Other Opinions and Aphorisms*. Philosophical Library.

Eisner, Elliot W. 1998. *The Enlightened Eye: Qualitative Inquiry and the Enhancement of Educational Practice*. Merrill.

Eliot, Thomas E. 1943. *Four Quartets*. Harcourt.

Fancourt, Daisy, and Saoirse Finn. 2019. *What Is the Evidence on the Role of the Arts in Improving Health and Well-Being? A Scoping Review*. World Health Organization, Regional Office for Europe. https://iris.who.int/handle/10665/329834.

Frey, Carl B., and Michael Osborne. 2013. 'The Future of Employment: How Susceptible Are Jobs to Computerization?' Working Paper. Oxford Martin School, University of Oxford. https://www.oxfordmartin.ox.ac.uk/publications/the-future-of-employment.

Greene, Maxine. 1995. *Releasing the Imagination: Essays on Education, the Arts, and Social Change*. Jossey-Bass.

Gupta, Shilpa. 2012. '1:14.9 (Thread Ball)'. *Shilpagupta*. Last modified December 2007. https://shilpagupta.com/114-9-thread-ball/.

Hetland, Lois, Patricia Palmer, Steve V. Siedel, Shari Tishman, and Ellen Winner. 2009. *The Qualities of Quality: Understanding Excellence in Arts Education*. Harvard Education Press.

Hong Kong Arts Development Council. 2024. Annual Arts Survey Result Dashboard, Performing Arts. *Hong Kong Arts Development Council*. https://www.hkadc.org.hk/en/research.

Kelly, Brian L., and Lauren Doherty. 2017. 'A Historical Overview of Art and Music-Based Activities in Social Work with Groups: Non-Deliberate Practice and Engaging Young People's Strengths'. *Social Work with Groups* 40 (3): 187–201. https://doi.org/10.1080/01609513.2015.1091700.

Korea Arts & Culture Education Service. 2024. 'President's Message'. *KACES*. http://eng.arte.or.kr/about#presidents-message.

Lai, Tsz Yu. 2024. 'Spotlight on Students 2023–24'. Interview by the AFTEC team, 12 March 2024. YouTube. https://youtu.be/x5LJV_HK8jE?si=zT6uKewVqU-ORdeD.

Lancaster, Kate (host). 2019. *First-Class Humans, Not Second-Class Robots – Andreas Schleicher on Learning and the Future of Work*. OECD Podcasts, OECD iLibrary. 23 June. Podcast, 14 min, 59 sec. https://doi.org/10.1787/87958706-en.

Lau, Chung Yim, and Cheung On Tam. 2022. 'Examining Performing Arts Education in Hong Kong'. *Arts Education Policy Review* 125 (3): 1–12. https://doi.org/10.1080/10632913.2021.2023933.

Leung, Gabriel, Lai Ming Ho, Tai Hing Lam, and Anthony J. Hedley. Supplement 9, 2009. 'Epidemiology of SARS in the 2003 Hong Kong Epidemic'. *Hong Kong Medical Journal* 15 (6): 12–16. Department of Community Medicine, The University of Hong Kong. https://hub.hku.hk/bitstream/10722/86739/1/content.pdf?accept=1.

Liew, Wei Li. 2024. 'Singapore's 15-Year-Old Students Score Top Marks in OECD's Creative Thinking Test'. LinkedIn, June 2024. https://www.linkedin.com/posts/

wei-li-liew-98051044_singapores-15-year-old-students-score-top-activity-7209552308576141312-vI1c?utm_source=share&utm_medium=member_desktop.

Lucas, Bill. 2016. 'A Five-Dimensional Model of Creativity and its Assessment in Schools'. *Applied Measurement in Education* 29 (4): 278–90. https://doi.org/10.1080/08957347.2016.1209206.

McMaster, Brian. 2008. *Supporting Excellence in the Arts: From Measurement to Judgement.* Department of Digital, Culture, Media and Sport, UK Government. https://cercles.diba.cat/documentsdigitals/pdf/E130091.pdf.

MedicineNet. 'Interstice'. 2024. *MedicineNet.* https://www.rxlist.com/interstitial/definition.htm.

Mulgan, Geoff, UCL STEaPP, and Demos Helsinki. 2020. 'The Imaginary Crisis (and How We Might Quicken Social and Public Imagination)'. UCL Science, Technology, Engineering and Public Policy Working Paper Series, April 2020.

Museum of Old and New Art. 2024. 'About'. *MONA.* https://mona.net.au/museum/about.

National Arts Council Singapore. 2024. 'Arts Education – Essentials of Teaching and Learning'. *National Arts Council.* https://www.nac.gov.sg/support/capability-development/training-opportunities/arts-education-essentials-of-teaching-and-learning-module-(em).

National Arts Council Singapore and SkillsFuture Singapore. 2024. *Skills Framework for Arts (Arts Education).* National Arts Council Singapore and SkillsFuture Singapore. https://www.nac.gov.sg/docs/default-source/skills-framework-documents/skills-framework-for-arts-(arts-education).pdf?sfvrsn=69556f56_4.

OECD. 2024. *PISA 2022 Results (Volume III) Creative Minds, Creative Schools.* PISA, OECD Publishing. https://doi.org/10.1787/765ee8c2-en.

Office of the Government Economist Financial Secretary's Office and Census and Statistics Department. 2021. *Hong Kong Poverty Situation Report 2020.* The Hong Kong Special Administrative Region of the People's Republic of China. https://www.censtatd.gov.hk/en/data/stat_report/product/B9XX0005/att/B9XX0005E2020AN20E0100.pdf.

O'Hanlon, Jacqui. 2023. 'Evidence Informed Decision Making About the Importance of Arts Rich Schools'. *Royal Shakespeare Company.* https://www.rsc.org.uk/learn/research/research-blog/evidence-informed-decision-making-about-the-importance-of-arts-rich-schools.

Oxford English Dictionary. 2022. https://www.oed.com/search/dictionary/?scope=Entries&q=imagination.

Perkins, David. 1994. *The Intelligent Eye: Learning to Think by Looking at Art.* Getty Publications.

Polly, Marie, Marcello Betotti, Richard Kimberlee, Geoff Pilkington, and Charlotte Refsum. 2017. *A Review of the Evidence Assessing Impact of Social Prescribing on Healthcare Demand and Cost Implications.* University of Westminster, London. https://www.socialprescribingnetwork.com/media/attachments/2022/02/22/review-of-evidence-assessing-impact-of-social-prescribing-1.pdf.

Pringle, Emily, ed. 2014. *Transforming Tate Learning.* Tate Learning, Tate Modern.

Qualifications and Curriculum Authority, Department for Education, UK. n.d. *Framework of Personal, Learning and Thinking Skills 11–19 in England*. https://dera.ioe.ac.uk/id/eprint/7268/3/PLTS_framework_v2_tcm8-936-1.pdf.

Quantumrun. 2020. 'Future of Teaching: Future of Education P3'. https://www.quantumrun.com/prediction/future-teaching-future-education-p3.

RAND Research. 2008. *Cultivating Demand for the Arts – Arts Learning, Arts Engagement, and State Arts Policy*. RAND. https://www.rand.org/pubs/monographs/MG640.html.

Robinson, Ken. 1982. *The Arts in Schools: Principles, Practice and Provision*. Calouste Gulbenkian Foundation.

Schön, Donald A. 1983. *The Reflective Practitioner: How Professionals Think in Action*. Basic Books.

School of the Arts Singapore. 2024a. 'About SOTA'. *SOTA*. https://www.sota.edu.sg/.

School of the Arts Singapore. 2024b. *Curriculum Booklet 2024*. School of the Arts Singapore https://www.sota.edu.sg/docs/default-source/curriculum-booklet/currbooklet2024.pdf.

Senge, Peter M. 1990. *The Fifth Discipline: The Art & Practice of The Learning Organization*. Doubleday.

Singapore Government. n.d. '21st Century Competencies'. Ministry of Education Singapore. https://www.moe.gov.sg/education-in-sg/21st-century-competencies.

Singapore Teachers' Academy for the aRts. 2024a. 'Home'. *STAR*. https://star.moe.edu.sg/.

Singapore Teachers' Academy for the aRts. 2024b. 'STAR Professional Development Framework'. *STAR*. https://star.moe.edu.sg/programmes/star-professional-development-framework/.

SkillsFuture Singapore. 2024. 'About SkillsFuture Singapore'. *Skillsfuture*. https://www.skillsfuture.gov.sg/aboutssg.

Society for Community Organisation. 'Children's Right Project'. *SOCO*. https://soco.org.hk/en/projecthome/child-rights/.

Sunah, Kim. 'Cultural Arts Education as Transformative Pedagogy'. Keynote address presented at the Knowledge Exchange Forum for *The Jockey Club Arts-Based Cross Curriculum Creative Learning Project*, The Absolutely Fabulous Theatre Connection, Hong Kong. 18–19 July 2022. See video at https://www.youtube.com/live/L8ZwcOmna2s?si=_MzqPinliO83qQ1Z&t=3306.

TALE Project. 2018. 'Tracking Arts Learning and Engagement'. *Research Tale*. https://researchtale.net/.

Tambling, Pauline, and Sally Bacon. 2023. *The Arts in Schools: Foundations for the Future*. Calouste Gulbenkian Foundation and A New Direction. https://www.anewdirection.org.uk/the-arts-in-schools.

The Absolutely Fabulous Theatre Connection. 2024. 'digiAFTEC for Schools'. *AFTEC*. https://www.aftec.hk/digiaftec-for-schools/.

The Chief Executive's 2022 Policy Address. 2024. 'East-Meets-West Centre for International Cultural Exchange'. The Hong Kong Special Administrative Region of the People's Republic of China. https://www.policyaddress.gov.hk/2022/en/p43.html.

The Hong Kong Special Administrative Region of the People's Republic of China. 2023. *The Chief Executive's 2023 Policy Address*. The Government of the Hong Kong Special Administrative Region. https://www.policyaddress.gov.hk/2023/public/pdf/policy/policy-full_en.pdf.

Twardzicki, Monika. 2008. 'Challenging Stigma around Mental Illness and Promoting Social Inclusion Using the Performing Arts'. *Journal of the Royal Society for the Promotion of Health* 128 (2): 68–72. https://journals.sagepub.com/doi/10.1177/1466424007087804.

VUCA-World. 2023. 'Where Does the Term VUCA Come From? Role of Nanus and Bennis'. *VUCA-World*. http://www.vuca-world.org/roles-of-nanus-and-bennis/.

Whitbread, Richard. 2016. 'Cultural and Arts Education Policies in Hong Kong: Two Wings of the Same Bird?' EdD dissertation. ProQuest (10245202).

Wong, May. 'Jockey Club Arts-Based Cross Curriculum Creative Learning Project Teachers' Focus Group'. Interview by GeoDimension InfoSolutions Limited, 2024.

World Economic Forum. 2023. *Future of Jobs Report 2023*. World Economic Forum https://www3.weforum.org/docs/WEF_Future_of_Jobs_2023.pdf.

Yau, Lynn F. C. 2016. *Arts Change Lives: Social Impact Assessment*. The Absolutely Fabulous Theatre Connection Company Limited.

Your Brain on Art. 2024. 'What is NeuroArts'. *Your Brain on Art*. https://www.yourbrainonart.com/what-is-neuroarts.

World Intellectual Property Organization (WIPO). 2023. 'Global Innovation Index 2023: Innovation in the Face of Uncertainty'. *WIPO*. DOI:10.34667/tind.48220.

Note: Although the author has made every effort to reach out to copyright owners for the materials included in this work, she recognises that some may not have been contacted. If you feel your copyright has not been acknowledged, please contact the author, and she will do our best to address it.

Index

Page numbers in italics refer to figures and tables.

AFTEC, 2, 36, 50, 55, 70, 86, 90, 91, 93, 176, 181, 183, 196, 206, 220, 229, 231, 263, 265; assessment and evaluation, 90–128, *95* table 5.1; 2009 to 2012, early years, 96–103; mood beads bottle, 98–99, *98* fig. 5.2; reflection journal, 99–100; annual dialogues, 100–102; 2013 to 2018, Middle Years, 103–22; social impact of, *113* table 5.2, *114* table 5.3, *115* table 5.4; and behavioural changes, 120–22, *121* fig. 5.10; 2019 to 2024, recent years, 122–28

arts: appreciation, 222–24; performing, 1, 3, 19, 48, 60–64, 67, 192, 206, 213, 219, 225, *241* fig. 9.8, *242* fig. 9.9, 245, 264; as spectacle, 23; twelve powers of the, 2, 3; and the UK, 5, 90, 151, 229, 232, 233, 250, 252; visual, 1, 3, 16, 22, 29, 34, 35, 168, 187, 192, 212, 229, 234, 249, 255, 260; and well-being, 139–45, *140* fig. 6.4, *142* fig. 6.5, *146* fig. 6.7

arts educators. *See* teaching artists

arts-in-education, 3, 5, 6, 9, 17, 23, 50, 70, 71, 87, 88, 219, 232, 248, 264, 266; key documents in, 17–18

Arts on Prescription project, 151, 154, 248

audienceship, 54, 267. *See also* Chapter 9

Australia: Museum of Old and New Art, 197; performance in creative curriculum, 180–83

Bravo! Hong Kong Youth Theatre Awards, 56–60, 88, 101, 171; Bravo programme, 104–20; and capacity building, *58* fig. 3.4; reflection and social impact, 103–22, *106* fig. 5.3, *108* fig. 5.4, *110* fig. 5.5

Calouste Gulbenkian Foundation, 5

capacity building, 55–60, 103, 104, 176, 263

Classics for Juniors, 50–52, *51* fig. 3.1

costume, *147* fig. 6.8, *148* fig. 6.9, 210, 256, 261–62

COVID: backstory, 130–31; and digitisation, 50; impact, 131–38, *137* fig. 6.3; and well-being, *140* fig. 6.4, *144* table 6.1, *148* fig. 6.9, *149* fig. 6.10. *See also* Chapter 5

creative learning, 3–8, *7* fig. a, 10, 22, 24, 42, 49, 56, 160, 165, 181, *217* table 8.1, 265–67; and Creative Learning

Project, 66–67, 122–26, 169, *217* table 8.2, 219, 228, 236, 237; practitioners, 4; and theatre productions, 50–52; and thinking skills, 224. *See also* Chapter 8
creative mindsets, 4, 6, *7* fig. a, 9, 199, 215, 250, 263. *See also* Chapter 7
creative practitioners (CPs), 4, 8, 66, 122, 123, 124, 216, 251, 256; and Development Web, 248, *249* fig. 9.12; and para-CPs, 251–52. *See also* Chapter 9
creativity: code, 22–24; and jobs, 26; and learning, 66; role of, 25–26. *See also* Chapter 1
cross-sector learning, 60–63, 65, 219, 264; and collaboration, 228, 229; and networking, 248
Culture, Sports and Tourism Bureau, 24, 157, 220

data explosion, 26–29

East-West Centre for International Cultural Exchange, 6, 158, 220
Education Bureau, 2, 16, 18, 23, 157, 220, 228; Commission, 16, 24
education reform (of 2000), 9, 15; the achievements, 18–19; the gaps, 19–20; gaps as maps, 20–22; status quo, 22–24
emerging translators, 53, 54

five core Chinese concepts, 16

gaps. *See* Chapter 3
growth mindset, 41, 121, 134, 135, 263

Hong Kong Academy for Performing Arts, 56, 64, 104, 153, 238
Hong Kong Arts Development Council, 18, 23, 158, 220, 241, *242* fig. 9.9
Hong Kong Jockey Club Charities Trust, 65, 88, 96

Human Resource Planning: audience and, 221–28, *222* fig. 9.1; context of, 218–19; insights into, 219–21; and practitioners, 237–40, *238* fig. 9.6, *239* fig. 9.7; and schools, 228–37, *230* fig. 9.4, *231* fig. 9.5, *234* table 9.1

Industrial Revolution, *31* fig. 1.3; first, 47; second, 30, 40; third, 30; fourth, 17, 25, 26

jobs, 26–35; and the arts, 34–35; data explosion and automation in, 26–29, *28* fig. 1.2; future, 30–34, *27* fig. 1.1, *30* fig. 1.3, *32* fig. 1.4, *33* table 1.1
Jockey Club Arts for Change Project, 65–66, *66* fig. 3.6
Jockey Club Arts-Based Cross Curriculum Creative Learning Project, 21, 66–67, *125* table 5.5; *126* table 5.6; *217* table 8.2; Year Two, 122–26

Key Learning Areas, 16, 18, 274
Korea: performance in creative thinking, 161, 175, 178; performance in creative curriculum, 183–85; and Bong Joon-Ho, 185; and Korea Arts & Culture Education Service (KACES), 185

LAMDA, *58* fig. 3.4, 59, 105, *111* fig. 5.6, 113–14, 120
Lead Creative Schools, 236, 251
Lee Hysan Foundation, 56, 59, 103
Leisure and Cultural Services Department, 48, 158, *207* fig. 8.12, 221, 241

McMaster review, 90–91
Medical Humanities, 151–52; assessment and evaluation in, 102–3; and cross-sector learning, 60–63, *62* fig. 3.5
museums, 215; and cognitive space, 199–202, 215; past and present,

193–99; as sites of creative learning, 193–202; Tate influence, 201–2

network, 183, 187, 189, 248, 267

pedagogy, 70, 72, 173–80
performing arts. *See* arts
performing venues, 215; Passoverdance, 213–14; physical space, 202–6, *203* fig. 8.7, *203* fig. 8.8, *204* fig. 8.9, *204* fig. 8.10, *205* fig. 8.11; physical to cognitive space, 206–12, *207* fig. 8.12, *208* fig. 8.13, *209* fig. 8.14, *209* fig. 8.15; as sites of learning, 202–11; Tate, 212–13
PISA creative thinking assessment, 159–60; Australia, 161, 180–81, *182* table 7.4; and gender, 171–73; Korea, 161, 183–85, *184* fig. 7.10; 2022 report into, 160, *161* table 7.1, 162, *163* fig. 7.1, *165* fig. 7.2; and science fair, 167–68, *169* fig. 7.4, *170* fig. 7.5; Singapore, 161, 186–89; and social economic status, 171–73, *172* table 7.3; and teaching pedagogies, 173–80, *174* fig. 7.6, *177* fig.7.7, *227* fig. 9.3, 232. *See also* Chapter 7
Plays for Young People, 52–54, *53* fig. 3.2
polymath, 29
poverty, *37* fig. 2.1, *38* fig. 2.2; and demotivation, 41; and imagination, 40–43. *See* Chapter 2
primary school, 8, 36, 51, 57, 66, 71, 83, 87, 116, 122, 124, 183, 188, 228, 232, 237; to secondary, 16, 56, 180, 225

Quantumrun: *The Future of Employment* report, 25, 26, 29, 35

RAND, 244–46; *244* fig. 9.10

Sai Wan Ho Civic Centre, 48, 72, 92, 138, 206, 257
Singapore: 6, 23, 228; and creative thinking, 161–62, 165–67, 173, 175–76, 178, 180, 185; performance in creative curriculum, 23, 185–89
sites of creative learning. *See* museums; performing venues
Sm-ART Youth, 36, 55–56; case study, 69–88; cultural outings, 82–86; environments, 72–79, *73* fig. 4.1, *75* fig. 4.2; parent-child collaboration, 79–82, *80* fig. 4.3; pedagogy, 72. *See also* Chapter 4

Tate Modern, 171, 195–97; learning, 199–200; influence, 201–2
teaching artists, 8, 9, 11, 22, 63, 64, 88, 89, 102, 186, 188, 201, 219, 221, 236, 237–40, 256
teaching environment, 72–79
theatre production, 105, *110* fig. 5.5, 122, 206, 261; and behavioural changes, 120; and COVID, 132; and creative learning, 50–60
training the trainers, 7 fig. a; 63–65, 88, 266

visual arts. *See* arts

World Economic Forum: *The Future of Jobs* report (of 2023), 25, 26, *27* fig. 1.1, 225, *226* fig. 9.2, 262

Young Theatre Makers, 54–55, *55* fig. 3.3, 88

www.ingramcontent.com/pod-product-compliance
Ingram Content Group UK Ltd.
Pitfield, Milton Keynes, MK11 3LW, UK
UKHW021829140426
5217IPUK00017B/1267